ALL THAT IS
WICKED

ALSO BY KATE WINKLER DAWSON

*American Sherlock: Murder, Forensics, and
the Birth of American CSI*

*Death in the Air: The True Story of a Serial Killer,
the Great London Smog, and the Strangling of a City*

ALL THAT IS
WICKED

A GILDED-AGE STORY of MURDER

and the RACE to DECODE the

CRIMINAL MIND

KATE WINKLER DAWSON

G. P. PUTNAM'S SONS

New York

PUTNAM
— EST. 1838 —

G. P. Putnam's Sons
Publishers Since 1838
An imprint of Penguin Random House LLC
penguinrandomhouse.com

Library of Congress Cataloging-in-Publication Data

Names: Dawson, Kate Winkler, author.
Title: All that is wicked : a gilded-age story of murder and the race to
decode the criminal mind / Kate Winkler Dawson.
Description: New York : G. P. Putnam's Sons, [2022] |
Includes bibliographical references and index.
Identifiers: LCCN 2022019068 (print) | LCCN 2022019069 (ebook) |
ISBN 9780593420065 (hardcover) | ISBN 9780593420072 (ebook)
Subjects: LCSH: Rulloff, Edward H. (Edward Howard), 1819-1871—Psychology. |
Criminal psychology—United States—History—19th century—Case studies. |
Serial murderers—United States—History—19th century—Case studies.
Classification: LCC HV6113.R85 D39 2022 (print) | LCC HV6113.R85 (ebook) |
DDC 364.3—dc23/eng/20220426
LC record available at https://lccn.loc.gov/2022019068
LC ebook record available at https://lccn.loc.gov/2022019069

Printed in the United States of America
1st Printing

To JWD,
who deserves the dedication in every book I write

Contents

Author's Note

xi

PROLOGUE

A Criminal Mind

1

CHAPTER 1

The Author

13

CHAPTER 2

Between the Lakes

39

CHAPTER 3

The Newspaperman

79

CHAPTER 4

The Greek Scholar

117

CHAPTER 5

The Educator

161

CHAPTER 6

The Alienist

199

CHAPTER 7

The Phrenologists

223

CHAPTER 8

The Neurologists

249

EPILOGUE

A Cautionary Tale

281

Acknowledgments

287

Bibliography

291

Index

297

ALL THAT IS
WICKED

Author's Note

As I began researching *All That Is Wicked*, I realized that this story would be a wonderful tale to use for the debut season of my new historical true crime podcast, *Tenfold More Wicked* (on the Exactly Right network). You might have heard Edward Rulloff's story during the first season, but *this* story is very different. *All That Is Wicked* is a deep dive into Rulloff's motivations, his controversial brain, and how it changed history. Through Rulloff's story, we'll meet the first generation of what would one day come to be known as mindhunters—men who hoped to pick apart Rulloff's psyche to discover *why* he killed . . . and how to prevent others from murdering in the future.

PROLOGUE

A Criminal Mind

All human beings, as we meet them, are commingled out of good and evil.
> —Robert Louis Stevenson,
> *Strange Case of Dr. Jekyll and Mr. Hyde*, 1886

I t's strenuous work to saw through a skull.

The job demands an anatomist with dexterity, diligence, physical strength, and a sharpened blade. But the rewards of such physical exertion are great: the brain uncovered beneath the thick layer of bone might prove invaluable to science. This one certainly did.

Tucked deep inside a steel-clad, brown building at one of the most respected universities in the United States sits the brain of a brilliant killer: Edward Rulloff. Curious visitors to Cornell University's psychology department in Ithaca, New York, marvel at the brain's massive frontal lobe. It's been on display for more than one hundred years—so long that small pieces have begun chunking off, dissolving slowly in the murky formaldehyde. Though few students ever see the brain itself, its reputation is hinted at across the campus in several small, almost invisible ways. In a whisper from an upperclassman about the university's macabre history. Or in the name of the popular Ithaca eatery, Rulloff's Restaurant.

There are seven other brains inside that glass display, each one claimed by an owner who earned a place in history. One was a noted naturalist, another was a groundbreaking scientist, and one was an influential political activist . . . but Rulloff's brain is overwhelmingly the biggest of them all; you can see that right away. It is in fact one of the largest brains studied in the world—easily among the top 1 percent in size, a ghastly and strange statistic that leads to other, darker questions. (*How do scientists know this? How many other brains are out there, waiting to be weighed and examined?*) While Rulloff ended his life in ignominy, this brain in a dusty glass jar is in fact an artifact of a once-lauded scholar, a nineteenth-century polymath who charmed his way to the upper echelons of intellectual society. The amiable academic deceived almost everyone he met (at least for a little while), pairing a clever remark with a wink and a grin. But the brilliant Rulloff also had a dark side. He confessed to murdering his wife, though he likely killed his infant daughter, too. His sister-in-law and his infant niece were poisoned while under his care as a doctor in upstate New York . . . and then he killed again when he settled in Gilded-Age New York City.

After his past was unmasked, Rulloff was tantalizing fodder for journalists—a murderer cloaked as an intellectual savant anonymously roaming the streets of 1800s Manhattan. He might have strolled past the lavish mansions on Fifth Avenue or skirted the perilous alleys of Five Points. Edward Rulloff's New York was a spellbinding world, one teeming with corrupt politicians, self-righteous academics, unscrupulous journalists, horrible poverty, and unimaginable wealth. In the den of iniquity that was much of

Manhattan in the late nineteenth century, Edward Rulloff presented himself as New York City's own Dr. Jekyll—fifteen years before the character slunk across the pages of Robert Louis Stevenson's famous novella. But Rulloff's adaptation of Mr. Hyde was more ghastly and more merciless than Stevenson could have imagined. Before America became transfixed by London's Jack the Ripper in 1888 or by H. H. Holmes in 1894, it was riveted by Edward Howard Rulloff and his gruesome murders.

Almost thirty years after his initial crimes, Rulloff was finally captured and convicted of murder. And that was where the next phase of his story—the one that is still debated and discussed even today—began. As Rulloff sat shackled to the floor of a dismal jail cell, awaiting execution, he watched more than a dozen men in suits and hats come in turn to meet him. They each sat nervously, clutching their papers and pencils. An author. A newspaperman. A phrenologist. An alienist. A physician. And others. To them, he was a fascinating, unique specimen to study. They were each convinced that Rulloff's mind—in all its twisty, enigmatic glory—was the key to unlocking the mysteries of psychology and the human brain.

One by one these experts stared as the charming academic unspooled his life story. *If he were truly evil*, they each thought, *shouldn't it be evident somewhere on his face, in his speech, in his mind?* People in the 1800s prayed for that sort of clue, but there were no such giveaways with Rulloff. He appeared intelligent. Cultured. *Sane*. So why did he do the crimes he was accused of committing? New modes of understanding the criminal mind would need to be developed to grapple with his contradictions, each man agreed.

Maybe Rulloff's brain could point the way forward.

Rulloff's case became one of the first "trials of the century" in 1800s America—he was the predecessor of the celebrity criminal, a bewhiskered forefather to Ted Bundy or Dennis Rader's infamous BTK, both serial killers when such a concept was just being developed. The international press anointed Edward Rulloff with celebrity status—the killer became a presence so ubiquitous in newspapers around the world for his time that their copy referred to him by last name only. Rulloff's notoriety earned him a place in history as one of the most intelligent killers in the annals of American crime, and his reputation for brilliance twice removed the noose from around his neck.

Journalists, the literati, and influence peddlers of various stripes in big cities across the land debated Rulloff's case on the front pages of newspapers: *Is a brilliant man's life worth saving, even if he's a wretched killer?*

No, most of the country in the nineteenth century replied.

But what if his ideas could change the world for the better? Might he be allowed to live?

. . . *Perhaps,* replied some of the most powerful men in America.

But who would be trusted to make those decisions? And could Rulloff's self-reflection, coupled with the analysis of experts like the ones assembled in his cell, help prevent *more* criminals from terrorizing the country? What might these experts learn from him?

A century later, the FBI would seek answers to those questions from other criminals. In the 1970s, agents with the Behavioral Science Unit of the FBI spent hundreds of hours interviewing some of America's most despised criminals to build profiles of the murderer and his victims. The list included notorious serial killers like Ted Bundy, Charles Manson, John Wayne Gacy, Richard Speck, David Berkowitz, and Edmund Kemper. The insights that came from studying the minds of these killers would provide invaluable intelligence for future investigations. Researchers learned that serial killers would often return to the scene of the murders, and that they might leave behind misleading clues to disrupt the investigation. They also discovered that many killers had troubled home lives but that few felt remorse or were even capable of remorse. In total, thirty-six violent offenders offered FBI agents the clues to subtle patterns that investigators had missed in the past, opportunities to prevent more murders. Those data, collected decades ago, are still being leveraged as the FBI provides support and training to America's law enforcement community to help identify killers and prevent future violence.

But the FBI agents weren't the only experts who wanted to collect data from those criminals. Over the past fifty years, journalists, psychologists, and psychiatrists have also entered the jail cells of these same killers to glean information that might help the public protect itself from some of America's cruelest murderers. These "mindhunters" came from various disciplines, each with their own strengths in understanding criminal behavior.

The investigators with the FBI's Behavioral Science Unit (now known as the Behavioral Analysis Unit) had backgrounds rooted in psychology, science, and police investigation. They delved into the minds of criminals and mined them for useful information. These investigators and their subjects, the serial killers, were part of a unique, nascent experiment never conducted before—we thought.

In fact, I've found that a previously forgotten group of experts in the 1800s preceded the work of the twentieth-century FBI agents by almost a century. The Gilded-Age investigators you'll read about in this book—Hamilton Freeman, Dr. John Gray, and Dr. George Sawyer, among others—were nineteenth-century mindhunters, plumbing the depths of the criminal brain for insights about the nature of evil and what leads a man to kill. These investigators were given a daunting task: evaluate what went wrong with Edward Rulloff and whether to end his life.

In this book, we'll find out what they uncovered.

The men brought to investigate Edward Rulloff were some of the most respected in their fields, and their evaluations of the most curious criminal mind in American history might sway public opinion and spark an outcry that could influence Rulloff's fate. They could send him to an insane asylum, doom him to the gallows . . . or perhaps set him free. They could even determine his academic reputation by legitimizing his self-led, "gonzo" scholarship and absolve him from being labeled a fraud. For the first time in his academic career, Rulloff enjoyed an audience with the kinds of esteemed scholars he dreamed of—men who could secure his legacy and profess his intelligence to the world. It was ironic, of course, that this court of intellectual examination was held as he sat in a dank jail in upstate New York.

The journalists, alienists, psychologists, scientists, and academics held immense power over Edward Rulloff's life as they squabbled over his mind. Each agreed that he was, perhaps, the most intelligent killer in American history. They were fascinated . . . but cautious. The wisest of them realized that with the right words, the right interactions, Rulloff might fool them, too, as he had fooled others so many times before.

In 1871, the mindhunters pondered many questions that were

required to make the right decision about Edward Rulloff. *Was he born wicked, an offspring of the devil?* asked the theologians. *Was he insane or a gifted actor?* wondered the alienists. *Were his ideas worth killing over?* pondered the academics. *Or perhaps he was simply misunderstood, a genius triggered by a raft of hardships,* suggested the journalists.

Edward Rulloff might have been something else entirely—a callous, coldhearted killer with a diagnosis that wouldn't have a formal designation for decades. These experts lacked our current tools to assign Rulloff an accurate assessment; they were fumbling as they tried to understand the malevolent enigma sitting cross-legged atop a shabby pallet on the jail cell's stone floor. The men prayed that their insights, gleaned from these in-depth interviews, might help identify more monsters like Edward Rulloff, even prevent them from killing.

As I researched Rulloff's family history and pored over his letters, I began to suspect that his actions were not governed by a mental illness and certainly not by the devil; in fact, he appeared to show the hallmarks of antisocial personality disorder. Edward Rulloff was very likely a nineteenth-century psychopath.

I asked several modern experts to offer an opinion on Rulloff based on the Hare Psychopathy Checklist, a diagnostic tool used to rate a person's psychopathic or antisocial tendencies, and currently the only scientific way to diagnose a psychopathic individual based on his or her behavior. Hare's checklist contains twenty descriptors: traits like grandiose estimation of self, pathological lying, cunning and manipulativeness, lack of remorse or guilt, and parasitic lifestyle. The subject is ranked on a scale of 0–2 for each item: 0 for neurotypicals (non-psychopaths). The higher the score, the higher the level of psychopathy (40 is the maximum total). Ideally a qualified, modern-day psychiatrist would have conducted a formal exam on Edward Rulloff; because that wasn't possible, the assessment for this book was based on extensive biographical documentation about Rulloff's life, including his many detailed interviews with contemporary experts, along with hundreds of his personal letters.

A very clear picture emerged about *why* this killer had led such a troubled life, as well as why he left behind a wake of agony for decades. Edward Rulloff would likely have scored in the mid-30s on the checklist, indicating a high level of psychopathy. As I uncovered details about his life and reviewed his reactions, I discovered that virtually *every* trait on Hare's list emerged.

Edward Rulloff's story resonates with us today because it is crucial to study the criminal mind, specifically the mind of a psychopathic individual. A disproportionate number of incarcerated men suffer from psychopathy—as much as 25 percent—while only 1 to 2 percent of the general male population do. Psychopathic individuals rarely respond to traditional methods of rehabilitation like medicine or therapy, yet they are responsible for a prevalence of violent crime. Researchers believe that intervening early in the life of child who displays traits of psychopathy can eventually save lives.

"These kids are more aggressive," psychopathy expert Dr. Craig Neumann told me. "These kids are more likely to be delinquents as they grow up, more likely to offend as they grow up now. The key with psychopathology or with medical disorders is the earlier you identify some form of pathology . . . the more likely you can provide some sort of treatment and be of help."

If psychopathy and its treatments go back to childhood, we also must return to the early days of Rulloff's story—or at least as far back as the historical record allows.

———

I tripped over tree branches and cracked stones lying just beneath a layer of snow as I struggled to safely arrive at the centuries-old farmhouse. It was February 2017 when I first arrived in Dryden, New York—a village less than fifteen miles from Ithaca and Cornell University.

It was very disconcerting, and a bit exhilarating, to walk across the ground that a multiple murderer stood on more than 175 years ago. As I approached Kathy Chadwick's home, I glanced up at the massive maple tree just feet from an old slate well. Edward Rulloff certainly peered up at this same tree so long ago, perhaps drinking from this same well. Trips like these are a visceral experience for an author, and I relish them. In some cases, nothing can supersede the value of being at a pivotal location you intend to write about. It was certainly a riveting, and sobering, experience for me.

Six Mile Creek was less than a hundred feet from the rear windows of the modest wooden house, but it was no more than a skinny trickle in the deep snow during my visit. Rulloff walked along that same creek as an ambitious young man married to the lovely daughter of the couple who once owned this house. I had hoped to trudge along the creek, too, once it thawed.

Ms. Chadwick greeted me as I was climbing the stairs of the front porch, slipping on ice along the way. This house is the origin

ALL THAT IS WICKED

of the story because some descendants of Edward Rulloff's former family *still* live here more than two centuries later. In fact, Rulloff was Chadwick's great-great-granduncle. She warmly greeted me (as did her large dog, Hannah) and led me up a short flight of creaky, old wooden stairs to a small room where Rulloff and his seventeen-year-old wife, Harriet, once slept. Later that week, another descendant, Craig Schutt, would help me navigate up a steep, snowy hill of the ancient cemetery nearby, where Rulloff's victims are buried. I met Craig Schutt three times, and he often remarked how I always insisted on visiting upstate New York during the worst part of winter.

It felt important to come here to walk in Rulloff's footsteps and meet his surviving relatives because at the heart of this book is a family, one almost destroyed by a monster. The Schutts endured so much pain long ago because of this narcissistic, cruel, and violent man. It's a reminder that every twisty true-crime story leaves behind real victims, real pain.

When I began this journey years ago, I tried to properly evaluate Edward Rulloff, to dissect his actions, assess his scholarship, and then present a comprehensive profile of this brilliant murder—and I think that I have done it. None of the details of his case were very pleasant, but I found Rulloff simply beguiling as I struggled to untangle the complexities of his psyche. I joined the nineteenth-century mindhunters of Rulloff's time as I hoped to discover how one brain could guide the actions of both a gifted scholar and a wicked killer. Rulloff was undoubtedly incredibly intelligent, yes. But ultimately, he was self-defeating, constantly sabotaging his own academic and intellectual ambitions. He stole from people— their trust, their goods, and their lives—and rarely offered anything in return, other than suffering. Rulloff spread misery through one family, like a contagion, for decades.

But in many ways, the Schutts were unyielding. He's gone. They persist.

I've lingered four different times over the long wooden desks in the glass room of Cornell University's vast archives in the Carl A. Kroch Library; I've photographed hundreds of unpublished pages in Rulloff's collection containing his personal correspondence and scholarship. I thumbed through the journals of his confidants and his legal advisers. I gently touched his death mask at the History Center in Tompkins County, and I even hoisted the glass jar holding his degrading brain.

I strolled through the town square in Binghamton, New York, that once hosted thousands of people, all gleefully praying to see the murderer hang, only to be turned away in dismay. I walked past the store that Rulloff had looted—and where he murdered an innocent man. I touched the trees of the backwoods where men hunted him. I stood in front of the old jail in Binghamton, where officers in the 1800s had unceremoniously shackled him to his desk as he scribbled his deeply researched theories on the origins of language. I located his apartment near Irving Place in New York City, a two-room flat along Third Avenue between Sixteenth and Seventeenth Streets.

The goal of these journeys was to offer more insight into the man at the epicenter of this story. Edward Rulloff captivated international readers for decades in the 1800s, and then his legacy simply vanished from history. Now I might be able to finally offer answers, some commentary about *why* Rulloff's criminal mind has entranced readers, scholars, and me for so long. Perhaps I can also explain how current researchers are hoping to prevent more psychopathic individuals and multiple murderers, like Edward Rulloff, from hurting innocent people.

Rulloff was recorded in the annals of history for his remarkable brain . . . but not in the way he had hoped. To understand Edward Rulloff's influence on neuroscience and how we now examine the criminal mind, it's important to first meet him inside his jail cell in 1871, just weeks before his scheduled execution.

1

The Author

My devil had been long caged, he came out roaring.
—Robert Louis Stevenson,
Strange Case of Dr. Jekyll and Mr. Hyde, 1886

On Tuesday, January 10, 1871, the journalist shuddered from the briskness of the air. Edward Hamilton "Ham" Freeman peered down the corridor of the jail, a white two-story building with less than a dozen cells, in Binghamton, New York (a town about two hundred miles northwest of Manhattan). The sheriff escorted him through the darkness with only the feeble light of a kerosene lamp to guide their way. The stone walls smelled stale, like yeast in a wooden bucket that had molded after weeks of neglect, and the building was damp and cold even by the frigid norms of deep winter in upstate New York. The heels of Ham's smart leather shoes clicked along the floor. In just a few months he would turn twenty-nine years old.

The guard directed Ham to a cell and slipped a key into the lock on an iron door. It swung open and there sat the journalist's subject, the infamous killer. Ham had been a small-town newspaper reporter for much of his career, and he was always on the hunt for a prominent story, one that might showcase his writing chops. This meeting would provide him with a unique opportunity.

Condensation dripped down the jail cell's walls as the cold outside air blew through the cracks. When Ham offered the prisoner a handshake, his nervous voice echoed down the miserable halls. The criminal offered his own greeting: *Edward Howard Rulloff.* Despite the cheerless surroundings, Edward's voice boomed with confidence.

Ham stood just feet from the murderer in the tiny cell. The newspaperman felt some measure of fear now that he was finally alone with Edward, face-to-face, locked in a room with this infamous man. Ham squinted at the fifty-one-year-old criminal's dark hazel eyes, which were bloodshot from reading all night by inadequate light. But Ham also couldn't help feeling giddy at the opportunity ahead. Despite all that had been written about Edward—his mysterious past, his academic feats, even the murder of which he was now accused—the killer had never told his own story. Now the notorious Edward Rulloff had selected Ham to record his intimate, personal history. It was a career-making opportunity.

It was also terrifying.

Ham had become intensely interested in Edward Rulloff—an enigma of a man described by some as "a monster imbued by the spirit of the devil"—as he'd observed the first few days of Edward's criminal trial in 1871. At first, of course, his curiosity was merely for the scintillating story at hand. And it was *very* scintillating. Ham jotted down every detail of the case, each fact about how Edward had murdered a man during a botched robbery. It was a dreadful crime, and just one of many of which Edward was guilty.

Yet as the trial progressed, Ham began to feel some shred of empathy for the defendant. Maybe it was the way the beleaguered man continually leapt from his wooden chair after a particularly damning accusation, only to be reprimanded by his attorneys. There was something indignant, almost plaintive, about his presence. Edward seemed utterly sure of himself, even in these dire circumstances. Ham was fascinated.

"I watched intensely every expression and every movement of the prisoner," Ham would later write for the biography. "I did not, could not, keep my eyes off from him."

With each day that had passed during the trial, Ham had felt more and more sorrow for the maligned genius who stewed just feet away from him.

"I took a painful, and melancholy interest in the trial, which increased as it progressed," said Ham. "I listened intently to every word he uttered when he rose oftentimes, despite the efforts of this counsel to keep him still, to speak on his own behalf."

Ham would shift uncomfortably on the wooden bench in the courtroom as rounds of applause erupted from hundreds of trial watchers both inside and outside. Edward Rulloff's trial was becoming a spectacle, and for days the throng challenged local sheriff's deputies to keep order. Ham described the audience's outbursts as "crude" to his friends. Throughout the trial, the author sat directly behind Edward, and the man on trial seemed to take a particular interest in him. However, Ham wasn't the only observer who was intrigued by the accused murderer.

"A large portion of the audience was composed of ladies, hundreds of whom stood patiently for hours listening with seemingly unwearied interest to the details of evidence, with the outlines of which they had long been familiar," wrote *New York*

Times reporter Edward Crapsey. Ham, too, observed the women in modest country dresses who crowded the courtroom.*

"Crowds attended the trial," wrote Ham, "a great portion of them being women, many of whom would early in the morning make their appearance before the closed doors of the court room, bringing their dinners that they might not, by their absence, lose their place."

For generations, women have been the dominant consumers of true crime; in current times, most readers, listeners, or viewers of these crime stories are female. Experts say many women hope to learn from the mistakes of victims, to absorb themselves in a world they hope to never enter. In some cases, they change their behavior based on that knowledge—they're more skeptical of male suitors and more cautious about venturing out alone. This was certainly the case with the audience of mostly proper ladies in Binghamton in 1871.

Edward Rulloff certainly wouldn't be described as "plain" in looks, but he fell slightly short of "striking" or "devilishly handsome." Yet there was an element of danger that drew these women to his trial every day. To them, Rulloff was irresistible—a riddle that might never be solved, a threat kept just out of reach. They flocked to the courtroom each day, sitting with legs politely crossed at the ankles as the gruesome details of the trial unfolded.†

---

* The predominately female audience might seem odd, but more than 150 years later, killers are still admired, even adored, by some women; there's a word for it in the lexicon of psychology: "hybristophilia," the sexual interest in criminals. Forensic psychologists note the incredible amount of attention many high-profile murderers command from women, even after their convictions.

† Forensic psychologist Katherine Ramsland, an author and a professor of psychology and criminal justice at DeSales University, found that there are many reasons that women are attracted to high-profile killers, including low self-esteem, the desire to change someone, the need for attention, and even something called "the perfect boyfriend"—an incarcerated man won't cheat and is unlikely to leave them.

Hamilton Freeman certainly understood the allure of Edward Rulloff. The author was himself quite handsome, with short brown hair parted on the right; a long, pointed nose; and a brow and a mouth that seemed to always remain in a grimace. Ham was the archetype of a small-town newspaper owner and editor—a hardworking local man who also secretly craved national recognition. His weekly paper, the *Democratic Leader,* was considered the leading source of local information in Broome County, New York; it covered everything from politics to gossip to crop prices. Ham Freeman was considered a capable, if somewhat unremarkable (and occasionally politically biased), journalist.

"He was a good writer, strongly partisan, perhaps, at times, yet his leaders were always interesting and refreshing," read a journal in 1900 about Binghamton's history. "(Hamilton) was (and still is) well informed on all subjects pertaining to Binghamton history, for he came from one of our respected old families."

Ham's family was prominent in nearby Lisle, New York, a village just twenty miles from Binghamton. His father was a successful lumber merchant, and after his death, young Hamilton moved to Binghamton for school. With his bright, active mind (and respectable pedigree), Ham quickly earned a reputation as a critical thinker with intellectual capabilities and education far beyond most of the folks in that small village. Ham's penchant for scholarship and family connections led him into the newspaper business where, at a relatively young age, Hamilton Freeman found himself with a front-row seat to the trial of the century—the case of the killer-savant that had captivated American readers and horrified fundamentalist Christians across upstate New York.

And now Edward Rulloff wanted to talk. To him.

Ham glanced around the cell as Edward settled himself. The

room was surprisingly well appointed with dim oil lamps, stacks of books, and an old wooden desk with paper lying to the side. Atop that desk was a pen leaning inside its inkwell. Edward had a creaky chair pulled close to his desk.

The writer surveyed his interviewee. Edward was well-dressed for a man who had been relegated to this dank jail for five months. His dark brown hair was short; he'd once boasted a long, scraggly beard, but the sheriff now insisted that it stayed trimmed to his cheeks. He was fully clothed, though according to the guards, Edward often preferred to sprawl in the nude on the cell's worn pallet. Edward's overall countenance was that of a respected college professor, a scholar accustomed to being adored by overzealous students. *Was this bookish, slightly eccentric, eminently respectable-looking man really a murderer?*

Ham was like a lot of men of his class and background at that point in the nineteenth century. He subscribed to the belief that a killer would look like . . . a killer. And what was that, exactly? Of course, any keen person would spot one immediately—a man (almost always a man) with a disheveled appearance and wild-eyed, almost rabid features. The evil in his heart and mind couldn't help but be evident on his person. But Ham noted that Edward Rulloff seemed calm, poised, and sophisticated. He spoke with grace, even eloquence. He showed flashes of intelligence and humor. Edward had a long track record of academic accomplishment (or, at least, academic pursuits) that showed him to possess a first-rate mind.

Simply put: Edward Rulloff didn't look or *sound* like a killer to Ham Freeman. But the newspaperman needed more data. The journalist considered whether Edward could be innocent, as he had claimed. And if he wasn't innocent, *why* was he guilty? Was

Edward Rulloff insane or born evil? Or was he something else entirely?

Hamilton Freeman would be just the first inquisitor in a long list of men seemingly besotted with the killer's mind, despite the malevolent character grafted to it.* In effect, he was the first mindhunter to try to plumb the depths of Edward's psyche—but he wouldn't be the last. Ham requested that Edward Rulloff detail his personal history—his family, his boyhood, and his development into a troubled young man. Did something in Edward's background predestine him to a life of crime and violence?

This interview was Ham's chance to find out.

It was also Edward's chance to control the narrative. Sitting before Edward was a journalist pledging to chronicle his life story for thousands of readers. Ham had no interest in interviewing anyone else for the book—just Edward. Edward's own story would be the *definitive* account . . . if the killer could convince Ham that he could be trusted to tell the truth. But Edward Rulloff could never be trusted.

During their first conversation, one of many that took place over six months, Edward revealed something to Ham. He could identify *exactly* when his life seemed to unravel—his ruin began with an encounter in early 1842 after he stepped off a packet boat and shook the hand of Henry Schutt.

———

* Ham chronicled these facts just like a pair of journalists did as they interviewed Ted Bundy more than one hundred years later to write their book *Ted Bundy: Conversations with a Killer*. Stephen G. Michaud and Hugh Aynesworth scribbled notes about Bundy as he talked about his childhood and teenage years; Hamilton Freeman would do the same as Edward spoke about his own history.

America in the 1840s was a country striving to progress. Out west, the Oregon Trail guided settlers along more than two thousand miles of harsh land stretching from Missouri through Idaho. Travelers were inspired by dreams of gold and rich farmlands, but they also hoped to escape economic struggles in the east and deadly diseases in the Midwest.

But even as the country stretched and expanded its borders westward (and even as big cities like New York City and Baltimore exploded in size), the landscape of America was still primarily rural. Farm life was the heart of American culture—in the countryside, families relied on their faith in God, their allegiance to their communities, and their devotion to one another to survive.

Indeed, hospitality (even hospitality extended to itinerant strangers) was a way of life in many of the villages and towns that dotted New England and the Northeast. It was normal and expected to offer a traveler who knocked on your door a night's rest or a warm meal. Rural families would set a place at their table for drifters and offer them a warm seat by the hearth. They trusted these itinerant men (and occasionally women) as they warmed themselves by the hearth; much of the time, that trust was offered on the basis of nothing more substantial than a simple handshake. Sometimes the townspeople offered the visitors work in the wheat fields, in cigar shops in town, or on boats that traveled up and down the canals in upstate New York. Good, honest men might volunteer to carry the transients on horseback to another village that might offer better opportunities. All this fellowship might have seemed naïve to someone reared in a big city, but generosity was a trademark of the countryside.

In the quaint towns that peppered the Ithaca area's landscape, the sunset highlighted their most appealing traits—the silhouette of cornfields lined by spiky pine trees; a coral sunset reflected from the surface of a small pond; hundreds of cornstalks gently swaying during a light breeze. The hamlets were charming, unpretentious; they held a type of innocence and optimism that simply couldn't survive in metropolises like Manhattan or Philadelphia, residents agreed. Their produce and meats were unspoiled, and their drinking water was pure; crime was low and educational opportunities were on the rise, even among young women. These country towns seemed idyllic, as if the devil had never paid them a visit—not even once.

But the country was changing, especially in quiet upstate New York. The nearby Erie Canal had been completed just seventeen years earlier, in 1825, a marvel of engineering and a savior to the region's (and the country's) economy. The longest canal in the world at more than 350 miles, the waterway connected the pristine Great Lakes and mighty Hudson River, offering a direct route to the bustle and commerce of New York City. In effect, the Erie Canal unlocked trade between the fertile Midwest and the commercial ports of the Northeast. Each shallow canal boat could carry as many as thirty tons of produce into New York City from farms as far away as Ohio, Michigan, and even Canada, dramatically lowering the costs (and increasing the speed) of transporting products.

The boats crept along the canal in 1842, moving so slowly that a waddling duck on land scooted along at a quicker pace. A mule trudged down the towpath nearby, lugging a boat behind with a rope. The boatman could peer out, his thoughts lost in the cloudy water as his barge slogged along. The water seemed yawning, intimidating, even though the captain knew perfectly well it was only four feet deep. Still, in the night, the waterway was like a black abyss, an "interminable mud puddle," wrote author Nathaniel Hawthorne.

The canal delivered so many wonderful things to the people of New York: fresh produce and meats, essential building materials like lumber and gravel, and immense prosperity—for some. But not all the cargo it transported was wanted. People, too, traveled across New York State via the Erie Canal—and sometimes, those people could be treacherous.

Henry Schutt wasn't inherently a distrustful man, even as the second-eldest sibling of a very large family. He might have been a little naïve. His mother and father had raised their brood of twelve (five girls and seven boys) to always welcome the wayfaring men who stumbled onto their sprawling homestead, Brookfield Farm. The farm consisted of a farmhouse and a barn sitting atop acres of land in Dryden, a village in upstate New York. Henry was accustomed to wandering laborers searching for work. He had always assumed that they had honest intentions—and his family hadn't been swindled in the past.

In the summer of 1842, the twenty-seven-year-old worked on a passenger boat called a packet—a small, shallow canal vessel that carted riders between stops along the waterway. Off and on they stepped at destinations between Albany on the Hudson River and Buffalo at Lake Erie. As Henry Schutt docked briefly in Syracuse, a man strolled down the towpath.

The stranger seemed about Henry's age, or just a bit younger. With gleaming, dark gray eyes and a ready smile, he was an engaging presence. Henry gave him a quick, silent evaluation. The man wasn't particularly tall, just about five foot eight inches, but he was solid, with broad shoulders and a compact frame. Canal work required a strong body, but the man also seemed well groomed, not messy like other men in need of work. The man's face had a flushed, ruddy complexion, as if he were perpetually abashed, even while wearing a grin.

"He said he came from New Brunswick [Canada]," said Ephraim Schutt, Henry's older brother. "He said he was German."

That was about all the information the boatman gleaned from the man, except Henry did learn his name: *Edward Howard Rulloff.* Edward told Henry Schutt that he didn't have proper employment and his savings were spent. Edward hoped to earn a living on the canal and then transition to a teaching career in a country village. He assured Henry and the captain who owned the boat that he possessed good moral character with industrious habits— he'd be a reliable deckhand. *Can I come aboard?*

Henry warmed to him almost immediately. He'd always admired hard workers; his father toiled daily and so did he. He watched Edward scurry around the boat, assisting passengers, helping secure the ropes as it approached the towpaths. Edward would even leap right into the murky water, wading toward the pathways with the boat not far behind. He was enthusiastic, effusive, and clearly very bright. He reminisced with Henry about his days as a schoolboy in Germany. Edward spoke eloquently, especially for a canal worker in rural New York. His voice was mellow and calm.

Soon, Henry Schutt and Edward Rulloff became good friends. When it was time for Henry to return to his family's home, the boatman asked his assistant to join him, to stay at Brookfield Farm and meet the rest of the Schutts. Henry wanted to help his new worker . . . and he thought the family might eventually endorse

Edward in his quest to teach. Henry Schutt was supremely optimistic.

Edward eagerly accepted the offer and they set out toward Dryden, about forty-five miles south of Syracuse.

The month of May in rural upstate New York can be glorious, and in that year of 1842, it was particularly beguiling. In late evening, the clear sky slowly faded from cobalt blue to black. Fireflies created funny little blips in the air as they floated past the willow trees. Constellations spread across the sky. Owls perched on branches of green-leafed maple trees, awaiting their fall transition to orange, yellow, and red.

But nighttime in the country could also be disconcerting, even when traveling alongside a (supposedly) friendly companion. There were few lights—just starlight and moonlight—fewer visitors to encounter, and many strange sounds echoing through the forests lining the grassy trails. It might make a man wonder, as he sat near a total stranger whom he'd suddenly invited into his life and home . . . *What do I really know about this Edward Rulloff, anyway?*

But for now, the pair traveled happily together toward Dryden and Brookfield Farm. No one in that small village could have known how much misery one man would soon cause them.

———

Six Mile Creek is actually twenty miles long, but the people in Dryden didn't quibble over the inaccuracy—it was just another quirky detail about their beloved home. The country village was settled in 1797 and named after English poet John Dryden. After the American Revolution, Dryden became part of the Military

Tract of Central New York—a government program that offered New York soldiers land as a reward for participating in the war. Commissioned and noncommissioned officers each received one lot. Still more veterans qualified for these lots after the War of 1812 and made their way to the small rural village, which was proud of the fact that "battlefield heroes" built the village of Dryden. Among the town's most notable families were the Schutts.

Descended from natives of Holland, the Schutts owned numerous properties in this agricultural community. Dozens of Schutts made Dryden home—they owned lumber mills, clothing mills, and farmland. The family's patriarch, John, the father of riverman Henry, was a pillar of the community. John Schutt co-owned several businesses with his brother, James, who had been a lieutenant during the American Revolutionary War.

John Schutt had himself been a sergeant with the New York militia during the War of 1812; afterward, he became a school-teacher in Dryden, well known for his wide-ranging intellectual arguments over politics or religion. The Schutt brothers had merged their acreage so they could remain neighbors, and by the mid-1800s, there were at least six families of Schutts living just miles from each other in Dryden. They were a convivial, close-knit clan: During the wintertime, they rode horse-drawn sleighs through the town for family visits. They named their children after one another. John's homestead, Brookfield Farm, was a focal point for family dinners, weddings, and funerals. The younger cousins nicknamed John "Uncle Jack" and called his wife, Hannah Krum, "Aunt Netche."

When winter arrived, the snow in rural New York State was spectacular. Bright white flurries covered wooden wagons parked outside bucolic farmhouses in tiny villages like Watkins Glen, Trumansburg, and Lansing. Religion, family, and hard work were the principles that rooted families in those communities. Just about everyone toiled from sunrise to early evening—they farmed wheat and corn, raised cows and sheep, worked inside factories and mills that produced everything from machinery and tobacco to paper and flour.

Men grew rich in the countryside, but it was still a hard life of daily toil. Servants were rare, mostly found only in the upscale homes downstate in Manhattan. Instead, farm families used homegrown labor to keep things running smoothly. Children born on a farm worked from the time they could lug a water bucket. Women were tough and steely, keeping their families fed and their homes in good working order. The Schutts had learned to lean on one another, and the way they saw it, there was no need to move from Dryden—everything they required was there. There were loads of Schutts in the small village, each faithful to the others and fiercely proud of their heritage and accomplishments.

"You see, my dears," patriarch John Schutt would tell his twelve children, "you descended from the moon."

When Edward Rulloff arrived at Brookfield Farm in May 1842 with their son Henry, John and Hannah Schutt welcomed him into their home. They could always use an extra hand around the farm. Rulloff was intelligent, they observed—he had hauled along hefty books on languages and philosophy. As the large Schutt family came to know Edward, they grew fonder of him. They were impressed with the twenty-three-year-old's accomplishments: Edward was well versed in Latin, Greek, Italian, French, German, Spanish, and Portuguese; he was even familiar with Hebrew and Sanskrit. His penmanship was also gorgeous, and he was proficient in belles-lettres, a category of writing that described literature written creatively, instead of being technical or informative. He could recall the Latin names for all the flora and fauna in the county.

But was clever Edward Rulloff perhaps too intellectually curious and scholarly to be satisfied by simple farmwork? John Schutt treated Edward cordially, but with some reservations. *Where was he from again . . . Germany? Could this foreigner really become a reliable farmhand?* Edward explained that he eventually hoped to earn a position as an educator in their village. Despite his reservations, John allowed Edward to work on the farm over the summer of 1842. It must have gone well, because that winter, the family introduced the young man to a neighbor who was willing to rent out one of the rooms of his house to Edward so he could run a small private school, one modeled after the one-room schoolhouse that was gaining popularity in small towns and villages across the newly developing nation.

A teacher in a rural village would often instruct students from several families of various ages in just one room, sometimes in a church or a community building. The lessons would last from 8:00 a.m. to 4:00 p.m., then the students would return to their farm chores. There were two class terms—winter, which ran from November through April; and summer, from May until August. Older boys might attend only the winter session if they were needed for harvesting season.

Edward organized his private school and began offering classes that winter of 1842. The Schutts strongly believed in educating their children, including the young women, and the family enrolled two of the Schutt girls in Edward's classes. Their second-eldest daughter, sixteen-year-old Harriet, was extremely bright as well as a beauty—tall, slender, with long, luxurious, light brown hair, pale skin, and hazel eyes. Some reports called her "flirta-tious," but others simply said she was effortlessly charming and perhaps a little naïve, her affections guileless and worn on her sleeve. But, beyond anything else, she was devoted to her family, especially her parents and her older brothers.

The hallmarks of a respected curriculum in the nineteenth cen-tury were courses in penmanship, reading skills, and arithmetic, all of which Edward taught to his pupils. Harriet seemed to be an enthusiastic learner, and she fastened her attentions on her dash-ing new teacher that winter as Edward piled wood in the small stove, determined to keep her warm. He couldn't help but notice her—almost from the beginning, he complimented her looks the way a man seven years her senior might do in pursuit of a potential young wife—and she smiled and returned his affections.

The fact that Edward was Harriet's schoolteacher was hardly of concern to the Dryden gossips; after all, a girl of sixteen was of marrying age, and one could do much worse than the up-and-coming new stranger in town. Edward was attentive, handsome, and hygienic—the trifecta of desired attributes for most teenage girls in the 1800s hoping to find a husband. Edward's intellectual mien and worldly manners stood in stark contrast to the other men in the village, who seemed coarse and even boring by com-parison.

"He had magnetized her," someone would later say.

By the fall of 1843, more than a year after Edward first met the Schutts, it was clear that Edward and Harriet were determined to be married. Edward appeared to be thriving professionally and seemed perfectly capable of supporting Harriet. In addition to teaching, he was also working for a local drugstore and apprenticing under a botanical doctor in Ithaca, learning how to treat patients with herbs and roots. Edward's stature in the village was on the rise, impressive for a young man who had hopped off a canal boat just the summer before. Yet the family was becoming more uneasy, particularly Harriet's brother Ephraim.

The more they got to know Edward, the more . . . peculiar he seemed. While Henry might have appeared naïve, Ephraim seemed overly suspicious. Perhaps as the oldest brother, Ephraim was more worldly. He was two years older than Henry and a full six years older than Edward. Very little fooled Ephraim Schutt.

While the ladies in the family considered Edward charming, Ephraim found him to be often volatile, as he shifted quickly from offering compliments to muttering complaints. When Edward was talking about something he enjoyed—his love of academia, for instance—his voice was mellow, and his conversation became lively and animated. But when Edward was troubled or something didn't conform to his strict standards of propriety or correctness, his voice distorted to a shrill and harsh tone. His brow grew dark, and his temper became short. There were rumors that he was a harsh, punishing presence with the boys in his schoolhouse. His actions there and elsewhere in the community could be deemed rude, even cruel.

If Harriet became too coquettish with another man, for instance, Edward might scowl at the girl, then switch to a cool dispassion, and when she finally apologized, he would flash a wolfish half grin, pleased that she relented. *What an irritating man,* thought Ephraim. He had no use for a mercurial brother-in-law, especially such a mysterious one. *Where was he from again?* No one really knew.

As the relationship became more significant, the Schutts delicately approached Harriet. *Are you sure he's the one for you?* they asked gently. But she refused to abandon Edward Rulloff, and she became furious at her brothers for trying to sway her.

Ephraim Schutt was exasperated, so he approached Edward and requested character references from his past life, people who might explain his curious personality and provide some comfort to an increasingly alarmed family. *What was his life before he hopped off that canal boat a year before?* Edward did not receive this request well: he was insulted, *outraged* at the notion that his reputation as an upstanding teacher wasn't enough to earn him a place in the family. After all, had his behavior ever been anything but just and proper? Was he not a learned and cultured man?

"Those damned Schutts over there," Edward could be heard to mutter. *They don't think I'm good enough for Harriet,* he'd tell anyone who would listen. But for now, there was no outright antipathy, merely a seething undercurrent of resentment.

In the end, Edward indignantly refused Ephraim's request to supply any character references, to the frustration of his future brother-in-law. The Schutts realized they had no idea who was preparing to marry their daughter. Had they known the truth about who he really was, the Schutts would have quickly banished Edward from Harriet's life, driven him from their small village—they might have even dragged him to a rope hanging from a tree.

That would come later.

———

Back in that jail cell in 1871, Edward quietly eyed Hamilton Freeman, pausing in his narrative of the injustices and indignities perpetrated against him nearly thirty years earlier. *Was the newspaperman believing this story?* Ham seemed interested, but not yet particularly sympathetic, to the plight of the blustering former schoolteacher. Edward knew his only hope was to elicit understanding and even empathy from Ham, to convince the writer that he wasn't the dreadful monster that he was often portrayed to be. Only then would Ham be willing to help him. To Edward, Hamilton's potential book about his life was more than a simple biography—within its pages would be the proof that, even if Edward died at the gallows, his scholarship would be transformative for generations.

Now Edward decided to tell Ham a surprising story—one that he hoped would convince the author that Edward was caring of, even doted on, his family.

It happened less than ten years before his arrival in Dryden, when a cruel schoolmaster had beaten Edward's beloved younger brother to the brink of death during an examination. Edward emotionally detailed how he nursed his brother Rulof back to health single-handedly, and how devastated Edward had been at nearly losing his sibling.

Edward was a convincing, expressive storyteller. As the convict unspooled the story, Ham saw him tear up, overcome with the injustice of his brother's injuries. Ham was struck by the man's seemingly genuine anguish at his sibling's plight, even all these years later. It was clear to Ham that Edward Rulloff cherished his family. It softened him, humanized him in the writer's eyes.

"From the fact of the kindness and sympathy which Edward then manifested for him, a more tender and unusual bond of affection between these brothers was then created, which time has never severed," Ham wrote. It would be challenging for Hamilton to view him as a coldhearted killer now.

The author began struggling to reconcile these two versions

of Edward Rulloff: Was he a kindhearted protector or a vicious killer? Ham was convinced that the two descriptions were impossible to intertwine. Perhaps more conversations would expose Edward's true character, thought Ham.

As Edward settled in to recount more details to the eager Ham, he smiled to himself. Edward Rulloff was such an excellent liar.

——————

It turned out Edward had been lying from the moment he smiled and shook Henry Schutt's hand on that boat in the Erie Canal in May 1842.

Edward Rulloff was a fraud, starting with his name. His real name was John Edward Howard Rulofson, born on July 9, 1819, and he wasn't German. His father, William Rulofson, was a poor Canadian farmer near Saint John in the province of New Brunswick—"a respectable, ordinary man," as Edward recounted to Ham—who died when Edward was just five.

His father's death left Edward's mother to raise three sons alone, except for infrequent input from an uncle when there were financial questions.

Edward grinned as he recalled his love of his mother to Ham. Priscilla Rulofson was perhaps the most crucial influence on his life—the person who cultivated his love of academia. And ambition. Edward's father had been a simple farmer—not particularly bright, successful, or wealthy. But Priscilla Rulofson was brilliant, and she had revered formal education for her children.

"She was a woman of more than ordinary intellect," Edward said to Ham as he smiled, "and I presume that whatever genius for study that any of us boys ever had, we inherited from her."

Edward rarely expressed admiration for women, so he must have really grown to respect his mother and how she reared him. She discouraged Edward from distracting himself with friends—she plied him with books and paper and pens, as well as oil for his lamp. He was very young when he became imbued with a love of learning, thanks to his mother. She insisted that her sons become proper gentlemen, and she had managed to secure tuition for an exclusive boys' academy in Saint John when he was thirteen.

"I am naturally of an ambitious and proud disposition," said Edward to Ham. "My family proper are all so."

In the early nineteenth century, there was no compulsory, public education system in the U.S. or Canada. Families hired governesses for private tutoring or sent older students to private academies—that's if they could afford those options. Edward adored his mother for showing interest in his love of languages. When he returned home to the farm during vacations, he devoured books at night—he slept only because she habitually extinguished his lamp, forcing Edward to rest. She hoped he would become a professional success, unlike his father.

There was little money, but books were an entertainment he could afford. He had few friends, just the company of his brothers. At the Saint John's academy, the courses fueled his love for research, writing, and reading.

"I was thrown among persons who brought the study of language to my attention," Edward said.

He had learned about religion solely from his mother until he picked up a book by the French philosopher Auguste Comte, considered by some as the founder of sociology, the scientific study of human society. Comte argued against metaphysical speculation—his philosophy deliberately rejected conventional religion. For a boy raised in a world steeped in religious iconography and traditions, this was heady stuff. Edward was bewitched by Comte's theories and devoured his books.

"I may be called a materialist or infidel, but I can only believe in what I know," Edward explained to Ham. "All there is of religion is faith."

Edward's parents were members of the Episcopal Church, and Edward claimed that he would become a Sunday school teacher after his graduation. The Bible entranced him, even at the age of fourteen. And he sporadically attended church as he grew older, but the visits were simply an intellectual study. After reading Comte's theories, Edward began moving away from his traditional religious beliefs and started instead to embrace more secular disciplines. He found himself entranced by languages and threw himself wholeheartedly into the study of Greek. Edward marveled over the beauty of the language, and he began to envision a new, different sort of life for himself. One where he could dedicate as much time and effort as he wished to learning about language and its origins.

What did a rural Canadian boy know about a life of the mind? Almost nothing. But scholars, he understood, "had the skill and industry to study and perfect the philosophy of language." Edward envied those men who were gifted with leisure time to perfect their theories, to hone their words to convince other scholars of their intellectual worth. That's what Edward wanted, too. But he feared he might never be afforded that freedom.

Despite those worries, though, academic life was too intoxicating to ignore. Greek language would become the foundation for his groundbreaking theory of the origin of human language; in the decades that followed, Edward would write about this theory in a manuscript that would serve as his sole focus for the remainder of his life—a theory that would ruin so many lives, including his own.

Edward Rulloff graduated from school at age fourteen with a certificate, but no chosen career. His stated desire was simply to be a "gentleman"—but already, a dream was coalescing in his mind. Obsessed with languages and with the life of a man of leisure, Edward dreamed of publishing the etymology of every word in the Greek New Testament, explaining their origins. Edward could do that, he believed, only as a student at a prestigious university under the tutelage of world-renowned liberal arts professors.

Edward wanted to stoke his obsession with learning, hoping to gain the respect that had eluded his father before he died. He hoped to make his mother proud of a son who had been offered little in life compared to his contemporaries. A conventional career choice, like a bookkeeper or clerk, didn't interest Edward. Making ink from oak trees seemed like a bore. Edward desperately needed to be challenged and stimulated almost constantly. A career in academia was the only remedy.

Edward requested a meeting with his uncle, the person who would dictate where the family money might be spent. He asked for tuition money. *No* was the curt response. If Edward refused to commit to an orthodox profession, then he could fund his *own* tuition. Edward was crestfallen.

"I should have gone to a university had I had the opportunity," he told Hamilton. "My father was dead; I was alone in the world; I wanted to be a gentleman. And what else could I do?"

Ham noted the bitterness in Edward's voice, his regret at not protesting more to his uncle. But the older man was stingy and old-fashioned—printmaking was a more admirable profession than academia.

Upon hearing this, Hamilton softened even more. The man sitting cross-legged on the pallet before him was offered virtually no chance at life from the start.

The future could not certainly have looked very brilliant or promising to this poor youth, thought Ham, *under a cloud of some kind as he certainly was, whose happiness had in some way been blighted.*

The brilliant student faced life with no real direction—dangerous circumstances for a driven young man with no role models. Edward's uncle refused to support him financially, despite his pleas. University life was not in Edward's future, all because of one man. Edward vowed to never allow someone to control his destiny again.

He mustered himself and soon searched for a job before finally settling down as a clerk in a well-known law office in Saint John. It afforded him just a bit of leisure time, a few hours a week that he used to immerse himself in chemistry, botany, Greek, and Latin. Edward also learned quite a bit about the legal system, paying special attention to criminal law. After a year, Edward left the firm for a job as a store clerk, and that change of jobs signaled the beginning of troubling behavior.

In 1839, when he was twenty years old, someone set a fire at the dry goods store in Saint John where Edward worked. Arson was the cause, but the young clerk—with character beyond reproach—wasn't suspected. Soon after, another fire burned at the store's new location, and then items began to go missing, including expensive cloth. When the merchants spotted Edward wearing a posh suit made from the stolen material, they confronted the young clerk.

Confess and I won't have you arrested, threatened his former boss. *No, I'll do whatever I like* was Edward's stubborn response. He chose pride over prudence, and he paid heavily for it. Police arrested Edward, and he was quickly tried, then convicted of theft. Edward spent two years in the Saint John jail, and the trajectory of his future suddenly shifted. If he hadn't gone to prison, perhaps the twenty-two-year-old would have remained in Canada, close to his family. He might have saved enough money for tuition for a proper university, to fulfill his dream of maturing in academia.

It was not to be.

———

Ham Freeman dutifully took notes as he listened, captivated, by Edward Rulloff's tale. Ham was already framing this chapter in his mind—the orphaned child, the frustrated academic pursuits of a brilliant mind—and the journalist suspected that these experiences all informed Edward's actions later in life. Did his troubled youth make Edward's adult missteps seem . . . if not *forgivable*, at least understandable? Perhaps Ham saw something of himself in the ambitions and intellectual yearnings of a young Edward? *There but for the grace of God go I?*

Edward sensed the effect his words and story were having on the young author. He could see the empathy etched on Ham's face. He continued his story.

After serving his prison sentence for theft, Edward Rulloff was released in the fall of 1841 and promptly disappeared. There was no systemized method of identification in Canada (and of course, nothing that could track individuals across international borders), so Edward found himself free to reinvent himself completely in whatever way he wished—and he did. Edward abandoned his family in New Brunswick, including his beloved brother Rulof, and traveled to America. After a brief stint in New York at a commercial school learning bookkeeping and penmanship, Edward traveled upstate, penniless and bitter, desperate to remake his life. In less than a year, twenty-three-year-old John Edward Howard Rulofson became Edward Howard Rulloff, the German Canadian drifter with eloquent speech and shifty morals. Soon he would step on that passenger boat moored on the Erie Canal in Syracuse and introduce himself to Henry Schutt. And from that moment forward, the Schutt family would not know a moment's peace.

2

Between the Lakes

Instantly the spirit of hell awoke in me and raged. With a transport of glee, I mauled the unresisting body, tasting delight from every blow . . .
—Robert Louis Stevenson,
Strange Case of Dr. Jekyll and Mr. Hyde, 1886

Edward Rulloff's marriage to Harriet Schutt took place in a beautiful winter ceremony at her parents' farmhouse in Dryden on New Year's Eve 1843, about a year and a half after they first met. The flames of candles sputtered as the fireplace roared, warming the modest farmhouse. Snowy owls stalked their prey from atop barn roofs. Wind whipped across sheets of ice on the ground, dragging powdered snow into swirls.

There were already signs of discontent in the relationship—cracks that would only deepen and widen in the days, months, and years to come. But by this point, the marriage seemed inevitable. Even though Harriet's family was now having serious reservations about her groom-to-be.

"Marry him she had promised and marry him she would,"

typed his biographer, Hamilton Freeman, "and so the parents gave a reluctant consent."

Various Schutts mingled throughout the house, including Harriet's eleven siblings, her brothers William and Ephraim among them. As they milled around the parlor and kitchen, Edward glanced around the rooms—none of *his* family was there. The most influential woman in his life, his mother, Priscilla, had died at age forty-four, the same month he arrived in Dryden. Edward felt some regret that he hadn't bothered to tell his younger brother Rulof about the nuptials; he would have liked to show off his seventeen-year-old bride. Harriet was certainly quite beautiful that day, luminous in her white silk wedding dress. But as Edward admitted to Ham, he knew they weren't beginning their marriage on a strong foundation.

"There never was much of any courtship or love about it," Edward said of his relationship with the young Harriet. "We rather slid into it."

No one seemed pleased about the wedding ceremony, particularly the bride's family. In the eighteen months since they first met Edward, the Schutts had grown suspicious, fretful, and even antagonistic toward him. John Schutt, the family patriarch, told his sons that Harriet was lost now, that he had "washed his hands of the crime, if she chose to marry that foreigner."

Her family now openly scorned Edward, and he had grown to resent them deeply. Edward cringed when the Schutts joked about how he joined the family.

"They thought that they could make a tool, a sort of servant of me, because I was poor, and they 'picked me up on the canal,' as they said," Edward told Ham.

The Schutts assigned him to menial farm chores, even though he believed he was brighter than them all. "I was their superior in every way," he said to Ham proudly. "I would not have stayed with them if I had not been poor and had no other place to go."

Edward told Ham that he had grown tired of the family's nasty remarks about his background and their unkind reception. Not only had Harriet's brothers consistently shamed him over his humble beginnings, Edward claimed, but he had also found himself trapped in the middle of their personal disputes.

"The different members of the family, especially the boys, would sometimes make me their confidant of their troubles and little grievances with the others," Edward complained. "And if I sympathized either way, or expressed an opinion, I was sure to get into trouble."

Edward insisted to Ham that there seemed to be no pleasing the Schutts.

"I have never forgiven their taunts and insults, both behind my back, and to my face," Edward told Ham. "They called me a pauper and made fun of my awkward manners. I knew I was better than they, and that my family was far superior." Still, allegiance to a family as established and respectable as the Schutts had its advantages for a young man in that part of the world. Edward was determined to make a go of it.

Hamilton noticed Edward's sensitivity when he described how poorly the Schutts had treated him. Ham sensed shame around his backstory. A pity, thought Ham, that such a bright man could be steeped in such self-doubt. The author lamented Edward's poor luck in life.

But was Edward really showing true vulnerability to the young journalist? People with psychopathy, researchers say, are often gifted at emulating a wide range of emotions—including embarrassment or tenderness—if they think it will help them gain an advantage in any given situation. Even the savviest psychiatrist might find it challenging to detect deception in a high-functioning psychopathic individual. That ability to echo feelings can be mistaken by victims for authenticity when it is simply manipulation . . . and it's a dangerous tool for psychopaths like Edward Rulloff.

On their wedding day, Edward's determination to marry Harriet quelled his pride . . . for now. He gazed at her as she smiled with her parents. But he noticed someone else admiring her, too. Her cousin Dr. Henry W. Bull stood near the family, quietly watching Harriet. Edward grumbled as the physician frequently strode around the property, smiling and chatting—he detested Dr. Bull. He was altogether too affectionate with the Schutt women, a blatant sign of disrespect toward their husbands, Edward thought. But Henry Bull was embraced by the family in a way that Edward resented . . . and possibly envied. The older women doted on Bull, and the younger women were outwardly flirtatious with the dashing doctor. As Edward paced the kitchen that cold winter wedding day, he watched as Harriet, still in her wedding gown, received what he called an "intimate" kiss from Dr. Bull while they lingered inside the pantry.

Dr. Bull called on the Schutt women frequently, and he often greeted each with a kiss on arrival to the farm. Edward was incensed as he watched the gesture during each visit during their courtship, but the physician's clandestine kiss with Edward's wife on his own wedding day was unique. Dr. Bull was secluded in the pantry with Harriet Schutt, now Harriet *Rulloff*. Edward silently sulked and then slunk away, not uttering a word.

Ham Freeman listened closely to Edward's tale, sensing that this incident was a turning point in the relationship between Edward and his new wife. Ham's pencil scribbled notes in the jail cell as the killer's eyes grew black and his fists clenched. *What happened then?* Ham asked.

"I smothered my rage," Edward said.

Ham gingerly asked if it were possible that the kiss was innocent, a sign of affection between relatives. Edward scoffed. Dr. Bull was handsome, wealthy, and unmarried, a compelling threat to a new husband during an era when wooing cousins wasn't unusual.* He was also older: Dr. Bull was thirty-one while Edward was just twenty-four. Did Edward have good reason to be concerned?

"I imagined that my wife liked him better than she did me," he complained to Ham. "I was disconsolate—I was wild. All sorts of ideas and plans passed through my head. After a few days, matters grew worse. I resolved to put an end to her existence and mine."

Ham retired to his home in Binghamton that night and, as he looked over his notes from the day, he considered Edward's jarring reaction to what appeared to be an innocuous kiss.

"The peace and happiness of this newly married couple," wrote Ham, "was soon embittered by that green-eyed monster, jealousy, which both when founded on facts, and in a diseased and willing imagination, has so often incited so many domestic woes and tragedies."

Hamilton certainly didn't hold Harriet responsible for Edward's rage, but he also didn't absolve her.

---

* In fact, it was legal for first cousins to marry in all states of the union until the Civil War era, and before the mid-1800s marriage between first cousins was often encouraged, especially among the upper classes, to strengthen family bonds and preserve wealth.

"Mrs. Rulloff may have been, and probably was, as pure as the driven snow," thought Ham, "and only at most a little imprudent or coquettish in her actions, as country girls sometimes are apt to be."

The author studied his notes each night—he considered Harriet's probable flirtation with her cousin, along with Edward's unhinged reactions to innocuous circumstances, and he drew a conclusion, one that pointed to a specific source.

"Whether Rulloff had any cause or reason to be jealous he *was*," wrote Ham, "and that demon having once taken possession of his soul he could not rid himself of it, increasing in intensity until it drove him on to be the fiend he has been represented."

Jealousy was to blame for much of this, concluded Ham after the first few interviews—it had caused Edward Rulloff to lose all perspective and wallow in self-doubt and pity. Experts say that many psychopaths are also diagnosed with narcissism. Narcissistic behavior often masks almost debilitating insecurities.

"Narcissists' attempts to elevate themselves at the expense of others may actually be the result of an underlying sense of insecurity, emptiness and unstable self-esteem that depends too much on status or recognition from others," reads a 2021 study titled *Narcissism Through the Lens of Performative Self-Elevation.* "They [narcissists] may have unstable self-esteem, be over-sensitive to criticism and rejection," according to the study, "and may have anxiety about their relationships and how well-liked they are."*

Insecurity and jealousy were often at the root of Edward

---

* It's a pattern that plays out among narcissistic serial killers studied today—from Ted Bundy to Dennis Rader to Edmund Kemper.

Rulloff's violent outbursts—much of his behavior appeared very narcissistic, such as his reaction to a kind gesture from the minister.

Harriet Schutt's family may not have known about the kiss she shared with their cousin on her wedding day, but they did note her husband's antipathy toward other men. The groom had fumed earlier when the minister of his wedding leaned over and kissed Harriet, right after their ceremony. The next day, Harriet's brother William married his fiancée, Amelia, and the same minister kissed her, too, after that ceremony. Edward turned to a friend and mumbled that if he were Harriet or Amelia, he would have *murdered* the minister for being disrespectful. He was outraged that they were not themselves offended.

"He was very angry," said a friend. "He said he would never take her anywhere again."

Privately, Edward's jealous behavior was already exposed. Shortly after Harriet's wedding, Amelia found Harriet sobbing in the upstairs bedroom after a vicious argument with her new husband. Harriet was so upset by the confrontation that she didn't eat for two days, and the Schutts worried that she might have made a grave mistake. Now that they were married, Edward seemed determined to control every aspect of Harriet's life . . . and her death. Just days after his wedding, Edward said to Ham, he was already plotting how he might kill Harriet and then himself.

"I did procure a vial of poison," Edward told Ham matter-of-factly. "And I did attempt to make Harriet take it first, and then I intended to dose myself, and we would die together, but she screamed so as to attract attention, and I pretended that I was only in fun."

Edward decided to suppress his rage and prayed that suave Dr.

Bull would finally stop his visits. Of course, he didn't. The close-knit Schutt clan was always traveling between one another's houses, and Dr. Henry Bull was no exception. When the physician would arrive and offer his greetings, Edward would abruptly excuse himself. His delicate ego was threatened by the physician's presence at every family event. Edward's suffering marriage became what modern psychologists label a "stressor," a circumstance that serves as a trigger for violent reactions from unstable patients, and in the spring of 1844, Edward Rulloff was the epitome of "unstable."

All this time—both before and then directly after the wedding—Edward and his new bride were living at the Schutts' Brookfield Farm homestead. The small home was a simple, rectangular design, less than one thousand square feet, with two fireplaces. A large, wooden barn stood just a few hundred feet away. It was warm, cozy, and convivial . . . but obviously now too small for the growing clan (and Edward's growing animosity). Once he and Harriet were married, and Edward's true nature began to be revealed, the Schutts began to make their concerns known.

At times, Edward described his bride to Hamilton as "giddy" and "light-headed"—but she was also spirited. Harriet wasn't shy about sparring with Edward, and he seemed to enjoy her challenges. But what was growing immediately clear to everyone around them was the lack of intimacy in their relationship, an absence of emotional connection. For this, Edward blamed Harriet's interfering family, as well as his wife's whining. It was enough to drive a man mad, explained Edward.

"Harriet was young," explained Edward to Ham, almost pleading with him to understand his point of view on the matter. "She was easily influenced, and her people rather prejudiced her against me. You know when a girl is much attached to her own family, they can very easily prejudice her against him if they have no respect for her husband.

"It was a perfect hell on earth to me," he concluded.

It was time to leave Brookfield Farm and take Harriet away from her family and the amorous Dr. Bull. He packed up their modest belongings, carefully wrapping his precious books and journals, and moved his wife away from Dryden. He hoped that the move might draw her closer to him, he told Ham.

"So, I procured a humble home," Edward explained. "An old store to live in, over in Lansing."

———

Edward explained to Ham that in the early spring of 1844, shortly after their wedding, he'd secured and began renovating their new home in Lansing, New York (a town about ten miles from Dryden). Edward said that Harriet was delighted with the prospect of setting up housekeeping on her own. The house was a converted feedstore with a tin roof and a row of high windows and loads of space; Harriet was relieved to finally be able to organize her home as she spent months selecting furniture and supplies.

Edward described in loving, lavish detail how Harriet decorated the house—it seemed idyllic, and they both seemed blissful. The neighbors found them to be a charming couple. *Would Ham be drawn into Edward's splendid version of his marriage?* He seemed to be.

"For a time all went, 'merry as a marriage bell' with this young couple in Lansing," typed Ham. "She made no complaints of ill-usage, nor did the neighbors observe any. . . . he appeared, for the first time in his life, to be getting forehanded with the world."

It's not hard to imagine that Edward's disposition must have softened once on his own, far removed from the Schutts and their scrutiny. But any empathy or affection or humanity he offered was always quickly rescinded. Edward was hoping to contrast for Ham his troubled life with the Schutts to their peaceful lives without the family's meddling—it seemed to be working. The author scribbled notes that framed Edward as an affectionate husband who simply needed to spirit away his wife for her to realize his worth.

Edward boasted to Ham of growing professional success in his studies of botanical medicine with local doctor William Stone, who taught Edward age-old methods of treating diseases with herbs and other organic medicines. Medical treatment in nineteenth-century America was a battleground between traditional, formally educated physicians and alternative practitioners with no such official schooling (relying instead on time-honored family remedies). Dr. Henry Bull, Harriet's cousin, was a traditional medical doctor—so Edward and Dr. Bull were at odds personally *and* professionally.

"With this physician [Dr. Bull], Rulloff, who was an advocate of the new botanical method, had hot and bitter disputes as to the merits of the two systems," noted Ham.

Edward sneered in his cell as he described Bull as "an ass, who pretended to be a regular physician." The Schutt cousin stirred an insecurity within Edward like none before. Edward relentlessly criticized Dr. Bull for his newfangled views on medical treatments . . . but privately, Edward feared that his own botanical concoctions were worthless.

"I really did not have much if any confidence in my skill as a physician," he said sheepishly. Edward was secretly becoming convinced that his mentor, Dr. Stone, was a swindler, and now by extension he was, too. He didn't display any moral compunction about the potential deception at the time. But when Edward recounted the tale to Ham decades later, he expressed shame, not because he bilked patients of their money but because he had relegated himself to a profession that was beneath him.

"Damn it, a fraud! I was a quack doctor too, and to tell you the truth, I was ashamed of myself," Edward cried to Ham. "I only undertook it as a flyer until I could get into something else that was more profitable and legitimate."

Despite his avowed loathing of the profession, Edward's reputation as a physician at that time was exemplary—he treated many grateful patients in Lansing. In fact, things initially seemed to be looking up for Edward once he had put some distance between himself and the Schutt clan. Edward's character, according to townspeople at the time, appeared to be beyond reproach, at least at first. He was also gaining a prominence as a scholar who spoke a variety of foreign languages with ease; Edward honed those skills by paying for lessons in Latin and Greek with older teachers in Ithaca.

He was learning other subjects as well, like the emerging science of phrenology—the detailed study of the size and shape of a person's skull.

Edward Rulloff not only studied phrenology; he also hired other phrenologists to examine *his* skull and issue a report. Their results revealed that he was remarkably intelligent, and according to those "experts," he was certainly a moral man. (Lucky for Edward.) Edward was examined by one final phrenologist *after* his death—and that "expert" came to a very different conclusion.

Edward became so well versed in phrenology that local schools paid for his lectures on the topic. Between this extra work and all his other work, he now had spending money, a luxury he hadn't heretofore experienced. In an uncharacteristically kind gesture, he used his additional funds to shower Harriet with small gifts and tokens of affection. One present he liked to offer her was an occasional orange—an exotic and expensive fruit, especially in upstate New York. Maybe there was some hope for this couple after all? Edward's future seemed positive, and his prospects might be improving since leaving Canada.

Yet despite everything seemingly going well in his life—his marriage, his emerging medical practice, his growing economic security—there was a gloom grafted to Edward that he was unable to shake.

"I was very unhappy, and discontented," he told Ham. "I was dissatisfied with the life I was leading, and with my prospects. I resolved at one time to raise the means and go west with my family."

Edward still yearned for an academic life, preferably one in a large city where he could find intellectual debates and stimulating collaborations. The rubes in rural New York never understood the value of a formal education, he thought—which was ironic because he didn't have one himself. Edward began saving some of his income, concealing funds from Harriet in hopes that she would be pleased when one day he might be able to offer her a new life; she would certainly be pleased to be the wife of an esteemed academic, instead of being the wife of a small-town doctor who flimflammed patients.

Edward's anguish over his waning academic prospects eventually poisoned his home life. Despite the distance from her family, their presence was never far from his mind. Whenever Harriet asked him about making the ten-mile visit to Dryden, Edward would dramatically fling open a suitcase, hurl clothes inside, slam it shut, and stomp out the door, threatening to leave her. And the specter of Dr. Bull was also still looming in their marriage. During one of his threats to leave, Edward snatched her beautiful silk wedding dress and frantically wadded it into a ball, screaming that he wouldn't leave it behind because "in three weeks she would have it on and be with Dr. Bull."

At eighteen, Harriet was barely an adult. But she had selected her path, and she accepted that her job now was to please her husband—as unreasonable as he might be at times. Such was the norm for nineteenth-century brides.

"The man is not created for the woman . . . but the woman for the man," preached one contemporary guide for wives. "How much soever of his own natural rights the husband is required to yield, the concessions of the wife are still more numerous, and justify the inevitable conclusion that matrimony involves, as a matter of the plainest necessity, not only a greater degree of dependence on her part, but also a species of inferiority."

Ephraim, Harriet's oldest brother, had of course recognized that his sister and her new husband were having difficulties even before the wedding—and his concerns were only elevated now. He'd never fully trusted his brother-in-law as some of the other Schutts had, but they were married now—she was Edward's, legally. Edward had dragged Harriet to Lansing, but when the Schutts were allowed to visit with her, Edward refused to offer them privacy. He ordered her around, and she seemed compliant much of the time, but dismal. Of course, Edward told Ham none of this during their interviews.

Ephraim and the others missed Harriet deeply, and he relished their infrequent trips. One afternoon, Ephraim heard her soft cries from behind a closed door at Brookfield Farm. He pushed into the room and glared at Edward, searching for an explanation. Her husband was standing near Harriet as tears ran down her face. Edward seemed to be struggling with self-control. Ephraim snapped at him, demanding to know why he seemed determined to make his wife miserable.

"He made no particular reply," remembered Ephraim. "I said to him that his conduct was very strange."

Ephraim adopted a very serious tone—his mood darkened to match Edward's somber attitude.

"Leave her to us," Ephraim demanded, if he couldn't treat Harriet with respect.

Edward seemed to sulk, resentful that he was being issued an ultimatum from one of the Schutts.

"He finally concluded to stay," said Ephraim.

If only Edward had just agreed to abandon Harriet, then his fate might have been different. Perhaps he would have borrowed a horse and wagon, loaded up his books and papers, and moved somewhere far away. Edward could have been free to pursue his lofty academic dreams, the ones that were clearly waning in the countryside. But Edward Rulloff stayed in Lansing and maintained a desperate grip on his wife and his in-laws—to his (and the Schutts') everlasting regret.

———

The horseback trip from Dryden to Ithaca was lovely—ten miles of picturesque fields filled with wheat and cotton, spotted with rolling hills and patches of forest. Maples fraternized with pines and spruces along the quiet trail. The footsteps of the horse were nearly silent, save the occasional clicks of its hooves as they kicked errant stones.

It was a time when a philosophically inclined rider might meditate on his choices in life or ponder future decisions or simply appreciate the peace. Unfortunately for William Schutt, that was not the sort of journey he would enjoy in July 1844, when his hysterical brother-in-law joined him on a horseback ride for a visit at William's home in Ithaca.

William was the fourth-oldest Schutt and the brother closest in age to Harriet; she was nineteen and William was twenty-six, the same age as Edward. And that similarity in age might be why William and Edward seemed to get along well. Unlike Ephraim, who presented as aloof at times to Edward, William appeared genuine. Both men had been married six months earlier and just twenty-four hours apart. It was William's new bride, Amelia, who had received the controversial kiss from the cheeky minister on New Year's Day, according to Edward. If Edward could identify with *any* Schutt, it would be William. But this would be a trying day for Harriet's weary brother. William half listened as Edward obsessed for hours over enduring six months of Dr. Bull's inappropriate flirtations with his wife.

"He thought Dr. Bull and his wife had had intercourse together," remembered William. "He said he thought he should leave her."

William seemed shocked by Edward's accusation, but then quickly settled into disbelief at his brother-in-law's self-doubts. Edward despised Dr. Bull—"He hated him," William remembered— and now Edward was beginning to resent his wife as well. *She's a sinner*, he exclaimed to William. Edward had recently spotted

Harriet and Dr. Bull at a mill near the Schutt farm. They were standing intimately, clearly trying to be discreet—it enraged him. Edward crept over and eavesdropped. He claimed he heard Dr. Bull wooing his wife.

"Harriet, you have been seduced. And I think you might be again," Dr. Bull reportedly crooned to Harriet. She apparently laughed it off, but Edward was livid.

What was William going to do about this? Edward demanded.

The answer: nothing. After all, with the Schutt family, blood was thicker than water. And despite Edward marrying into the family, Dr. Bull was a cousin by blood and therefore beyond reproach. William refused to exclude Dr. Bull from the farm—and he offered Edward little sympathy, even if they were friends.

Dr. Bull *was* a flirt, William admitted. The physician insisted on also greeting William's wife, Amelia, with a kiss. His younger sister, Jane, and even their mother were recipients.

"I think Dr. Bull kissed them all around," said William.

But it was simply an innocent social ritual—and a frequent one, because Dr. Bull lived less than four miles from the family's farm. As Edward glowered, William assured his brother-in-law that he was overreacting. *How could William defend Dr. Bull and abandon his own brother-in-law?* Edward was incredulous at William's disloyalty after how much Edward had contributed to the family.

William believed his brother-in-law's behavior was foolish and irrational, and he tried to pacify him. But Edward was apoplectic with anger, threatening to leave Harriet in a storm of expletives the likes of which the countryside had never heard. William braced for a confrontation as they arrived in Ithaca. And then suddenly, Edward's mood shifted.

"That evening, he thought he would go back to her," sighed

William. Edward's vacillating feelings over his marriage were exhausting. The gifted teacher, who at twenty-six years old had dazzled college professors with his study of languages, struggled to pacify his own anxiety and insecurity.

Never leave my side, he demanded.

———

But it wasn't only Dr. Bull who stoked Edward's anger. He had plenty of simmering resentment and violence even without the dapper doctor stirring it up, as Harriet's sister Jane observed a few months later. Harriet and Jane were only two years apart (they had both been Edward's students when he taught at the Dryden schoolhouse a few years earlier). Jane had also lived with the newlyweds at her family's farm before Edward had whisked her sister away in early 1844, so she had spent quite a bit of time with her brother-in-law—and Jane found Edward tolerable much of the time. He seemed to provide well for her sister: a nice home, a stable life, and a rising income. But Jane's opinion of Edward Rulloff would soon darken.

About a month after the couple was married, Edward listened quietly as Jane and her sister chatted in the Rulloffs' small kitchen in Lansing. Harriet lifted a heavy marble pestle and poured some peppercorns into a large stone mortar. The pestle was intimidating—it weighed about twenty pounds. A pestle was a crucial instrument for a doctor who prescribed herbs, so it was one of Edward's most important tools. Harriet pounded the peppercorns, preparing them for dinner as she chatted with Jane. Edward fidgeted nearby, eyeing his wife's feeble technique with the massive pestle.

"She didn't pound it fine enough to suit him," recalled Jane. "He proposed to do it for her."

Edward lunged toward the pestle, but Harriet pushed back, insisting that she finish the job—a wife should always appease the most finicky of husbands, according to her mother. Frustrated, Edward snatched the pestle, wrestled it away from her, and then flung it against his wife's forehead. Harriet staggered and shook.

"It knocked her back several steps," remembered Jane.

Edward stared at Harriet for a moment, seemingly shocked at how hard he had hit her. He examined the contusion left on her forehead as she steadied herself. Jane stood in silence as Edward began to offer an array of apologies to Harriet as she tried to recover.

"He said he didn't intend to strike her so hard," said Jane.

Harriet glared at him—she knew her husband so well. *You did it on purpose,* she snapped back. Edward ignored her accusation and she refused to accept his apology. Jane was quiet as the husband and wife turned their backs. Their unstable marriage was slipping into open hostility. Soon, Jane Schutt's reaction to her brother-in-law shifted from concern to terror when she heard details of another violent encounter between the couple.

Three months after their marriage—before they moved into the renovated store—the Rulloffs roomed at a boardinghouse over a tailor shop in Ithaca. It was a lovely, sunny day—Mary Schutt, Harriet's eleven-year-old sister, had been visiting, and their brother William was scheduled to pick her up before nightfall so the girl wouldn't have to walk back to Brookfield Farm alone. But William was running late, and Edward was furious. He wanted young Mary to leave immediately, a punitive demand leveled at the family for being thoughtless. Edward maintained that the Schutts had "taken advantage of him for years," and he was done being kind.

Angrily shoving his young sister-in-law toward the stairs, Edward demanded that the girl walk the ten miles home to Dryden alone in the dark. Harriet refused to let Mary leave. Edward stared at his wife and ordered her to follow him to the upstairs bedroom. In the horrible fight that followed, blows were dealt on both sides, the specter of Dr. Bull was raised yet again, and the threats culminated in a chilling statement from Edward.

"Rulloff said that before he would leave her to another, he would serve her as Clark did his wife," remembered Jane O'Brien, the landlady. "He would chop her as fine as mincemeat."

About twelve years earlier, in 1832, shoemaker Guy Carlton Clark's wife, Fanny, had begged deputies in Ithaca to arrest her husband after he nearly knocked her eye out during a fight. A habitual wife beater, Clark vowed, "I'll kill you for this." Released after serving ten days in jail, he hacked her to death with an ax. At his trial, Clark declared, "I swore I would kill the damned bitch, and I have killed her."

Edward smirked at Harriet and at Jane O'Brien, vowing to follow in the infamous Clark's footsteps. It was a dreadful declaration, but one that Harriet didn't seem to take seriously because of Edward's ongoing pattern of histrionics and manipulation. Edward had become more violent as his relationship with Harriet deteriorated, but while this escalation was disturbing, it was not necessarily a marker for psychopathy, according to researchers.

"Psychopaths . . . are not always physically or sexually violent," writes psychologist Scott Johnson. "They take advantage of others but may do so without violence."

Dr. Craig Neumann, an expert on psychopathy, explains that there are two categories of psychopaths. "There's a manipulative type of psychopaths, who instead of using overt aggression and violence will tend to use cunning and deception," he told me. "The manipulative psychopath may be likely to fundamentally ruin your financial future. And there's also an aggressive type of psychopath." This is the type who lashes out physically when challenged.

But some psychopaths can be both manipulative *and* violent—in fact, that versatility helps them achieve their goals. Edward Rulloff depended on a varied menu of emotional abuse and physical abuse to control Harriet. When his wife didn't react to his threats or his overt physical violence, he flopped down on his knees with his forehead resting on the bed, pivoting to psychological warfare. He wailed, he wheedled, he pleaded. To Harriet, her husband seemed exhausted. Something turned in her. This time, as had happened every time before, Harriet relented. She sat near him and laid her hand gently on his dark hair.

"You're mine forever, dear Edward, whether you live with me or not," she sweetly told him.

The anger defused, Edward stumbled downstairs and requested a horse and carriage so he, Harriet, and Mary could return to the family farm. As they pulled away from the home, Jane O'Brien prayed for their safe journey, but Edward was gone just briefly. He returned to the boardinghouse only a few hours later—alone—after being ejected from Brookfield Farm by William Schutt. His brother-in-law had spent the last year trying to be cordial. But he was finally fed up with Edward's constant jealousy over Dr. Bull, and William was furious after hearing about Edward's callous demands that young Mary walk miles alone in the dark, and the subsequent argument. William had had enough. Edward was in effect banished . . . at least for a short time. But while William would eventually relent, Edward's resentment lingered.

Jane O'Brien sensed Edward's simmering anger. "He said he sometimes felt like destroying the whole family," remembered O'Brien. Edward Rulloff had offered the people around him many lies for several years, but this was not one of them.

Sometime after this carriage incident, Harriet returned to Edward, and the two attempted to rebuild their marriage and their life together. But friends believed that the relationship between the two was never the same.

"She never appeared as cheerful as usual," said Mrs. O'Brien. Edward resented Harriet's entire clan, but he was especially disgusted with William Schutt, whom he blamed above all others (excepting, perhaps, Dr. Bull) for the alienation of his wife's affections. But as 1844 turned to 1845, the family reached an uneasy détente, and after years of discord, the Rulloffs finally had some pleasant news to share with the Schutt clan. On April 12, 1845, Harriet gave birth to a baby they named Priscilla, after Edward's deceased mother. The little girl seemed to soften the couple—there were fewer arguments, at least publicly. One disturbing note to consider: Harriet became pregnant just two months *after* Edward tried to kill her and she seemed pleased with the prospect of parenting a child with him. It was just another example of how Edward must have manipulated her into compliance. He understood that a baby would help him tighten his control over his wife. Harriet was unlikely to abandon him, because she would do so in disgrace.

Shortly after Priscilla was born, Edward and Harriet brought her to visit her uncle William and aunt Amelia in Ithaca. William's wife was also pregnant, with a little girl due in a month.

The families seemed to be growing closer, thanks to frequent visits and William's benevolence, but Edward struggled to ignore his resentment toward William, whom he still viewed as disloyal for refusing to ban Dr. Bull from Brookfield Farm. Sure enough, Dr. Bull was due to visit William's home later that day. Edward was grim as he waited for his wife's cousin to arrive.

"Rulloff sat at the window looking out and took up the child and told Harriet to go with him," remembered William. "He didn't want her to meet Dr. Bull."

Edward's insecurities were exhausting, and William pleaded with him that day.

"I then said I was tired of hearing about these troubles," said William, "and if he couldn't omit the subject, I didn't want him to come."

William issued an ultimatum—if Edward couldn't resolve his concerns about Dr. Bull, his brother-in-law would no longer be welcomed. William refused to listen to any further complaints—he would stop placating Edward amid these ridiculous accusations about an affair between Edward's wife and her cousin. That conversation became critical because, within weeks, William Schutt's wife and baby would be dead.

———

The noise was appalling—a guttural, violent cough that seemed to drag on for hours. Amelia Schutt was a petite, meek woman, but today she sounded like a wounded animal, desperate for the suffering to end. She was also panicked over the health of her newborn daughter, Amille, who was just a few days old.

Amelia's husband, William, was frantic. She seemed to be suffering from "childbed fever," a common bacterial infection that was a dreaded and often fatal affliction of new mothers. William's mother, Hannah, blamed Amelia's illness on "going out too soon" after childbirth—it was just as good a reason as any for a postpartum death. Whatever the cause, Amelia's health was in steep decline and William was desperate for help. Luckily, he knew someone with the requisite knowledge of plants, herbs, and healing.

Sadly, it was his brother-in-law, Edward Rulloff.

Edward, Harriet, and little Priscilla were nearby, chatting with Harriet's parents in Dryden during a three-week visit when William arrived, panicked and desperate. Edward stood by and listened as William wailed over his wife and child. *Come help them,* he begged his brother-in-law the botanical physician.

Hannah Schutt assured her son that Edward would visit Amelia in Ithaca the next day. Hannah was under no illusions about her son-in-law. Like the rest of her family, she loathed him—he seemed to make her daughter miserable, and this was a disturbing revelation from a woman who was inherently tough but famously kindhearted, always willing to help someone down on their luck. Still, Harriet's discontent was hard for a mother to ignore.

"I saw that she was unhappy," remembered Hannah.

She had hoped during this visit to convince Harriet to return home with her new child and leave her menacing husband in Lansing. But when William arrived, desperate for medical help (and Edward was the only one with the skills to assist), Hannah realized that she, William, and the whole family had to trust Edward. At William's request, and against her better judgment, Hannah accompanied Edward to Amelia's bedside.

Why did they put Amelia's life in the hands of a man they all loathed?

"I felt anxious for her to get well," said Hannah bitterly.

As the horses trotted along, Edward turned to his mother-in-law and issued a startling statement about William's wife.

"It was wholly indifferent to him whether she got well—that William had misused him about Dr. Bull, and that thing would yet mount to the shedding of blood," Hannah recalled. The fact that Edward would think such a thing at a desperate hour—let alone say it to Amelia's mother-in-law—was a window into just how frayed relations had become between Edward and the Schutt clan. But Hannah Schutt had long ago grown accustomed to her son-in-law's melodramatics, so she ignored it as she escorted Edward to care for Amelia and her newborn.

Edward treated Amelia first with a vial of botanical medicines. And now the baby was also desperately ill—little Amille's body was suddenly racked with convulsions, and as she jerked and heaved, the family begged Edward for assistance. Edward fed the baby some powdered herbs in milk, but despite his ministrations, both Amelia and her infant became sicker. William was beside himself with grief, but Edward ordered him to keep calm. All they could do was sit there and watch as both William's wife and his daughter began to slip away.

The baby died first, on June 3, 1845, and then Amelia passed away two days later. The grief was too much for William—he was devastated. As the reality of their deaths settled, Hannah Schutt, the stalwart matriarch of the family, turned to Edward for an explanation and then braced herself for another disturbing conversation.

"He said it was strange that I had raised so many children without losing any," she remembered, "but my gray hairs would yet go down in sorrow to the grave." Shocked, Hannah watched her son-in-law closely and asked him what, exactly, he meant by that.

"William's wife and child have gone," Edward declared with a smirk; "who will go next?"

He then offered his mother-in-law a vindictive prophecy about Harriet and his own two-month-old daughter, Priscilla.

"Harriet and her babe will go next," he snarled.

It was a cruel statement to a grieving grandmother. But Hannah sensed something more behind his callous words—anger. She realized that Edward was still furious with William for banishing him from the farm earlier that year. She had hoped that the relationship had healed—clearly, it had not.

But astoundingly, despite his incriminating words, the Schutts apparently didn't suspect that Edward had poisoned Amelia and Amille. In the nineteenth century, mothers and infants died in great numbers from a host of poorly understood causes; murder was not usually among them. Their obituaries were printed in the *Ithaca Journal* under the heading: DIED.

"In this village on the 3rd, Amille Rodolphe, infant of Wm. H. and Amelia Schutt. On the fifth, Amelia, wife of Wm. H. Schutt, aged 19 years."

As the Schutts planned for a double funeral, Edward, Harriet, and Priscilla stayed nearby another two weeks to help with the preparations. During the funeral, Edward showed no signs of a guilty conscience—he was appropriately supportive and frequently solemn. Even the most skilled alienist (psychiatrist) would have struggled to discern his guilt from innocence.

In 1871, almost thirty years after Amelia and baby Amille's deaths, Hamilton Freeman failed to detect any remorse as he heard the story from a much older Edward Rulloff—only indignation at how he'd been treated by the clannish Schutt family. Ham had been talking with Edward for days now, and he was starting to get a sense of the man's rhythms and patterns. The interview about William's wife and daughter had been especially terse, yes—he'd started to see flashes of that famous Rulloff anger that the Schutts had been so anxious about decades earlier. But Edward flatly denied murdering Amelia and Amille (and he maintained that he had forgotten any conversations he might or might not have had with his mother-in-law, Hannah Schutt, that day).

"I do not remember of telling the old lady that I would bring her gray hairs in sorrow to the grave . . ." Edward insisted to Ham. "She was a very good old woman, but ignorant and suspicious, and easily influenced."

Later that night, Hamilton Freeman retired to his home in Binghamton. He pulled out his wooden chair and began writing on a proper notepad, scribbling "poison" and "vile rumors."

"We do not believe there is any truth in these reports," concluded Ham. "1st. There was an entire absence of motive to perpetrate such a crime. 2d. If anything of the kind had been done it would have been at once suspected, and an investigation held."

Ham was correct—there was no investigation done at the time, and Edward was never formally accused of killing Amelia and Amille. He might have been blameless, given that maternal and infant mortality were achingly common in those days. And even if their deaths resulted from Edward's remedies, it didn't necessarily follow that they were maliciously given. Accidents caused by administering too much medicine were also frequent in the 1800s, because measuring deadly narcotics was tricky. And yet, an acquaintance would later remark just how adept Edward seemed to be with poisons, as well as with tests for detecting poison. Edward Rulloff made mistakes, but he was never prone to mistakes with medicine. Could it all just be a coincidence? How could it be when he seemed to confess to his mother-in-law? Edward—the temperamental, mentally unstable, psychopathic brother-in-law, with an axe to grind against William and the means to put a murderous plan into action—just happened to be the apothecary on call when William's wife and child died? No, I don't think it's likely. It seems clear that Edward intended to kill Amelia and Amille.

But Ham Freeman didn't agree and he pledged to his book's readers that he would winnow fact from fiction with the unbiased ear of a journalist.

"I purpose to write a truthful account of the life and remarkable career of EDWARD HOWARD RULLOFF," Hamilton Freeman typed. "I shall relate some of the incidents of his early life and shall endeavor to trace subsequent facts and circumstances, which influencing his mind and conduct, led him on step by step to that anomalous career of study, and of crime . . ."

Ham was trying, with his unique access, to offer his readers a neutral evaluation of the most famous (and infamous) contemporary killer to face the noose in America. Like the mindhunters (and journalists) who would follow in his footsteps more than a century later, he thought his access would give insight into the thoughts and motivations of this man, insight that could not be gained by any other means. But Ham's own motivations were perhaps more mercenary than scientific. He saw in Edward Rulloff the chance to pen not just a newspaper article but an authorized biography and firsthand account (through Edward's eyes) of these crimes that had so captivated a nation. In effect, he was trying to compose a nineteenth-century true-crime narrative. If Ham could pull off this coup and write a truly balanced look at Rulloff's life and (alleged) crimes, the resulting book would likely secure his family's financial future.

Ham's newspaper, the *Democratic Leader*, was a little more than a year old, but Ham had already considered selling his interests to his partner if the biography of Edward Rulloff was successful. The labor of maintaining a daily paper was too tiresome. Literary fame and fortune in the book publishing world was a much more appealing prospect.

Ham quickly dismissed accusations from the Schutts that Edward had murdered Amelia and little Amille; Edward denied it, and the evidence simply wasn't there. Edward was a brute, sure, and his behavior toward the Schutt family had probably been atrocious. But the fact remained: Years after the deaths, Amelia's body was exhumed, and the toxicology report was inconclusive. No hard evidence linked Edward to the deaths of William Schutt's wife and child.

Of course, there were other unsolved deaths from that time—deaths that were even closer to Rulloff's home. As Ham continued to type, he steeled himself for the questions he knew he would have to ask Edward the following day. Questions about Edward's own missing wife and child: it was inevitable.

Harriet and Priscilla had disappeared almost thirty years before—their bodies had never been found. Ham's readers, all of America, were desperate to know their fates . . . but Edward had stayed silent for decades. The Schutts suspected that Edward had murdered them . . . but for what reason? Despite their fights, Harriet seemed to have loved Edward.

If Ham could secure a confession from Edward as he sat shackled in the Binghamton jail in 1871, then Ham's biography would be a bona fide sensation. But was Ham charming Edward to get an admission of guilt . . . or was he playing right into a psychopath's hands?

———

The next day, Edward Rulloff reclined on his thin pallet as Hamilton slid into his usual wooden chair in the cold jail cell, pencil in hand. Edward seemed particularly fatigued this morning. Over the past month, Ham had occasionally glanced over at Edward's academic papers on his desk—the jailed man continued work on his own intellectual pursuits, even while locked away in this small room. *What was he working on so feverishly?* Ham couldn't really understand the details, but he could tell that Edward's hand occasionally became tired—his smooth strokes turned sloppy and slanted, sometimes too messy to be readable. He felt a deepening empathy for this old man in this frigid cell. But Ham remained focused.

The author gingerly turned the conversation to Edward's last encounter with his wife. *What do you remember about Harriet that day?* The writer was startled by the killer's physical response.

"The cold drops of perspiration stood upon the man's forehead," wrote Ham. "And tears rolled down his cheek while he related this."

Edward Rulloff recalled eyeing Harriet as she tidied up their house in Lansing, New York. It was June 23, 1845, and there was a beautiful summer sky as the daylight faded. Edward's two-month-old daughter, Priscilla, cooed nearby as a cup of composition tea sat on the table. The twenty-six-year-old braced himself for yet another argument with his young bride; their rows had become obnoxious, loud feuds that usually resulted in his stalking off, refusing to resolve the issue. And their quarrels had a similar theme lately—Edward hoped to move his little family out west, but Harriet wasn't convinced.

Edward had felt for quite a while now that he was languishing in a sad little town in upstate New York—trapped, with no real prospects for research and no chance of advancement. Three weeks earlier, he was offered a position as the head of a prestigious academy in Ohio, a step toward the academic career he coveted. Harriet, however, stubbornly refused to leave New York's countryside and her family. She made it clear that she deeply resented her husband's hubris—*Who did he think he was, putting on airs like this?*—and she didn't even want to consider the opportunity.

Harriet infuriated him—her lack of respect and outright disobedience dismissed his values. Of course, underlying her obstinance was likely a strong sense of self-preservation; after all, in Lansing she was just a ten-mile carriage ride from her family. When things got difficult between the two of them (and they always, somehow, seemed to be difficult), she could always go away for a few days until Edward cooled off. Where was she going to escape to if they moved to Ohio? Another row began, and Edward didn't expect this discussion to end well.

It certainly wouldn't for one of them.

Edward cried to her that he had always been an outcast, treated like a common peasant when it suited the family. When he was useful as a doctor, he was their savior, Edward screamed, but the large family was emasculating—they treated him as a wretch. And he was still profoundly unhappy with his career as a botanical physician. This job would be his opportunity to transition to the academic life he knew, deep down, he was destined for.

Edward glanced beneath the diaper line draped across the kitchen. Little Priscilla was lying in a crib, wiggling around. Two weeks had passed since the double funeral of Amelia and Amille Schutt, who were now buried in the same casket in Ithaca.

Edward took a breath and began a new argument to Harriet. He had secretly saved money for the trip west—perhaps he could go now, and Harriet could follow with Priscilla soon? He understood that Harriet might not want to leave New York immediately. She could stay here, in Lansing, and keep the house going until he returned for her. His young wife glared at him, exasperated.

"No," she declared. Harriet would *never* go to Ohio with him, or anywhere far away from her family, for that matter. And if he left without her, she refused to keep house for him. She would pack up their things in Lansing, borrow a horse and cart, and she and Priscilla would return to her family's farm in Dryden.

"She was tired of living with me, anyhow," Edward recalled. "Her mother was anxious for her to return home."

Edward was enraged. He didn't know what to do, how to stop her from leaving. He tried to make her realize that his career, their future, was dependent on seizing this new opportunity out west.

"I could not make a decent living there. . . . I was poor, and too proud to have the neighbors and people generally know how poor I was," Edward said.

They screamed at each other, and the argument started tracing a familiar pattern as he accused Harriet of lusting for Dr. Bull— *She preferred her own cousin to her husband, and so did her family.*

She might favor the doctor, yes, she admitted.

Edward was irate. He let loose a string of horrible profanities before glancing at his daughter and turning to Harriet.

"I think I said she might go to hell if she chose to," recalled Edward, "but that she should not take the child, that I would take care of that."

Harriet snatched up Priscilla and backed away from her husband. He lunged at her and tried to strip the baby from his wife's arms, but she clung too tightly as Priscilla wailed. Edward's eyes darted around the room before he spotted that hefty marble pestle, the same heavy tool he had hit her with last summer. He reached for it as Harriet sobbed.

Sitting in the jail cell with Edward, hearing this story, Hamilton felt his chest tighten; this was the long-awaited confession from America's most infamous killer. He scribbled notes quickly while Edward wept.

"I must have struck very hard—I was a young man and very strong, and the blow broke her skull," Edward said. "She fell senseless with the child still in her arms, which was crying. Oh! that dreadful hour! That horrible moment which I would have given worlds to blot out! It makes me—*yes, even me*—shudder sometimes when I think of it."

This dramatic confession stunned Hamilton with its vivid description of brutality. Edward had just admitted to murdering his wife, in front of their child. Edward wailed as Ham watched him, dumbfounded. He hardly knew what to say.

After a long silence, Hamilton spoke and gently implored

Edward to continue. The killer quickly glared at Ham, causing the author to sit back with surprise.

"He fixed upon me a fiendish glare which *made me shudder*," Ham later typed.

Ham had witnessed the shift that modern forensic psychiatrists have found is common with psychopaths—the ability to adjust their countenance to fit their audience and their own needs. At a moment of vulnerability, Ham had pressed Edward too firmly for details. The murderer demanded control during their interview, and he used quiet intimidation to regain it.

"[I wished] I was a mile away from him instead of being locked in that narrow prison with him," wrote Hamilton.

Moments after Ham cowered, Edward softened his demeanor and continued. He described how Priscilla was crying near her mother's body, so he administered a narcotic to quiet her. That scene concluded the story.

Edward was quiet, and now Ham was reticent to push him further. Edward refused to reveal anything more about the fate of his infant daughter—it was as if she had vanished from his narrative. Ham bravely attempted to press him once again.

"That is no one's business," Edward snapped back.

Priscilla Rulloff vanished in June 1845, never to be seen again. There were rumors that Edward had sent his daughter to live with his wealthy brother in Pennsylvania, but Ham suspected he was silent about Priscilla's true fate out of pride.

"His personal self-respect would never allow him to acknowledge that he murdered, in cold blood, a sweet little infant," wrote Ham.

Ham was now finally able to confirm—for his readers, and for his own satisfaction—that Edward Rulloff had indeed murdered his wife. Ham wasn't definitively convinced that he had killed his daughter. In fact, he prayed that Edward had not. But Ham was still confused about *why* he would murder Priscilla. For the author, there was no simple answer to that question. I believe that Edward *did* murder Priscilla—there is no easy explanation for how she would have been spirited away (more on that later). But Edward made clear to Ham that he had killed his wife . . . and he responded to Ham's horror with a sinister reaction.

"He said then, with a significant smile, 'I had raised Harriet up and placed her in a position so I could examine the wound,'" wrote Ham. 'The pestle broke the skull and sunk into her brain. She bled some, but not much.'"

Edward's "significant smile" while describing the death of his wife would haunt Hamilton Freeman for the remainder of his life. *What did it mean? Was Edward not aware of how horrid he seemed?* Yes, Edward clearly was aware—he just didn't care. And he might have taken pleasure in murdering the woman he believed had defiled their marriage and doomed his academic career. Ham was determined to record the rest of the confession, so he calmly continued his notes as Edward described the outcome.

"I knew I was a ruined man," Edward told Ham. "Everything that had before been bright and hopeful turned black and forbidding in my mind."

The humble house was silent now as two bodies lay in the room. Edward listened to the ducks on the pond nearby. He sat silently on his bed all night and fretted—*What should he do now?* He could call the neighbors and confess, or perhaps he could die by suicide. Edward stood up and fingered the vials of various poisons he kept for his medical practice. He closed each of the shutters in the house. Edward resolved to take his own life; he wrote a letter, detailing what happened that day. He stirred up his deadly concoction, brought it to his lips—and then paused. *No. Death would deprive the world of his knowledge. Of his marvelous brain. There had to be another way.*

"I had my reasons for not committing suicide as I intended," Edward said. "I had ambition to live for, and responsibilities."

Edward's inflated sense of self-worth is yet another hallmark of psychopathy. He would deprive the world of his brilliance if he took his own life. Edward began to plot as he glanced around the bedroom and pulled out his largest chest. He dragged it close to Harriet's body. Priscilla lay nearby. Edward retrieved a pair of shears from the drawer and snipped off a lock of his wife's hair before placing it inside an envelope. He folded his daughter's small blanket and set it aside. Rags assisted in the cleanup of blood once Harriet was placed in the trunk.

An hour later, Edward rapped on his neighbor's door, requesting the loan of a horse and cart. Thomas Robertson agreed, though reluctantly—it was a sweltering day, and he was concerned about the health of his horse, but Thomas had never had any trouble with Edward (and country life was all about being a good neighbor, after all). The farmer agreed to meet Edward at his house in the early afternoon to deliver the horse and wagon. Just as Robertson and his son arrived, Edward was shoving the chest through the front door.

"Shall I help you load it?" asked Robertson.

"If you please, sir," was Edward's response.

Robertson struggled. He guessed that his end of the trunk weighed about seventy pounds. The men finally heaved the chest over the side of the wagon. Edward snapped his whip and the horse pulled away before Edward hopped on top. He drove slowly, listlessly toward the southern shore of nearby Cayuga Lake. He could hear metal clank in the back from the heavy flat irons he had laid in the wagon. He took winding roads, routes that seemed senseless. Edward told Ham that he imagined everyone he encountered knew what happened and he fretted.

"I was so completely confused and overcome by the horror with which I was filled," Edward cried to Ham, "that had anyone charged me at the time with the crime, or arrest me, I would instantly have confessed all."

He considered driving into Ithaca, parking the cart with the chest on the street, and buying some potash, a potassium compound often used in fertilizer to break down soil. Edward planned to bury the contents in the chest, with the potash on top, hoping they would dissolve and disappear.

"I was not [a] good enough chemist then to know whether it would, so I abandoned that idea," he recalled.

He was desperate not to be caught, and he seemed to improvise quite well. Edward drove all night until he reached the shore of Cayuga Lake, just before dawn. He hopped down from the seat in the wagon bed and opened the trunk. He spotted a small boat to steal and made two trips to load it with Harriet's body. Edward was coy with Ham about this detail—*Did he return to the cart to pick up weights to attach to Harriet's corpse or did he return for Priscilla's body?* Within thirty minutes, Edward was rowing toward the middle of the lake. He was sweating, red-faced—he could hardly control his breathing.

"I rowed a long way, until I found a spot where I thought the water was the deepest," Edward remembered.

He tied the weights to Harriet's body, and likely that of

Priscilla. Again, Edward chose his words very carefully, determined to remain vague with Ham.

"I then carefully placed what I had with me in the water," he said. "It sank rapidly to rise no more."

———

Hamilton listened as Edward wept again over his remorse for the murders. As he recounted the horrible events, his anguish seemed sincere.* Edward blamed his past physical abuse of Harriet on his jealousy over Dr. Bull—and his actions that fateful June day on temporary, emotional anger. Edward had been stricken by an impassioned psychological break, thought Hamilton, just like another well-known genius who had made news many years before for a similar crime.

In 1849, Dr. John White Webster, a professor at Harvard Medical School, had impulsively murdered a colleague after being harassed over a financial debt. Webster was an outlier—*Harvard professors didn't commit murder, after all*—and the case made national headlines by defying social norms and exposing depravity that had been hidden in the upper echelons of academia and society. Ham believed that Edward's case was similar. Rather than a premeditated crime, Edward's actions had been an act of passion. In fact, that could be the *only* explanation in his case, concluded Ham after hearing the story.

---

* It almost certainly wasn't. His false contrition was another trademark characteristic of a psychopath, a way to manipulate a sympathetic victim like Hamilton. In the three decades after their disappearance, Edward had never expressed true compassion or even sadness over the loss of his wife and child—until this moment.

"A disappointment in a love affair in early life shocked the tender cords in his sensitive nature, embittered the later years," Ham typed in his manuscript, "and drove him from society to become a literary recluse."

Edward Rulloff, according to his biographer, suffered from a broken heart and unrelenting jealousy; he wasn't plagued by a twisted psyche or afflicted with a curse from the devil. Ham was convinced that Edward's life story was tragic, yes—but ultimately understandable. Any man could find himself drawn to the breaking point if the circumstances conspired against him in a similar way, Ham explained.

"There is no man suddenly either excellently good or supremely evil," wrote Ham.

His interviews and musings on the Edward Rulloff case became a book: *The Veil of Secrecy Removed,* self-published in 1871. A fascinating document of Rulloff's case and of the psychological prejudices (and blind spots) of the time, Ham's book also revealed the inner thoughts of a writer who feared he would never truly understand his infamous subject. The words "psychopath" and "personality disorder" didn't yet exist, of course. But Ham's unease about the man he'd been in such proximity to for weeks on end is evident on every page. Something felt insincere about Edward's story and his motivations, but Ham doesn't have the language to explain his confusion. Instead, he keeps coming back to the way he was dazzled by Edward.

"There was a personal magnetism about the man that irresistibly drew me to him," wrote Ham. "There was a charm about his manner and conversation which when he chose to exert it, made me forget for the moment his past history, and that I was talking with a man charged with the crime of murder."

Armed with modern data, Ham might have suspected what twenty-first-century psychiatrists do—Edward Rulloff had psychopathy, and he was leveraging one of its traits (charm) to achieve a singular goal: his freedom. Later, that goal would switch to securing his academic legacy, but it wasn't time for that yet.

In his interview with Ham, Edward was *finally* able to shape his own story by dispensing carefully chosen bits of information— and he thrived on control. Edward was careful because he needed the power of Ham's pen; journalists in the 1800s held enormous influence over the public. And Edward was still convinced that public opinion, not necessarily a court of law, was where he would find justice.

Of course, superficial charm is also a trait on Hare's modern psychopathy checklist: the tool many psychopaths use to take advantage of victims, like journalists. *The Veil of Secrecy Removed* is an unusually intimate profile of a disturbing relationship between a brilliant, glib psychopath and an impressionable writer—a cautionary tale for current journalists who should avoid being drawn into a psychotic killer's web.*

But of course, Hamilton Freeman couldn't have known any of that in 1871. All he realized was that he'd just gotten the scoop of a lifetime—his own ticket out of the sleepy upstate New York town and into his own literary fame. Though Ham didn't yet realize it, he was being used by Edward just as much (if not more) than he himself was using the murderer. After all, Edward

* There are contemporary examples to draw from: Author Norman Mailer championed the parole of a convicted killer in 1981 because he considered Jack Henry Abbott to be an outstanding writer, based on letters that they had exchanged for two years. Mailer helped secure Abbott a book deal and even agreed to hire him as his research assistant. Abbott slowly, methodically gained the trust of Mailer and his circle, but within weeks of his parole, Jack Abbott murdered someone else.

Rulloff's attempt to change the narrative and escape the gallows for the third time in thirty years was still underway. Ham had played a part, yes. But Edward was about to welcome another writer to his jail cell in Binghamton, a notable newspaper journalist from Manhattan with a much larger audience than Hamilton Freeman could ever hope to attract.

Reporter Oliver Dyer's admiration and fascination would shift Edward Rulloff's legacy within academia, and perhaps dictate his fate on the gallows.

3

The Newspaperman

Even as good shone upon the countenance of the one, evil
was written broadly and plainly on the face of the other.
—Robert Louis Stevenson,
Strange Case of Dr. Jekyll and Mr. Hyde, 1886

I t was late January 1871 when newspaper reporter Oliver Dyer strolled through the Binghamton jail with the confidence of a writer who had happily investigated more intimidating criminals than Edward Rulloff. The sheriff guided Dyer along the dark corridor as one of Edward's two defense attorneys, George Becker, followed behind. Dyer was a spiritual man who relished profiling deviants, something he had ample opportunity to do as a journalist for one of Manhattan's most popular and lurid newspapers, *The Sun.*

Edward would prove to be a fascinating profile for Dyer: a murderer unwilling to atone for his crimes, who perhaps even reveled in them. Dyer had reviewed the earlier newspaper articles about Edward's missing wife and daughter. The journalist examined Edward's thirty-year record of countless felonies. Those culminated in the 1870 murder of an upstate New York warehouse clerk, a local man whose only mistake was confronting a masked robber. This crime—not the murder of his wife and child and perhaps two other members of the Schutt family—was the offense he stood accused of in the courtroom in 1871. But despite all the evidence of his guilt, Dyer arrived at the cell that day with an open mind. Just weeks earlier, Edward had confessed to Hamilton Freeman that he murdered Harriet back in 1845 (even though he had been vague about Priscilla's fate), but Ham was still busy on the manuscript, so the author kept the killer's secret . . . for now.

Dyer knew the accusations against Edward were serious. But like Hamilton before him, Dyer was beguiled, bewitched even, by Edward's mind. If the claims were true, if he really was an intellectual powerhouse, didn't that perhaps mitigate his crimes? Shouldn't a man's contribution to the world be considered when deciding his fate? The newspaperman hoped to introduce New York City readers to a complex villain—part scholar, part devil—a fusion sure to frighten even the most stalwart tycoon sitting safely inside his Fifth Avenue mansion.

Dyer himself was a blending of identities, a combination of devout Christian, pugnacious street reporter, and studious former schoolteacher, all of which resulted in a thoroughly American creation: a member of the self-made media intelligentsia. Dyer had risen from humble means to become a confidant of kingmakers in New York, and he could boast having the ear of great men like U.S. president Ulysses S. Grant and future New York governor Samuel J. Tilden. By age forty-seven, Dyer was a brilliant scribe and orator who had earned a national reputation that Hamilton Freeman could only pray to gain one day. But while Ham hoped to offer book readers a sympathetic portrait of a murderer's deteriorating mind, Dyer proposed to dissect a genius's curious ideas about languages, as well as reveal the provenance of Edward's obsession with his own research.

That research, which posited a central unifying origin of all languages, was informed by Edward's own years studying classical Greek, Latin, and modern languages. His ideas were bold. Daring. Audacious. Dyer recognized that Edward, like himself, was a self-educated man with big dreams, who'd struggled to rise above the station to which he'd been born. Was Edward perhaps innocent of the crimes he'd been accused of? Or if he *had* done something wrong . . . was there possibly a justification for his actions?

Edward had dismissed as childish and reductive all previous journalistic attempts at interpreting his wild new ideas about language. *No writer is clever enough to capture my concepts* went his refrain. But Oliver Dyer offered something Edward had been craving: an astute, educated admirer who had a platform for sharing his intellectual theories with the wider world. Dyer's first interview in *The Sun* with Edward would transform the killer from a craven specter stalking upstate New York into a spellbinding, possibly misunderstood philosopher who captivated much of America.

By 1871, *The Sun* was one of Manhattan's most prominent newspapers. Founded in 1833, the paper adopted the slogan "It Shines for All" because the paper focused on stories that appealed to working-class New Yorkers, including the throngs of immigrants who stepped off boats moored in the port daily. *The Sun* was sold for just a penny, and it sold well—so well that it inspired the advent of the penny press, tabloid-style newspapers that were cheaply produced en masse.

The Sun was the first newspaper to report on tawdry events like crimes, deaths, divorces, and deaths by suicide. Sure, it showcased crude, prattling journalism when compared to more erudite papers like the *New York Times* . . . but it offered readers something they craved, and it did so with verve and style. What's more, *The Sun* served an important political and governmental function in fast-growing New York City: it was a vital way to connect and build lower- and middle-class communities that were swiftly gaining power and influence by virtue of their burgeoning numbers. At *The Sun*, Oliver Dyer was a headliner, a popular and persuasive writer noted for his tenaciousness and versatility.

"Oliver Dyer whose range of ability was so great that while one day he wrote for *Bonner's Ledger* advice to distressed lovers," read a book about the newspaper's origins, "the next day would find him penning for *The Sun* an exhaustive article on the methods employed in building a railroad across the Andes!"

Dyer was also a prolific innovator; he was the first person to introduce stenography to America after he studied the system in Europe, and he later became the first shorthand reporter in the United States Senate. Dyer had once studied law, but he settled on a career in journalism to passionately advocate for righting what he saw as the wrongs in the criminal justice system. There was plenty of crime in New York, but it seemed manageable compared to other large cities. The city's population reached one million people between 1860 and 1870, and yet its crime rate remained relatively low compared with the rest of the country.

"New York City, the densest, most crowded, most—or one of the most—corrupt, filled with immigrants, should have had high rates [of dangerous crime]," wrote one current researcher about this period in the city's history. "Yet it recorded some of the lowest rates of the era."

The research concluded that the low rate of crime in New York was tied to the emergence of so-called "civilized society"—the social mores and values that were upheld as virtuous and honorable (at least in public) by government officials, leading citizens, and, yes, the media, including newspapers like *The Sun*. Indeed, guides in the late 1800s were available with advice for men on how a proper gentleman might behave toward women.

"In the familiar intercourse of society, a well-bred man will be known by the delicacy and deference with which he behaves towards females," read the 1860 edition of *The Gentlemen's Book of Etiquette and Manual of Politeness*. "That man would deservedly be looked upon as very deficient in proper respect and feeling, who should take any physical advantage of one of the weaker sex or offer any personal slight towards her."

But of course, New York City was still struggling with illicit enterprises, including brothels. Lower crime did not mean no crime.

In 1870, a pamphlet called *A Gentleman's Directory: New York City* was sold for one dollar to male visitors hoping to explore the city's more sordid side. The thirty-two-page guide printed details about specific saloons, public houses, and brothels, including ratings that seemed focused on "agreeability."

"No. 116 W. 26th St. is a parlor house kept by Sarah Wilbur," read the guide. "This house is most elegantly furnished, the proprietress is a very pleasant and agreeable lady, and of a fun-loving disposition. She has seven lady boarders, who are very affectionate and agreeable. Gentlemen seeking for pleasure will be very agreeably entertained. This is a first-class house."

The guide even advertised nineteenth-century condoms called "male safes," which were imported from France: "a perfect shield against disease or conception, made of both skin and India rubber."

Oliver Dyer personally despised the shabby saloons and brothels peppered throughout New York City during the 1860s and '70s, so much so that he had targeted their owners in a series of scathing, widely read articles that set the precedent for true crime investigative stories in newspapers. Dyer's pieces braided dramatic narrative with exhaustive research in devilishly effective tales. One titled "The Wickedest Man in New York" earned Dyer international acclaim for unmasking a career criminal in Manhattan, a dance hall owner named John Allen.

"The wickedest man in New York goes by the name of John Allen," wrote Dyer. "The best bad are always the worst. Take him for all in all, our wickedest man is a phenomenon." Dyer was fascinated with Allen's compartmentalized life, how he employed sex workers, yet insisted on reading them the Bible daily. Allen's crimes were more of the moral nature than violent—he ran a brothel where the city's most notorious criminals in the Fourth Ward spent their wealth. But Dyer marveled at the dissonance between the two sides of Allen's personality: devout Christian, family man, and formally educated businessman who nonetheless thrived in his seedy underworld of nightlife and sex work. The dichotomy of Allen's character challenged Dyer's notion of the "born criminal." John Allen was a man with many faces.

"This wickedest man is the only entity appertaining to the shady side of New York life which we have not been able to fathom or account for," wrote Dyer. "Why a human being of his education should continue to live in a Water-Street dance-house, and bring up his children there, is more than we can comprehend."

After the exposé was published, Allen was jailed and the

dance hall shuttered, illustrating the potency of Oliver Dyer's pen. His evisceration of Allen's criminal empire was impressive enough that it later inspired writer Herbert Asbury to include an account of Allen's life in the author's jolting, sensational nonfiction book: *The Gangs of New York*. But unlike Asbury, Oliver Dyer had long since grown bored with telling tales of what he thought of as the vulgar hoodlums who lurked in the alleys of Five Points late at night. He had little interest in the Irish American gangs that controlled many of the shadier areas of New York. Instead, he'd started asking deeper questions. *What caused men to commit acts of evil? And did evil acts overshadow all that was potentially good or useful in a man's life?* Dyer's deep religious beliefs compelled him to push beyond the surface-level facts of a case to unearth the motivations and purposes driving these dark forces of America's underbelly. He sought access to their spiritual depths—or, in the case of Edward Rulloff, the origin of his criminal impulses. While Dyer was a vocal and influential champion for crime victims, he also believed that a man's usefulness *could* be divorced from his immorality. Perhaps Edward Rulloff's innovative ideas about languages could help society, more than his execution could satisfy American law?

Dyer had a meeting with Edward's defense attorney, George Becker, during his murder trial in January 1871 and formally requested an interview with the prisoner. At first, Becker wasn't encouraging. Edward had firmly refused to see all journalists except Hamilton Freeman.

"Rulloff had an immovable will of his own," wrote Dyer in the first of three articles. "[He] had determined and declared that he would not talk with anybody."

Edward insisted to his attorney that all writers were fishy, their motives dubious. But what seemed more likely was that Edward had finally turned sensible: he hoped to avoid being trapped by factual inconsistencies in his story while still on trial. Dyer sat across from Becker at a wooden table inside Becker's office as he gently pressed the attorney, insisting that he only wanted to query Edward about his theory on the origin of human language and the manuscript he'd been working on for years—a document that was nearly completed. *Wouldn't Edward like to see his linguistic ideas shared with the wider world?*

Dyer smiled at Becker. The journalist was distinguished, with a full beard, flowing brown hair, and a long face. The result was a visage that resembled an odd fusion of Presidents Grant and Lincoln. Dyer fancied himself an amateur linguist, and he'd become fascinated by the short excerpts of Edward's manuscript that had appeared in Hamilton Freeman's paper. Dyer insisted to Becker that he could translate his client's complex, sometimes convoluted theory to the common reader—someone like the meat-market butcher in Manhattan who regularly skimmed *The Sun*. This proposal pleased the attorney, and Becker dispatched quickly to the jail to inform Edward of Dyer's intentions. As the reporter waited in Becker's office, he thumbed through a copy of Ham's paper, scribbling notes on his pad. An hour later, Becker hurried back into his office with news of an agreement from Edward, but with caveats.

"Rulloff had finally consented to an examination of his manuscripts, and also to a personal interview with us on philology," wrote Dyer, "and on nothing else. We were particularly advised that any attempt to touch on any other subject, and especially either on the facts of his life or on religious topics, would bring the interview to an immediate close."

Certainly was Dyer's response—he would follow the restrictions Edward requested. But in Dyer's experience, once someone started talking, it was easy to keep them talking, and Edward was no exception. The killer shared a wealth of information about different aspects of his life, including his childhood, his crimes, and his religion, giving context about his motivations and his psyche. Ham Freeman had learned all of this, but he was still writing his book, so those details had not been published. The public had not yet met *this* version of Edward Rulloff. By the time Oliver Dyer finally exited the dank, chilly jail cell, the world would be offered an even deeper and more nuanced portrait of Edward Rulloff. Dyer's articles were far more reaching, far more erudite than Ham's stories, and he knew they'd make a stir at *The Sun*. But the clever newspaperman might have realized the extent to which he, himself, was being used and manipulated by the cunning killer. In the end, Dyer's stories became a powerful tool to save Edward's own life and secure his academic legacy.*

In 1871, as the sheriff, the defense attorney, and the newspaperman approached Edward's cell, the prisoner leapt from his pallet. His left hand snatched a kerosene lamp off his desk, as bits of light bounced around the stone walls. Dyer glanced at the shadows of large iron locks and thick bars on the tiny windows—no need to plot an escape from this jail. The cells—and the guards—were unforgiving, as was the fetid air.

A warm glow spilled through the lamp's glass, and as Edward

---

* Over the years, psychopaths and journalists have often enjoyed reciprocal relationships. Notorious serial killers including Ted Bundy, Dennis Rader (also known as BTK), and Arthur Shawcross (the Genesee River Killer) have sat across a table from journalists, each hoping to retrieve something from the other. The criminal is given the opportunity to craft his own account of his life (and perhaps relieve some boredom), while the journalist might be offered an exclusive that helps shape their career.

shoved his right hand through the small opening of the iron door, he warmly welcomed Dyer inside. The journalist nodded and turned to the sheriff, requesting to enter because the bars would inhibit a proper interview. The sheriff agreed, and his key turned. He fetched a chair as Dyer walked in and sat down across from Edward; the killer slid onto his bed. Their knees touched as they watched each other. The writer quickly surveyed Edward's short stature, his strong frame, and the thick sinews of his neck (an odd observation that would become more relevant later). Dyer silently commiserated with Edward, as a fellow writer. He seemed startled by the terrible conditions in his cell.

"His keen hazel eyes looked swollen and bloodshot," Dyer wrote later. "The corridor in front of his cell was too dark to read or write without a lamp, and his cell itself was dark as night."

Edward's apparent stress might have also been the result of news from George Becker that the murderer was in danger— rioters outside the jail were determined to inflict vigilante justice on the man they believed responsible for at least seven deaths over the past thirty years, including four members of his own family.

"Mr. Becker was notified that if the jury acquitted Rulloff, there were two hundred men in complete readiness to hang him [Rulloff] the moment the verdict of acquittal should be announced," said Dyer.

Oliver Dyer understood the one question that had plagued many New Yorkers: *Would Edward Rulloff escape?* This was a concern because Edward had in fact vanished from a jail cell before. A lynch mob was growing outside the jail to prevent that from happening once again, despite the increased security. Edward put aside his fears for his own safety and smiled at the journalist. Despite his insistence that their interview remain focused on his work in linguistics, Oliver Dyer's intellectual admiration was too tempting to a narcissist.

———

On the afternoon of June 24, 1845—the day after Edward Rulloff's disposal of the remains of his wife and presumably those of his infant daughter—there came a knock on William Schutt's door in Ithaca, New York. Harriet's younger sister Jane opened it to find a red-faced, sweaty Edward. He quickly brushed past her into his brother-in-law's house.

Jane glanced outside and didn't spot a horse, or a carriage driver retrieving water for a long return trip. Edward had quietly appeared at the doorstep, like a shadow. *What could be the purpose of this visit?* Relations with William and the whole Schutt family were so strained that Edward didn't often stop by, and certainly not without his own wife and child.

Where are Harriet and Priscilla? Jane asked. Edward quickly replied that a neighbor had invited the Rulloffs on an impromptu trip to visit to a nearby town. Jane eyed Edward as sweat gathered on his sideburns—he was characteristically nebulous with details.

"He thought he should go and stay five or six weeks and might return," recalled Jane.

This wasn't completely unexpected—the Rulloffs enjoyed taking short respites, especially during the hot summer, though staying away for more than a month seemed a little surprising. Jane surveyed Edward, and he grimaced as his face grew even more flushed than usual.

"Don't my face look red?" he asked Jane.

"I said it did," she said. "He said he had walked five miles very fast, and it made his face red." Jane noted how unusual it was for Edward to turn up on foot unexpectedly, and without his family, but country hospitality being the rule, she didn't linger on that detail and instead offered him some water. Edward, with his customary rough manners, abruptly declared that he was starved. Skipping the polite formality of allowing Jane to serve him food, he "went down to the cellar and ate ravenously, taking his food into his hands," said Jane.

While all this seemed slightly strange, Jane wasn't terribly alarmed. She and the whole Schutt family had grown used to Edward's awkward behavior. He told her that Harriet was at home in Lansing, and he prepared to return to her and baby Priscilla.

On his way out, Jane picked up a pile of tiny clothing from a table—outfits made for Edward's deceased baby niece that were now painful reminders for her father, William Schutt. Jane handed Edward the stack, suggesting that he might find the items useful for little Priscilla. Her brother-in-law declined the gift, finished his food, and quickly left.

Back at home in Lansing, Edward hastily prepared to flee. He rented a horse and cart. He swiftly loaded up two trunks, which he'd filled with books and other valuables. Edward Rulloff hoped to vanish one final time, to start a new life out west in Ohio, just as he had planned. But some perverse instinct caused him to circle back to the Schutt family one more time.

It's tempting to think of criminals with psychopathy as brilliant masterminds—Edward was certainly extraordinarily intelligent academically, but he wasn't an *intelligent criminal* and it's important to make that distinction. I explained this section of the story to Dr. Craig Neumann, detailing how Edward returned to the Schutt family several times after the murders. He didn't seem surprised.

"Here's the thing with personality pathology—often the psychopath may do something that is deceptive and cunning and get away with it, but in the long run, they foul their own nests," Neumann said. "We are fundamentally a social species. And the reason we are is because of our social interconnectedness. The psychopathic orientation is fundamentally to use individuals as resources. That is only going to get you so far."

Edward Rulloff viewed the Schutts as his most stalwart resources—they had aided him in the past, *so why not now?* Edward's lack of emotional awareness prevented him from understanding that they might be suspicious. Neumann said that psychopaths are likely to bring about their own demise because they lack the ability to adapt in society—they're borrowing "emotions" from others, but they continue to stumble during many interactions that they can't manipulate.

They are often self-defeating, and there are modern examples to examine. Edmund Kemper turned himself in because he was not receiving the media attention that he craved. Ted Bundy was caught because of a simple traffic violation. Dennis Rader sent a computer disk to police that could be traced back to the serial killer. Edward Rulloff also seemed to crave risk, like other psychopaths— and he put himself unnecessarily in danger.

When Edward rapped on William Schutt's door once again, his brother-in-law greeted him and invited him in. After a short chat, Edward reached inside his vest's small pocket and revealed a gold band made for a lady's delicate finger, a ring worn by Harriet for several years. It had in fact been given to her by her brother

William. Edward held it in his palm. *Do you want it?* he asked William.

No, give it back to your wife was William's reply. *Why wasn't it on her finger now, in fact?*

Edward insisted that Harriet had given it to him several weeks earlier because she no longer wanted it. William and Jane stared at their brother-in-law and pondered his bizarre behavior. Once again, Edward appeared mystified by human emotions. He assumed that, by offering William the ring, he would ingratiate himself to his brother-in-law. It only caused more suspicion.

Edward reluctantly returned the ring to his pocket, quietly sipped his tea, set down the cup, and then quickly left. William and Jane Schutt were left uneasy.

"I have never seen his wife since," remembered William.

———

August 2, 1845, was a hot, sticky day, late summer in the country. Ephraim and William Schutt sat inside Hale's Store in Ithaca, a cheap dry goods store that peddled everything from local produce and toothbrushes to French prints and extra-superfine Welsh flannels. Beads of sweat dripped from their temples. They heard heels clicking on the wooden front steps as a man opened the screen door.

Edward Rulloff. He smiled and offered a handshake.

Shocked, the Schutt men eyed their brother-in-law. Ephraim and William had not seen or heard from their younger sister or her two-month-old baby for six weeks, ever since Edward's hasty and strange departure back in June. The Schutts were becoming worried. Rumors had started to swirl around Ithaca and Lansing about Edward, terrible stories. The Schutts refused to believe it, at first. Edward Rulloff was a terrible husband, as well as a nasty, profane man, but he was not a murderer. *Was he?* William shook Edward's hand uneasily.

"Where have you been?" William asked.

"Between the lakes," Edward calmly replied.

"Where's your wife and child?"

Edward smiled and repeated: "Between the lakes."

The brothers glanced at each other and pressed Edward for details. He replied that they were staying "between the lakes" near Geneva, New York, about fifty miles from their home in Lansing, at the head of Seneca Lake. He had left them there—it was a long journey to Ithaca on a horse and cart—and he explained that his wife and child would remain away for an extended time. Perhaps he'd even take his family off to Ohio, after all, so he could pursue that position at the prestigious academy. *There was nothing to worry about. Everyone was fine.*

As the tale unspooled, William grew increasingly tense. Harriet had told her brother numerous times that she would *never* leave home. What might have changed? And why had she and Priscilla vanished? It made no sense.

But then, if Edward were guilty of harming his wife and child, why would he return to visit his wife's family? And where had he been for the past six weeks? It turned out, as he'd later explain to the journalist, that he'd made his dreams of escaping to the West a reality. But for some reason, he had not gone to the teaching job in Ohio—perhaps the absence of his wife and child would have been too obvious. Instead, he'd traveled all the way to Chicago, veiled as just another anonymous immigrant. Once there, he'd sold the contents of his trunks for thirty dollars. But then, after the first flush of excitement had worn off, Edward found himself frustrated with no work, no rest, and aching regret.

"I was constantly haunted by some terrible visage either awake or asleep," he cried to Ham during one of their visits. "Remorse, remorse pursued me everywhere." Was it guilt that drew him back to Ithaca, an impulse to come clean to the Schutt family? There were, and are, a myriad of theories.

Former Ithaca district attorney Samuel Halliday would later interview Edward and report his assessment to readers. Halliday offered some poignant observations that seemed to confirm some of Edward's psychopathic traits, including evidence of pathological lying.

"Rulloff was a great actor," remembered Halliday. "Nothing seemed to throw him off from his balance or to disturb him. . . . It may be he had the power of will to enable him to dismiss for the time being all thought of his then predicament."

Halliday had a theory about why a killer would return to the area where he was under suspicion, as Edward did when he visited William Schutt not just once but several times after murdering Harriet and Priscilla.

"It is a well understood fact that there is a kind of indescribable fascination to a criminal about the place where he has committed a crime, and however far he may go away still he wants to come back," contended Halliday. "Leading and long-experienced detectives all assert that if a crime has been committed, and the criminal is known and has run away, it is not necessary to go after him; all one has to do is to keep perfectly still, and in time he will come back to the very scene of his crime. Such seemed to have been the impelling influence that compelled Rulloff to return."

Halliday described a character trait that researchers at the

FBI's Behavioral Science Unit discovered more than a century later and it clarified the nuances between different classes of criminals. In the 1970s, FBI profilers began classifying the crime scenes of serial killers based on whether they were "disorganized" or "organized." Some of what agents John Douglas and Robert Ressler learned about organized killers came from Ressler's interviews with serial killer John Wayne Gacy, who murdered more than thirty men in Chicago in the 1970s. Ressler believed that the organized murderer such as Gacy carefully planned his attacks; Gacy was usually highly intelligent, meticulous, and left behind little evidence, all to maintain control. Agents concluded that this type of murderer was often very difficult to catch because he is forensically savvy, as opposed to the disorganized killer.

The disorganized criminal, on the other hand, is spontaneous, and his crimes are likely to be opportunistic. The disorganized killer is more likely to leave weapons at the murder scene; he is messier and leaves behind more forensic evidence; he is generally easier to find and capture. And crucially, the FBI realized through their interviews, some disorganized criminals enjoy returning to the scene of the crime to relive the details. Most criminals are disorganized, thankfully for law enforcement. But the organized murderers often make history in the media, like serial killers Dennis Rader, Ted Bundy, Israel Keyes, and Joel Rifkin.*

As neat as these categorizations are, Edward Rulloff defies *easy* classification. His behavior seemed both organized and disorganized at different times. The murder of Harriet and Priscilla didn't

---

* Ed Kemper, an organized killer, explained to FBI agents that he had "seen one too many stories of one too many people" being caught by police by returning to the scene—he vowed not to make the same mistake. But Kemper wanted attention and when he realized that the police might never catch him, he turned himself in and confessed.

seem premeditated, but the meticulous care he took to clean the crime scene and remove the bodies was distinctly organized and painstaking. So why did he return to Hale's Store that day? That wasn't the act of an organized murderer, as Samuel Halliday believed; rather, I believe it stemmed from self-preservation.

After years of leaning on the Schutts for resources, Edward had nowhere else to go. His bravado and brashness outweighed any common sense he might have once had—another common trait among psychopathic individuals. Their hubris might get them so far, but it ultimately leads to detection. Throughout history, some criminals have risked being caught by allegedly taunting police and the press, infamous killers like Jack the Ripper, "Son of Sam," and the notorious BTK killer. Dennis Rader's taunting letters, sent to law enforcement and even surviving victims in the months and years after his crimes, were acts of self-sabotage that eventually led to his capture. Why risk being detected?

"The beating heart of his identity was that he was a serial killer," author Katherine Ramsland told me after interviewing Rader. "And he wanted to be a famous one. He wanted to be Jack the Ripper. There have been metaphors to try to characterize this sense of when a psychopath has a goal. They're like on a speeding train; they don't think about negative consequences. They're just completely bent on the reward, no matter what."

Edward Rulloff was similarly confident that he could manipulate his brother-in-law, another display of his immense hubris. William eyed Edward and insisted that they retire upstairs to his lodging house. Edward followed him up the staircase before William slid the latch to the lock on his bedroom door. He swung around and interrogated Edward with a series of pointed questions.

"I asked him if he had heard of a report there was about

his murdering his wife and child," recalled William Schutt. "He said he had not. He seemed to be somewhat surprised that they should think any such thing."

Edward's pained reaction to being accused of murder seemed to quell William Schutt's suspicions, at least for the moment, so he invited his brother-in-law to stay. But Edward grew restless, complaining that his eyes were aching from many sleepless nights. William responded kindly, as he had many times before.

"His eyes were sore, I wrapped them up in cloths," said William. "I asked him what troubled him. He said it troubled him to think that the people had that opinion of him that he would murder his wife and child."

It was clear that Edward was guilty of *something*; it was unclear of what. Finally, the family landed on a plan. William walked over to an old wooden desk and retrieved a fountain pen and some slips of paper, along with an envelope. His idea: they would force Edward to write a letter to Harriet, post it, and then he would stay with them in Ithaca until they could read her response, which could take weeks. This plan was an incredible exercise in patience for the Schutts and a source of anxiety for Edward. He knew that when Harriet failed to respond, he would certainly be arrested.

Edward reluctantly agreed to write the letter; he penned a note, scribbled an address on the front of the envelope, sealed it, and handed it to another Schutt brother, Ephraim, to deliver to a nearby post office. As Edward waited for his brother-in-law to return, he paced along the wooden planks of the back porch. For some reason, the family left only Harriet's sister, Jane Schutt, to watch him. They were in the same room for a while, until Edward smiled and requested a glass of water. While she was gone, Edward made his escape.

"He walked back and forth for a while as if he wanted to get rid of me," Jane said, "then went on to the front stoop, and then went off suddenly. I sent word to the store that he had left."

Edward Rulloff was gone once again, and this time the Schutts were certain that he wouldn't return voluntarily. They rushed to Edward's abandoned home in Lansing, bringing the sheriff. There was no sign of Edward or his family—but neither were there damning clues of a murder.

"The bed was in disorder," reported John F. Burdick, a neighbor who volunteered to help the family. "Saw a skirt at the foot of the bed laying in a circle, also stockings, shoes, elastics—some dishes on the table unwashed . . . one or two diapers lay near the door."

The men discovered no blood, no weapon, and no significant signs of a struggle—just poor housekeeping. There was little evidence of a cleanup in the house, but Ephraim Schutt did notice something disquieting.

"I know [Edward] had a cast iron mortar that would weigh 25 or 30 lbs," remembered Ephraim. "He had flat irons; on search [I] could not find anything of them."

This scene was still enough to dismay the Schutts. Ephraim, ever the commander of the Schutt brothers, immediately began to arrange travel plans—he would track Edward Rulloff across America, if needed. Ephraim's brother William secured a warrant from a local magistrate, paperwork that assigned him power to arrest Edward Rulloff and return him to Ithaca in shackles to face trial. This all seemed improbable, even foolhardy . . . he could be anywhere. In the mid-1800s, anonymity was easily attained; a criminal could simply hop on a train and travel throughout much of the country. With no systematized method of identification, it was nearly impossible to locate him or prove his real identity. Photography had been introduced just a few years earlier, in 1839, and it was primarily used for scenic views of cities, not personal portraits. There was no contemporary photo of Edward Rulloff until decades later—the Schutts feared that Ephraim would be luckless on his frantic search.

But Ephraim Schutt was dogged. He quickly hired a private horse-drawn carriage to take him to a train station in Geneva, where Edward claimed he and his family were staying, almost forty miles northwest of Ithaca. Ephraim guessed that Edward would head west, and he figured that using the railway would be his safest and fastest way to escape. Ephraim arrived in Geneva early the next morning and searched multiple train cars, but with no luck. The next nearest railway was in Rochester, less than fifty miles from Geneva. Ephraim bought a ticket, rode the train, and stepped out onto the platform in Rochester, and ran down toward a car assigned to immigrants. He swiftly searched that car and was prepared to give up when, miraculously, he spotted a stocky, ruddy-faced man with broad shoulders holding a bundle in his hand: Edward Rulloff. He stared back at Ephraim and quickly turned on his heel toward the door of the car to jump out, but it was too late. The wheels of the train squealed and began to roll, trapping the two men in the train together.

Edward slumped down and tried to crawl, hoping to vanish among the sea of scowling faces in a cramped car. Ephraim scanned the faces of each person until he found his brother-in-law. Edward panicked and tried to run, but Ephraim snatched him by the collar and dragged him to another car. Edward screamed at Ephraim that Harriet and Priscilla were in Ohio—he had been lying before when he claimed they were in Geneva. He explained that he quickly left Ithaca because he was anxious to be reunited with them.

Ephraim listened to Edward. At this point, he didn't believe a word that his brother-in-law offered. But he was becoming worried sick about Harriet and baby Priscilla—*Where were they?*—and sticking with Edward seemed to be the best, maybe the only, chance he had of seeing them alive again. He decided upon a course of action that might seem confounding, even foolish, to modern ears: Ephraim glared at Edward and insisted that they travel west together, so he could see Harriet and Priscilla for himself.

The duo continued on the train to Buffalo, and there they planned to take a steamer on Lake Erie that would eventually lead them to Cleveland, Ohio, more than three hundred miles away from Ithaca. Ephraim thought it prudent to spend the night at the Mansion House Inn in Buffalo, though Ephraim never slept. "He took off his shoes," explained Ephraim. "His feet were blistered badly."

Edward sprawled out on the bare floor and closed his eyes. Ephraim offered little sympathy and even less trust as he turned the lock to the door; Edward slept as Ephraim stood guard outside his door all night, determined to return him to the sheriff in Ithaca if they didn't find Harriet and Priscilla in Ohio. The next day, Ephraim dragged Edward along by his shirt as they waded through a large crowd on the gangplank boarding the steamer. The throng heaved forward, and Ephraim lost his grip on Edward. In an instant, his brother-in-law was gone once again.

Ephraim frantically searched the horde for Edward, but to no avail. He thought Edward must be on the steamer to Cleveland, but he couldn't be sure. Ephraim scooted off the gangplank to sort out his next steps, and as the steamer pulled away, he spotted a figure on the boat. Edward. Free again.

Ephraim tried to think like his sneaky brother-in-law—there was still a chance that he might find Edward if he could get to Cleveland before the boat did. He hired a livery team and rushed to the dock in Cleveland, arriving before the ship did and plotting his next steps.

Ephraim composed himself as he stood on the wharf, watching as the steamers floated in, both carrying hundreds of immigrants. He showed a law enforcement officer his arrest warrant for Edward and offered him cash to help hunt him down. As the pair began searching the boats, Ephraim peered inside an old, cheap dining saloon and pointed to a man squatting on the floor. The officer rushed over.

"Is your name Rulloff?" the officer asked the man crouching behind a box.

"No, sir," Edward calmly replied.

"Yes, it is," snapped Ephraim, exhausted from the multiday search.

The officer quickly arrested Edward, placed him in shackles, and walked him aboard a steamer heading back northeast on Lake Erie to Ithaca. Ephraim shoved Edward into a cabin and locked the door, above Edward's pleas. Ephraim slid onto a bench on the back deck alone before relief washed over him—and then sorrow. He now believed with certainty that his beloved sister and niece were most certainly dead, and Edward Rulloff was guilty of murder. As the steamer chugged along the eastern coastline, Edward beckoned the officer who had helped Ephraim to arrest him. Edward was cunning—he whispered to the officer:

"My friend, it is alright; my wife and child are living. You see

I am a poor devil. Look at me! My wife's family are wealthy and proud and despise me only because I am poor. My wife loves me, and I her, and we have concluded to leave her family, and go where they will know nothing of us."

The officer surveyed Edward—he seemed sincere. After more sobbing, Edward begged the officer to release him and spare him from certain mob justice once he arrived in Ithaca. The townspeople there were brutes, he insisted. As the officer reached for the door handle, Ephraim arrived back at the door and shoved him aside. Edward's countenance shifted almost instantly when he realized that his opportunity to escape had been dashed by his brother-in-law.

"[Edward] assumed an air of 'injured innocence,'" wrote biographer Hamilton Freeman; "he played the martyr, became silent and moody, and refused to enter into any explanations, or to tell where they were."

But then suddenly, Edward's tone switched once again; the killer was gifted, as many psychopaths are, at posturing to suit his needs. Edward sensed an opportunity as he whispered promises to Ephraim through the steel door. *Just release me and I'll talk.* Inexplicably, Ephraim cautiously agreed as the boat reached the center of Lake Erie. If Harriet and Priscilla were indeed dead, as Ephraim feared, then they deserved a proper Christian burial. Ephraim hoped to force Edward to tell the truth, for once. Ephraim unlocked the door, unfastened his shackles, and marched the killer to a bench on the upper deck near the pilothouse; together they gazed across the lake as the steamer slowly moved toward certain justice for the Schutts in Ithaca. Ephraim turned to his brother-in-law and struggled to control his rage.

"You came into our family in poverty and distress," he pleaded.

"You were kindly—very kindly—received. I am now entirely satisfied that you are guilty. What can you say for yourself?"

Edward was quiet before he offered Ephraim an unusual proposal. He would save the Schutts the pain of a public trial and jump overboard right now—his death would relieve everyone of more suffering. Ephraim watched Edward—he was so deceitful. For several years, Edward Rulloff had deceived the Schutts. Not this time.

"Fine," Ephraim said snidely. "But you're too much of a coward."

Edward didn't reply as he sat by stoically. Ephraim scoffed and snatched him by the collar, then quickly walked Edward back to the room before locking the door. By this time a crowd had gathered around the room because the passengers had heard the rumor that a murderer was on the ship—a child killer, the most despicable type of criminal. The captain admonished Ephraim for sparing Edward's life.

"That damned wretch has murdered your sister," yelled the captain. "My friend, if this was my case, I would hang him to the yard-arm."

Ephraim Schutt silenced the growing mob. He, more than anyone, wished to see Edward hang for killing four members of his own family, but vigilante justice was not *real* justice. Ephraim would spare Edward's life so he could face a jury in the hopes that he would reveal where Harriet and Priscilla's bodies were hidden.

Ephraim would soon regret his decision.

———

Four months after Ephraim Schutt captured his brother-in-law in Ohio, Edward Rulloff's trial (the first of several) began in Ithaca, New York. The Schutts all sat shoulder to shoulder in the courtroom's gallery. Edward was charged with murdering Harriet, not Priscilla—the district attorney contended that few would believe Edward could kill his own child. Harriet and Edward had a troubled marriage, as many people would swear to on the stand.

The Schutts listened as Judge Hiram Gray offered the jury two choices—they could convict Edward of murdering Harriet Rulloff *or* kidnapping her, but not both. The jurors needed to agree on whether she was dead or alive. If he were convicted of kidnapping, Edward would spend only a decade in prison, not severe enough for most sitting in the gallery. A murder verdict would doom Edward to the gallows.

The trial began in January 1846, with Edward representing himself—he pointed to his previous legal experience working at a law firm in Canada, and the judge agreed that he was qualified. Edward deftly cross-examined witnesses, including his in-laws. Edward debated with the judge graciously and he argued brilliantly; he reasoned that until investigators could locate the body of his wife, he could not be held responsible for her death. But of course, Edward denied that he had killed anyone—he was being persecuted by a spiteful family who loathed him.

"Rulloff himself made a speech, laboring evidentially under intense excitement," relayed a local newspaper. "He had found rumors rife . . . that he had planted the dagger in the breast of a child . . . he had poisoned—poisoned. He had not outraged the feelings of the community. The community had outraged *his* feelings."

Edward's passionate defense echoed across the walls of the courthouse . . . would a guilty man protest *this much*? thought some spectators. Edward inserted the concept of reasonable doubt into every argument, and he smartly avoided testifying. The prosecutor listened to Edward's claims and became dismayed because

Edward was right—they had not located Harriet's body, and her relationship with Edward was known to be acrimonious. *She might have simply left me,* argued Edward. Investigators uncovered no evidence to the contrary. Each Schutt shifted uncomfortably in the witness chair as he or she outlined Edward's abusive behavior and violent jealousy.

The jurors debated the evidence for days until they reached a verdict: *guilty,* declared the foreman—but of kidnapping, not murder. He would not hang. The judge sentenced Edward to ten years in prison. The Schutts were outraged; Edward, strangely, seemed unconcerned.

"He received his sentence not with defiance, but with a cool indifference," wrote Richard Mather, an academic who would later study Edward's complicated theory about languages, "an amused smile at the judge's advice to prepare for a future life, and a laugh with his counsel as he sat down."

But psychopaths are experts at masking their emotions—especially fear—out of self-preservation, so Edward's composed reaction was certainly just for show. While the Schutts appeared defeated, Judge Gray was incensed. His professional edict was to remain impartial, but Gray was convinced of Edward's guilt. After Edward was returned to the Ithaca jail, Judge Gray quietly surveyed each juror. The men collectively replied that they, like Gray, were also certain of Edward's guilt. The judge stared at the group incredulously and asked:

"How, then could you find him conscientiously guilty of abduction?"

"We did not know if we should ever get a chance at him again," replied one juror, "and we were bound to convict him of something."

There was not enough evidence to legally hold Edward for murder, but the jurors felt desperate to keep him in prison. Gossip spread across Tompkins County in the aftermath of the trial, and the lies terrified the Schutts. There were rumors that Harriet and Priscilla had been sold to a nearby medical college for use in anatomy classes. A newspaper in Vermont reported that a recent flood in Ithaca had exhumed a trunk from Cayuga Lake. Officials discovered the mangled bodies of what seemed to be a woman and child inside, but neighbors were certain that Edward had returned to his home with his trunk. Edward reported the same thing to Hamilton Freeman. It was another distracting, false lead.

The Schutts authorized the Tompkins County Sheriff to offer a $300 reward "for the discovery of the bodies of the wife and child of Edward H. Rulloff, or of the body of the wife alone—and a farther reward of $100 for the discovery of the baggage of the said Edward H. Rulloff."

The horde of outraged locals received even more fodder when the attorney who had advised Edward during his kidnapping trial claimed that Edward told him that he had cut the throats of both his wife and daughter. On his deathbed, S. B. Cushing declared that his client had wrapped the bodies with wire so they could never be unfastened before attaching a heavy iron mortar to Harriet and a flat iron to Priscilla.

"According to this alleged confession Rulloff chloroformed his wife, opened an artery, took up a board in the floor and allowed the blood to flow through upon the ground underneath until she died," wrote attorney Samuel Halliday. The former district attorney argued that slicing Harriet's throat would have created a torrent of blood, yet the Schutts discovered no blood inside the Lansing home.

The truth is, we'll never know what happened to the remains of Harriet Schutt or whether little Priscilla lived and thrived with Edward's brother; there are odd coincidences. Rulof Rulofson had a daughter also named Priscilla, born just five months after Edward's daughter, in Calais, Maine. It was this fluke that ignited rumors purporting that Priscilla had been sent to her uncle's homestead after her mother's murder.

I've pored over evidence for years about Priscilla's disappearance; I believe, for several reasons, that Edward likely murdered his daughter. His neighbors noticed when he left with the trunk and when he returned with it—they reported that he received no visitors before they watched him leave the Lansing home for the last time. When did Edward have time to transport Priscilla to his brother's home almost seven hundred miles away without being noticed? He didn't have the money or the resources for that trip. He claimed that Harriet's murder was a spontaneous crime of passion. When did he arrange for her to be taken by a trusted friend to Maine?

Craig Schutt offered me another observation.

"The baby would have been crying," he told me. "She was still nursing."

Edward told Ham that he fed Priscilla a narcotic to stop her crying, which was likely true. But without someone there to monitor Priscilla, she would have awoken at some point. Wouldn't a woman be needed to calm her? None of that seems likely. Perhaps if Harriet's murder were planned, then whisking Priscilla to Maine was possible, but not in this case. I believe that Edward fatally poisoned his daughter and then disposed of her body in Cayuga Lake, as he did her mother.

In 1846, Judge Hiram Gray sentenced Edward Rulloff to a

decade in Auburn State Prison, the maximum punishment allowed for kidnapping. The entire Schutt family demanded that
Edward immediately face the gallows. Ephraim remained silent,
regretting his decision to stop the vengeful passengers aboard the
steamer the previous year. Ephraim refused to make another mistake. The law had failed him and his family—but vigilante justice
could offer the Schutts some level of retribution. The family raised
a lynch mob, hoping to break into the Ithaca jail before Edward's
transfer to the prison. The men sawed down a large tree and built
a battering ram to knock down the door—it was so unwieldy that
it took twenty people to pick the thing up. But they were too late;
the sheriff had transported Edward to protect him. The killer was
saved by the law once again.

Edward Rulloff soon became the newest inmate of the Auburn
State Prison, a maximum-security facility about forty miles north
of Ithaca. His new home was an imposing building designed to
resemble a medieval English castle, with a grim exterior that inspired fear in those who passed by it and terror in those who were
confined inside. Prison life was a terrible trial for most inmates at
Auburn; many convicts were sentenced to hard labor in the nearby
fields, and yet Edward Rulloff seemed to thrive there as, once
again, he remade himself—his innate skills at inventing became
invaluable.

"The keen perception of the keeper very soon discovered that he
had in him a prisoner of remarkable ability," wrote Hamilton Freeman, "with a genius of great versatility in mechanical arts as well as
literary pursuits." Edward Rulloff became a proficient carpet designer, part of his work program inside the prison, and he was hired
by a contractor to create designs worth about $5,000 a year (of which

he received a percentage).* Edward also received money in the mail from his younger brother William, who was now an acclaimed photographer in San Francisco. William refused to visit his brother in Auburn, but he later claimed he would always be grateful for Edward's guidance and protection when they were younger.

Edward ordered dozens of books to stack inside his cell, along with writing materials to use on an old wooden desk. The guards trusted him, and the warden seemed impressed with his academic pursuits. In some ways, prison offered Edward his greatest desire: a life of quiet, focused study and reflection. Day and night, Edward reignited his passion for philosophers, especially Plato, an obsession which began when he was a young student in Canada. When he wasn't toiling at his prison job, he was perfecting his Greek and even deepened his knowledge of Sanskrit.

"A lot of education in the 19th century was based upon the study of Greek and Latin, and that's actually a rather challenging thing to master," Cornell University linguistics professor Michael Weiss told me. "If there was a kind of magical key to understanding the sound and meaning in these languages . . . then that would have made a lot of people's lives a lot easier in that period."

One night, Edward was awoken by a revelation about the origin of language, a particularly popular topic amongst nineteenth-century linguists.

"He saw in his mind's eye the outline," said Ham Freeman,

---

* Some career criminals do thrive in prison and offer something back to society, even if it is in their own self-interest. Serial killer Edmund Kemper has narrated more than five thousand hours' worth of audiobooks for the visually impaired for the Volunteers of Vacaville at the California Medical Facility, a state prison at Vacaville, where he is currently incarcerated. He touts it as one of the most important things he's been involved with.

"which some bright angel whispered to him was to be not only the talisman of his fame and future . . . he could atone for the past, that mankind would forget and forgive his sins."

In the quiet of his prison cell, Edward began refining a unique theory about language called philology. A subfield of linguistics, philology is the study of language in historical and oral sources. Edward had long maintained a broad fascination with languages, and now he was honing his studies to reveal a specific thesis: he believed he had discovered a universal, unified theory that linked the origin of all languages along one singular path of development. He believed the study of language was a methodical science, like analyzing algebra—there was a relationship between words that could be understood using only his logic. Language didn't evolve from a primitive communication system, according to Edward. It was specifically designed; he detected a universal pattern across languages, one that would allow him to teach all languages to anyone—a Frenchman might learn Italian in a short period of time by learning the pattern that governed it, for example. It was a tantalizing theory, and Edward seemed to be proficient both at research and at penning that research in a cohesive way.

Edward's theory was still in its nascent period as he toiled on his manuscript by a little oil lamp hanging on the grating of his cell door. But he was starting to put his ideas into words, and he grew more excited as he found connections that seemingly bolstered his theories.

"Things which are opposites in meaning, are named from the same roots, in which the elements however are reversed," he wrote. "Take the words *stir* and *rest*, for example, the meanings of which are opposites. In *stir*, the roots is composed of *s, t, r*; in *rest* these are reversed—*r, s, t*." It sounded crackpot, almost insane, when taken out of context. But he was convinced his ideas would unlock the key to a universal theory that unified all languages under one common umbrella.

"No other man lived with a higher or nobler ambition than I," he insisted to Ham Freeman.

He obsessed over each word, revising every sentence ad nauseam. While in prison, Edward was introduced to several students of theology at a nearby school, including a bright seminary student named Julius Hawley Seelye. Seelye would eventually become an author, a congressman, and the president of Amherst College. The pair exchanged numerous letters, each delving deeper into Edward's evolving theory, but they also discussed Edward's philosophy about life.

"From the invisible animalcule to the leviathan of the deep, one order of creatures is constantly preying upon another," wrote Edward to Seelye, "and can subsist only by doing so."

Edward recited knotty passages in Greek and offered astute context afterward. He presented Seelye with multiple theories, some of them sounder than others. Edward speculated on the language of Homer, the Greek poet who authored *The Iliad* and *The Odyssey*.

"He was the center of a system which was perfected under that name," wrote Edward. "I believe with others that no one man was the author of all that is ascribed to Homer." Edward's insightful theory was echoed by others but was far from accepted science at that point in the 1800s. Edward believed that the phraseology of Homer was developed by multiple people, not a single man.

Modern linguists now believe that to be true, but it wasn't a mainstream theory in the 1850s when Edward was in prison. He was so bright, a scholar with loads of potential—and finally his mind was being given the opportunity to grow and develop.

Edward, a self-taught languages expert from a humble background, might have been gifted, but he couldn't suppress his violent nature, even in letters. When Seelye criticized some aspects of his theories, gently pushing back in the way that academics do when challenging one another, the imprisoned scholar replied with a frightful reaction.

"I think I perceive that you regard my discovery in language as of trifling or doubtful importance—and it may now be that you will never live to see reasons for correcting the impression." The tone of Edward's letters reflected his volatile temperament while observers noted a man with a dual personality: a model inmate with a deep desire to better the world with his innovative theory on languages, but one who shouldn't be threatened. Edward's impulse to react rashly was concerning to Seelye, even as a young student of religion.

Despite the horrid conditions, Edward thrived in Auburn and in 1856, after ten years, he composed a series of letters to his attorneys to prepare for his release. He appeared optimistic about his future as he swiftly recorded his ideas each night, readying himself for a new start anywhere but upstate New York.

In 1871, reporter Oliver Dyer watched Edward Rulloff weep—not for his wife and child but for his own wasted intellectual capacity. As Edward began to describe his theories of the origin of the human language, his demeanor lit up in a way it never seemed to when remembering his long-dead family. The prisoner wiped his face with a bedsheet. Dyer stared at the disgraced scholar through the dim light of the flickering oil lamp hovering nearby. *Tell me about your work*, the newspaperman urged Edward.

"Why did you cry over it?" softly asked Dyer.

"To think that fate should lead me into so many complications and perplexities which interfered with my prosecution of the work," Edward cried, "and when . . . driven almost to despair again, I have finally rallied to the work once more; and so have gone on with it, year after year."

His theory of one unified language—and, specifically, writing a book that outlined the theory for a general audience—had become the driving force in his life. Edward's compulsion to complete the book had become an obsession. In his mind, any action he must undertake to finish that task—lying, cheating, worse?—was justified. Experts in antisocial personality disorders believe that those mired with psychopathy feel forced to act in their own self-interests, less by obsession than by a compulsion for self-preservation. Sometimes they resort to violence to remove obstacles, but there is also an element of manipulation. FBI agent John Douglas found this uniformly with the killers and psychopaths that he interviewed for the Behavioral Science Unit in the 1970s.

"Every killer and predator represented many layers of subtle distinctions," wrote Douglas in his book *The Killer Across the Table*. "Yet we can say that all of these men had internal conflicts between grandiosity and inadequacy. All had a sense of personal entitlement that removed from them the obligation to heed society's laws and conventions."

Edward Rulloff relished his sense of entitlement and his demand for control. Once again, he was leveraging a nascent relationship with a journalist to influence public opinion. And it worked; Oliver Dyer's widely read articles in *The Sun* not only legitimized Edward's theories, they also offered a sympathetic portrait of a man once vilified in national press. Edward had successfully reframed his own narrative for the public, one as a brilliant scholar languishing behind bars when he could be contributing to important scholarship.

"As the door of his cell was closed and double-locked on his, we thought Rulloff exhibited a worried and depressed aspect, and a nervousness bordering on hysteria," Dyer wrote. "Were it not for his persistent studies, the chances are that he would go insane."

Dyer concluded that Edward was *not* insane but obsessed . . . and perhaps unjustly incarcerated. Edward constantly complained to both Hamilton Freeman and Oliver Dyer that he was a victim of circumstance.

Edward explained to Dyer emphatically and passionately that he was compelled to commit these horrible crimes because of his own complicated, brilliant ideas. He had to remove obstacles to those ideas.*

"Is it because you regret the facts of your life?" asked Dyer.

"I have done many things under stress of circumstances which I am sorry to have done," replied Edward, "but before God I have never done anything in my life which, under the same circumstances, I would not do again."

Edward Rulloff was inherently contradictory—during interviews with Hamilton Freeman, he bemoaned his reckless decision

---

* Self-serving complaints are also a trademark of psychopaths, according to forensic psychologist Dr. Katherine Ramsland, citing her experience with Dennis Rader. "Psychopaths are all about: 'I'm the victim.' They blame others," Ramsland told me. "They're always whining about their circumstances because it's all about them."

to murder his wife, but to Oliver Dyer he insisted that he would murder once again to achieve his goals. There were nuances in his behavior with both men. Ham had been visibly horrified by Edward's description of Harriet's murder, so Edward feigned contrition. But Dyer seemed in awe of his scholarship, so Edward framed himself as a man committed to his theory, at all costs. Another person's life was worth sacrificing—and this didn't seem to outrage Dyer.

Edward spent his life explaining his belief that God didn't exist, yet he was shrewd enough to realize that a pious man, like Dyer, wouldn't empathize with an atheist, so he adjusted.

"You believe in Providence then?" Dyer asked.

"That is a wonderful question," Edward replied. "I look into the stars, and I see no bottom. I have this conviction: that religion must be a matter of faith, and not of knowledge; that God's decrees are inscrutable."

The *New York Tribune*'s editorial board applauded Edward's thoughtful answer.

"A more admirable answer than the last—from a man evidently groping in the dark, as Rulloff is—could scarcely have been given," read one of Dyer's articles. "His last remarks, on bidding adieu to Mr. Dyer, was 'I should prefer to live and finish my work, but I am not afraid to die.'"

Edward certainly felt ill-used by the legal system and by society at large . . . and people were listening. Dyer's articles in the influential *Sun* would convince some of the country's leading politicians and orators to defend Edward. What fascinated (and terrified) Oliver Dyer's readers was how *sane* Edward seemed, and in fact psychopaths *are* sane. Psychopathy isn't classified as a mental illness but as an antisocial personality disorder. It would be another eighty years before character disorders were formally recognized in the *DSM* (*Diagnostic and Statistical Manual of Mental Disorders*). In the 1870s, a killer with Edward's characteristics would be labeled "morally insane," a neurotypical criminal without delusions or hallucinations—not mentally ill, but certainly amoral.

His time with Edward would invariably influence Oliver Dyer's career. In less than a decade, the writer would become an ordained minister, a godly man who spoke out passionately against lynch mobs that were targeting President James Garfield's assassin. *No one is wholly evil,* concluded Dyer after meeting Edward—there are nuances within our morality. The killer was not a monster, but a man. And yes, his ideas *should* save him from the noose because no one that promising should be wasted on the gallows.

Now two journalists—first Hamilton Freeman, now Oliver Dyer, both with national reach—had been seduced by a violent, manipulative psychopath. Edward Rulloff was a pathological liar, and few were skilled enough to recognize it. Yet several men, more astute than the pair of journalists, were scheduled to visit Edward—more Gilded-Age mindhunters seeking to understand the mysteries of his baffling brain.

4

The Greek Scholar

*I set out through the lamplit streets, in the same divided ecstasy
of mind, gloating on my crime, light-headedly devising others
in the future, and yet still hastening and still hearkening in
my wake for the steps of the avenger.*
—Robert Louis Stevenson,
Strange Case of Dr. Jekyll and Mr. Hyde, 1886

Richard Henry Mather had kindly eyes that drooped just slightly at the corners; his smile was framed by a round face and an Imperial beard, the muttonchops-plus-moustache style of facial hair so popular in the nineteenth century. The thirty-six-year-old was plump, short, and unimposing—balding but handsome. Mather resembled nothing so much as an admired professor whose patience soothed anxious students attending Amherst College in Massachusetts, which was exactly what he was.

Smartly dressed as usual, Mather walked toward the jail in Binghamton in April 1871 to visit the still-incarcerated Edward Rulloff. Mather was curious about the man after reading so much about him over the past many months and years—especially his intriguing and utterly new linguistic theories. As an expert in Greek and German at Amherst, Mather took particular interest in

Edward Rulloff and his unique ideas. Mather had admired Oliver Dyer's series in *The Sun* the previous month, which presented Edward's complicated theory of the origin of languages in rich, vivid detail. Was there something of substance here? Mather was determined to find out.

He'd heard much about Edward Rulloff, and not just from reading *The Sun*. Mather's colleague at Amherst, Julius Seelye, recounted his letters with Edward from back in the 1850s, when Edward had been serving time in the Auburn State Prison. Seelye was now a professor of mental and moral philosophy at Amherst, and within a few years, he would rise to the university's presidency. Seelye had recommended Mather's visit; he insisted that Edward's theory would fascinate Mather. On the strength of Seelye's recommendation, Mather had traveled more than two hundred miles from Massachusetts to his hometown of Binghamton to meet this strange, compelling man.

It was like a visit Seelye himself had made, back in the mid-1850s, when Edward had been serving a ten-year prison sentence for "kidnapping" his wife in 1845. During that visit, Seelye had presented to Edward a copy of the book *Plato Contra Atheos*. The writings were a translated summary of Plato's famous argument in Greek for the existence of God. Edward requested to borrow it and assured him that he would return it with comments on the translation; Seelye discovered that Edward had assessed the translation very thoroughly, and he had been dazzled. Decades later, Edward was once again developing scholarship on languages—honing his theory while shackled to the floor of a jail. Both Seelye and Mather found that feat to be remarkable.

"The whole was done by him in his cell," wrote Mather, "yet it was a piece of scholarly work, such as few professors could excel writing amid the resources of their well-equipped libraries. In point of penmanship, it was exquisite and like a finished engraving."

Mather was curious about Edward's own stance on the meaning of life. In October 1858, Edward had written Seelye an eloquently composed missive detailing his ideas about the existence of God.

"I look in vain for certain evidence of any higher agency controlling the course of things," wrote Edward. "What I see is only a world of conflicting passions and of clashing interests, producing strife and contention, and everywhere resulting in the heartless destruction of one creature for the benefit or preservation of another and with such an order of things I must say I have no sympathy whatever."

This was a different, more pessimistic response from his reply to Oliver Dyer, who had asked the same question. To Dyer, Edward teased that he *did* believe in God: "religion must be a matter of faith." But while Dyer required some courting to become useful to Edward, Seelye seemed to welcome a debate about Divine Providence. I suspect that Edward's true take on religion could be found in his comments to Seelye.

Edward might have entranced a young Julius Seelye, but Professor Mather would not be so easily swayed. The professor, a noted writer who edited Greek textbooks for universities, was armed with an incredible breadth of knowledge about languages. Mather was currently toiling over a volume about the ancient Greek historian Herodotus.

At nine in the morning, Richard Mather shook the hand of Edward's advocate before they both entered the unwelcoming corridor of the Binghamton jail, the same hallway that journalists

Ham Freeman and Oliver Dyer had walked down just a few months earlier. Inexplicably, the defense attorney had to struggle to convince Edward to accept the meeting; by this time, the killer shunned all visitors, except the few he deemed gullible and malleable (Freeman) or sympathetic and influential (Dyer). When the attorney explained to Edward that Mather was a highly regarded professor of Greek, he reluctantly agreed. Edward both feared and revered educators—they could reject his life's work, resulting in certain public ridicule, but he also knew that Richard Mather's endorsement of his academic mastery might offer Edward a chance at legitimacy and clemency.

As Mather stood near the sheriff by his cell, Edward approached the latticed iron door with trepidation. He was concerned that Mather would listen to his theory for just a moment before dismissing it out of hand; being misinterpreted was the killer's greatest dread. Edward very politely requested that Mather stay for a lengthy visit, to allow time to clarify his ideas. Mather didn't reply, simply requesting the sheriff to allow him inside the cell. The sheriff slid the massive metal bolts and swung open the door. Mather stepped inside the long, narrow granite-built room with high ceilings. Each loud noise generated an echo that bounced from wall to wall.

Edward dragged over two rickety wooden pallets and politely offered to take Mather's hat. The professor smiled, handed over his hat, and then explained that he had reviewed Edward's criticism of the translation of Plato's piece, from his time with Seelye. Mather used this to establish a baseline for Edward's understanding of Greek—now he wanted to delve into his scholarship further. *What else had he studied? How deep did his knowledge go?*

These weren't just abstract questions to Mather—they were imperative, and they'd inform everything that would follow. In fact, Mather was not merely evaluating Edward's knowledge; he was also interrogating the killer's intelligence, and therefore his value to society. Erudite, learned men in the 1800s were revered; in a time when formal education was often reserved for the elite, a knowledge of language was a status symbol of sorts as well as a mark of intelligence and breeding. Men of high intelligence controlled the country—and the threat of losing one to the noose seemed senseless to someone like Mather, no matter the crime. *Was Edward Rulloff elite?* Hamilton Freeman and Oliver Dyer seemed to think so. Mather would investigate for himself, and the evidence would be in the words Edward spoke, and the writing he labored over.

More than 150 years later, researchers are still studying the writings of criminals to find the hints of genius, and the traces of psychopathic tendencies, inscribed within their written communication. In 2018, three researchers in different disciplines—communications, psychology, and law—hoped to reveal whether "psychopathic tendencies leave a trace in online discourse." Psychopaths exhibit manipulation and callousness in person, but do they also follow linguistic patterns in their everyday online communication? They sure seem to, researchers discovered.

"Our findings across three types of online communication (email, Facebook, and SMS text messaging) support previous research, showing that discourse patterns of participants higher in psychopathy showed evidence of narcissism, psychological distancing, produced less comprehensible text, and used more words indicative of an interpersonally hostile style, including more anger and swear words," the report found. In other words, psychopaths are often less erudite and more antagonistic in their written communication style.

However, this study wasn't focused on the high-functioning psychopath, who is likely to subvert some of these unsavory characteristics; Edward Rulloff was certainly a high-functioning psychopath, so some of these features may not have applied to his writing. But the research did pose an interesting theory—no matter how glib or manipulative someone with psychopathy might be, they are likely to be eventually exposed. The trick, say experts, is discovering their penchant for violence or manipulation before it's too late. If the public can be taught to spot psychopathic behavior, people might be able to avoid falling victim.

Richard Mather didn't seem bothered by Edward's horrid crimes—instead, he was fascinated with his use of language, with both his writing style and his context. And maybe, just maybe, he was beginning to be drawn in by the probable psychopath's tried and true manipulation techniques. Mather was becoming enamored of Edward Rulloff, just as Hamilton Freeman and Oliver Dyer had been before.

"I had desired to learn how he had acquired his knowledge of the old languages," Mather said. But he was also drawn into the biographical and narrative details of the killer's life.

Edward grinned as he recalled much of his life story: he had not gone to university, but as a boy, Greek language had bewitched him, and since then he had studied it intently. Edward insisted that Mather assess his abilities, but the professor replied that he had not brought along any suitable textbooks.

"To which he rejoined that many of the classical authors he

knew by heart," wrote Mather. Edward quoted Homer and Sopho-
cles with great accuracy, noting that he was particularly fond of *The
Iliad*. He criticized a selection of well-known comments about certain passages of the ancient Greek epic poem.

"He did it with such subtlety and discrimination and elegance
as to show that his critical study of these nicer points was more
remarkable than his powers of memory," wrote Mather.

Mather marveled at the man sitting cross-legged on the shabby
pallet before him, who responded to his queries like a polished
Greek scholar. But Mather felt another emotion growing as well—
empathy for a tortured soul given no real chance in life. While
Edward talked about his past, his intellectual passions, and his
interests, Mather took note of the man's appearance.

"He has a singular face, not villainous or grossly sensual, nor is
it scholarly," Mather scribbled on a pad. "The features are strongly
marked and full of sinister meaning. It is a face that you could not
forget, and yet would not care to think about. His eye, which is
dark hazel, I had heard was the striking feature, but it did not
impress me so, perhaps because it showed struggle and suffering."

As Edward described the conclusion of his time at Auburn
State Prison fifteen years earlier, he seemed almost wistful, Mather
recalled, because his incarceration had marked a significant personal departure. While it had been lonely, it had also been the last
time he'd had the chance to devote himself fully to a life of the
mind.

Edward Rulloff was optimistic, even jubilant as he packed up his
belongings in his small cell in Auburn State Prison on January 25,

1856. The wind pushed against the stone doors of the building, and hard snow covered the ground as guards stood outside. Edward glanced at his cot, reflecting how Auburn's curious punishment system had helped him immensely.*

For more than a decade, Edward had been safely contained in these walls. But the Schutt family, whom he'd treated so terribly in so many ways, had not forgotten. Edward was still so despised in rural New York that his wife's family had received offers from hundreds of people to help lynch him upon his release. Edward knew that it wasn't going to be safe for him to resettle in the area. That cold Saturday morning, Edward expected to shake hands with the warden one last time and then leave upstate New York immediately.

Instead of release papers, however, the sheriff of Tompkins County handed Edward a document and asked that he read it over—it was another arrest warrant, this one from an indictment filed eight years earlier, while he was in prison. Harriet's family had spent years pressuring the district attorney to file new murder charges, and the DA had finally acquiesced. Edward's escape to a new life would have to wait.

Edward scoffed as the metal cuffs snapped around his wrists. Rather than leaving into freedom, he was loaded onto a wagon bound for Ithaca, and as he slid along the wooden bench, he seemed unsurprised to find that the Schutts were behind this turn of

---

* Elam Lynds, the first warden of the penitentiary, created the "Auburn Plan," which among other things required that prisoners work and eat together in silence. Convicts in striped uniforms shuffled across fields in lockstep, with their heads bowed. Each man had his own small cell, a type of solitary confinement regardless of behavior. The Auburn system served Edward nicely—the monkish quiet and hours of silent self-reflection proved productive for the academic.

events. The prosecutor planned to try him for the murder of his wife once again, even though Harriet's body had never been found.

A grand jury quickly indicted Edward on murder charges, and as the district attorney gathered evidence for his case, Edward plotted. Ever primed for an intellectual match, Edward had studied the law intently over the last several years. Prison guards at Auburn had spotted legal books lying alongside Edward's usual tomes on Latin and Greek in his cell. He was prepared for this day.

Edward insisted that his attorneys appeal the indictment, and Judge Ransom Balcom with the court of appeals was assigned the case. Edward represented himself, despite pleas from his attorneys; the killer rose in court and handed Judge Balcom the writ of habeas corpus he had composed himself, arguing that there could be no double jeopardy in his case because he had previously faced trial for killing Harriet, and a jury found him guilty of kidnapping, not murder, owing to a lack of evidence. Edward argued convincingly that he could not be tried twice for the same crime—and he was correct.

"The prisoner insisted that his trial, conviction and punishment for the abduction of his wife were a bar to all proceedings upon the indictment against him for her murder," read Edward's summary. District Attorney John A. Williams turned to Balcom and offered virtually no argument. Despite public sentiment that Edward must pay for his crimes, the fact remained: he had already been through the legal process once for Harriet's murder, and the law agreed. The judge glanced down at Williams and reluctantly replied:

"Rulloff is right."

The following day, Williams abruptly dropped the murder

charge connected to Harriet, to the outrage of the Schutts. Edward quietly gloated inside the Tompkins County jail—his wife's family had floundered once again.

Williams's decision sent the people of Tompkins County into fits. They wanted vengeance, and they demanded Edward's life. They stalked outside the jail in Ithaca as Edward sat silently inside, frantically making changes to his beloved manuscript. Edward refused to be deterred, despite facing a lynch mob.

But unbeknownst to the public, Judge Balcom had offered DA John Williams a clever solution (and an unethical hint) that could revive the case against Edward: "You must summon another grand jury and indict him for the murder of his child."

Edward had faced trial previously for murdering *Harriet*, not Priscilla. John Williams faced immense public pressure as he carefully prepared a case to ensure that Edward would remain in jail. He quickly drew up another murder indictment, this one accusing Edward of killing two-month-old Priscilla, and presented it to a panel of justices of the peace. But with no body, investigators couldn't establish precisely *how* Priscilla died, so the indictment described the various methods Edward *might have used* to murder her.

One of the most horrific theories asserted that her father kicked her to death. "[Rulloff is suspect of] the casting and throwing of her, the said Rulloff infant daughter of said Edward H. Rulloff, to the ground as aforesaid, as also by striking, beating, and kicking [Priscilla] . . . in and upon the head, stomach, back and sides of her . . . with both the hands and feet of him . . ."

Or, the indictment speculated, Edward might have strangled her with a silk handkerchief or bludgeoned her with a weapon. The former botanical doctor also could have poisoned her. "[T]he

quantity of two drachms of the said arsenic," read the 1856 indictment, "[Rulloff] did put, mix and mingle into a certain quantity
of milk . . ."

The prosecutor then offered a motive, one illustrative of the
terror felt by the people of Tompkins County: Rulloff did not have
"the fear of God before his eyes," the indictment read. "He was
moved and seduced by the instigation of the Devil."*

In 1856, the devil was certainly a central character in the public
perception of Edward Rulloff—at least in the countryside. Newspapers across America declared that Edward was purely evil; even
in the pages of Manhattan's *New York Tribune*, one of the country's
most progressive papers, editors marveled how Edward's scholarly
appearance never exposed his depravity.

"He has by no means a murderer's look about him," read the
editorial section. "Yet his development indicates strong animal
passions."

The case was so sensational that Edward insisted he couldn't
receive a fair trial, so it was moved from Tompkins County to
Tioga County, about thirty miles away. Ten months after he
was released from Auburn, he stood up in court and pleaded not
guilty for the murder of his infant child, Priscilla, twelve years
before.

According to accounts of the trial, Edward was cold and unconcerned as neighbors and friends filed past his table and sat
down in the witness chair. The trial was a litany of the complaints

---

* Putting the devil on trial was not new in America in 1856—less than two hundred
years earlier, the Salem witch trials were one of the most pertinent historic examples. The "witches" were accused of attempting to overthrow Christianity and the
church. By the conclusion of the hysteria, nineteen people had been executed and
more than two hundred people accused.

against Edward from more than a decade before: A confidant testified about his worry for Harriet after Edward expressed vitriol toward Dr. Henry Bull, her cousin and suspected suitor. The Rulloffs' former landlady described how Edward wrestled with Harriet over poison and then slapped her as she begged for forgiveness. The farmer who helped load the trunk containing Harriet's body and, presumably, Priscilla's body onto a horse and cart testified to Edward's cool demeanor.

Edward glared at his former in-laws, seated on the other side of the courtroom on October 28, 1856. Ephraim Schutt described how he found Harriet crying after Edward had hit her. William recounted his brother-in-law's complaints about Dr. Bull, while Jane Schutt testified amid tears that Edward had almost killed her sister by striking her in the forehead with a stone pestle. Finally, Edward's mother-in-law, Hannah Schutt, walked past him. He stared ahead as the sixty-year-old woman sat down in the witness chair, refusing to meet her eye.

"I am the mother of Mrs. Rulloff," Hannah said quietly. "I saw that she was unhappy."

She recounted the night that her son William's wife and infant daughter died, and afterward the callous threats Edward had made about her family. Ephraim Schutt recalled Edward's conflicting stories about the location of his wife and child; he described how he pursued his brother-in-law to Ohio and dragged him back to New York to stand trial, only to be dismayed by his light sentence. The Schutt family's fury at the justice system was evident to all spectators in court.

Edward Rulloff sat quietly and listened as his defense attorneys made their legal arguments. They refused to offer an emotional defense, just a simple legal argument—without a body, there was simply no crime. His attorneys offered no explanation for Priscilla's location, whether dead at the bottom of a lake or alive with Edward's brother. None of that mattered, they argued, because there was no proof of corpus delicti. The prosecutor was flummoxed.

As in the first trial, there was no physical evidence offered. But this jury didn't waffle about his guilt or innocence, as had the panel that convicted him as only a "kidnapper" more than ten years earlier. Jurors returned quickly, and they convicted him of murdering his daughter, despite a lack of proof of murder; Edward was immediately sentenced to death. The Schutts rejoiced because they would *finally* see him hanged. Edward reacted coolly and ordered his attorneys to immediately appeal his conviction as he was sent back to the jail in Ithaca.

The New York Court of Appeals delayed its decision for seven months as the convicted killer sat chained to the floor of the jail, staring at seven locks that were fastened to his cell door. Auburn State Prison had been more tolerable to the academic, with its thick walls and silent corridors. Here, though, the echoes from other prisoners in jail (and the frequent crowds shouting outside it) kept him awake at night.

"He'll soon be dead," chanted the villagers outside the building. It seemed that justice might finally be served. But then something curious happened: Edward turned on his charm offensive yet again . . . this time, with deadly results.

———

During his months in the Tompkins County jail, Edward Rulloff had befriended his keepers—he was often affable when needed— and the guards offered him quite a few privileges, including a writing desk, books, paper, and pens. To ingratiate himself to the sheriff, Edward offered to educate the young students in Ithaca in writing and languages; those teenagers readily agreed to spend time across from a murderer—and their parents also agreed.

Edward was a devil cloaked in the guise of a brilliant academic, but he was now available for private tutoring. A stream of teenagers lined the corridor of the jail almost daily. As Edward sat cross-legged, he flipped through German books and made suggestions regarding penmanship as he awaited word from the district attorney about how he planned to proceed with more charges.

"Believing this indictment to be the last device of those he considered his enemies," wrote *New York Times* reporter Ed Crapsey, "he went back to Ithaca Jail, convinced that it was more of an annoyance than a danger, and that without a doubt he would be able to break this new net within a few weeks."

But "a few weeks" turned into months as DA John Williams slowly developed his case for the murder of Priscilla Rulloff; Edward grew anxious in 1857, but he stayed distracted as pupils filed in and out of his cell. There was one, a teenager, who paid attention to Edward more keenly than the others. He listened intently, with a smile, as Edward recited Plato. It was a familiar scene—Edward had charmed Harriet Schutt in much the same way when she was his young student more than ten years earlier.

The eighteen-year-old admirer was Albert Jarvis, and Edward seemed immediately entranced by the young man's attention. Al was described as extraordinarily attractive—tall, thin, with dark hair and a perfectly symmetrical face. He seemed innocent and eager as he handed Edward a gift.

"My attention was attracted to him first by a present of some fruit he made me," Edward recalled. "He was then a bright, active boy . . . the attachment which he began to have for me attracted the attention of his parents, who did not object to our intimacy."

In modern times, "intimacy" is often associated with a sexual relationship, but this wasn't the case in the 1800s. "Intimacy" simply signaled that they had developed a close friendship. But Edward's reckless decisions were evident in his choice to befriend Al Jarvis because the teenager's father was the undersheriff (deputy sheriff) of the county, Jacob Jarvis, and the family lived just above the jail. For more than six months, he worked with Al on his studies— only minimally distracted by the clanking of the chains each time he crossed his legs. Edward taught the teenager to speak German, Latin, and French. They became closer with each lesson—Al became Edward's prized pupil.

"I used frequently to employ him to do little errands for me in the village," Edward said, "such as to procure paper, pens, books, candles, etc. . . . . I found him an apt pupil."

But Edward Rulloff had also attracted someone else's gaze. Jane Jarvis, Al's mother, strolled by the outside of Edward's steel door, coyly smiling at the prisoner. She brought him gifts and complimented his scholarship. She was plain, but Edward found her amiable, and she seemed like a good resource for use later. Edward made sure to be gentle when he talked with her—he kindly complimented her, much like he did with Harriet. Edward understood how to woo a vulnerable woman; while Harriet had been young and naïve, Jane Jarvis appeared woeful thanks to a hopeless marriage. Edward told author Hamilton Freeman that Jane Jarvis's husband was physically abusive—Edward had witnessed it from inside his cell.

"The father was a brute," insisted Edward. "He sometimes beat her and threatened to shoot her . . . she had no love for him—how could she have? He became jealous of me and would sometimes come in front of my cell door and abuse me by the hour, calling me everything he could think of."

Jane Jarvis warned Edward that her husband often feigned sleep and then he would quickly brandish a pair of pistols he had hidden under his pillow, just to frighten her. It must have been terrifying to be married to a cruel man who held so much power in a small village. Spending time with Edward must have seemed like a respite. But people with psychopathy are brilliant at searching your soul for what's missing (like safety and kindness) and then taking advantage of that. Deception is a constant, deliberate practice.

Of course, none of that might have been true. Edward's attempts to frame himself as either hero or victim were consistent through the years, depending on his audience. While Edward received appreciation from some villagers for his tutoring sessions, Ephraim Schutt was terrified for Jacob Jarvis and his family.

"Jarvis was warned in vain of what might result from this intimacy between his son and the prisoner by Mr. Ephraim Schutt, who had come to fully understand the character of that monster," wrote Crapsey.

But Ephraim's pleas were ignored. Edward had spent more than seven months in the jail in Ithaca, toiling on his manuscript, entertaining curious guests—and preparing for his escape using an adoring pupil. Edward seemed to be grooming Al Jarvis for something . . . and it was likely to turn out badly for everyone.

Most people in Ithaca viewed Al Jarvis as a dutiful young man—one journalist described him as a "young man of most correct habits and excellent promise." But that might have been a facade. The teenager seemed to have been primed for a criminal life before he even met Edward.

"It is entirely certain that he had in young Jarvis a very susceptible subject. Jarvis was a thief from childhood, and at one time served out a sentence in the jail over which his own father was a keeper," wrote attorney Samuel Halliday. "Everything connected with Rulloff seemed to have been surrounded with such strange circumstances."

So, Albert Jarvis wasn't as virtuous as many people imagined; Edward called him "impulsive and rash." The eighteen-year-old was a fledgling hoodlum when he first stepped inside Edward's cell, but he still had time to escape that fate. If his father was abusive, perhaps Al was acting out, or perhaps his defiance had resulted from boredom. Or Al might have just been a young man who relished danger. He certainly experienced that with Edward Rulloff.

No matter his motivation, Al Jarvis desperately wanted to ingratiate himself to his tutor, a man who could teach him about philosophy . . . and criminal enterprise. On May 5, 1857, Al quietly removed his father's keys from his jacket after his parents left for the evening. He sneaked down to the jail and swung open the huge steel door. Al unlocked each of the iron shackles.

Edward Rulloff was free once again.

"I was overcome with his kindness," Edward told Hamilton Freeman. "It was so unexpected."

That seems ludicrous—Edward had spent months grooming Al for this escape. The young man handed Edward some gold and silver pieces he received presumably from Jane Jarvis and bid him goodbye. Edward hugged him . . . and vanished, thanks to an abundance of trust offered to him by the undersheriff's son and wife.

Jane and Al had even arranged for transportation.

"Late one evening a team of black horses was driven up to the jail door," wrote Halliday. "Rulloff's cell door was unbolted by an accomplice in the jailer's family, and he walked deliberately out and was driven away."

Of course, a killer escaping from police custody is nothing new. Almost 120 years later, Ted Bundy also vanished from custody . . . twice. The first time happened in 1977, when Bundy was jailed in Aspen, Colorado, charged with first-degree murder. He was representing himself, so the judge offered him use of the law library on the second floor of the courthouse building, where he could walk freely without wearing leg shackles or handcuffs. The guard went outside to smoke a cigarette, and Bundy jumped from the second-story window and ran to the mountains.

"I had no plan. I had nobody helping me. I had no money. I had no nothing," Bundy told prison psychologist Al Carlisle. He simply saw an opportunity and took it. Six days later, he was back in custody, and he was transferred to the Garfield County Jail in Glenwood Springs, Colorado. Six months later, Bundy lost up to twenty-five pounds and crawled through a small grate in his ceiling. At that point, he simply walked out of the jail, wearing civilian clothes. He boarded a plane to Chicago and eventually ended up in Tallahassee, Florida, where he sexually assaulted and killed his final three known victims before being caught. A psychopath on the run is dangerous to anyone he meets along the way—so it was very concerning when, in 1857, Edward Rulloff disappeared from a locked jail cell.

Ithacans knew about Edward's escape by morning, as the sheriff and his officers attempted to mollify the town with calming reassurance that the killer would be returned shortly. Undersheriff Jacob Jarvis discovered that his son (and likely his wife) aided in Edward's escape; he was left behind, furious and humiliated. The sheriff interrogated dozens of locals who might have helped Edward flee—after all, the killer used a team of horses with a driver. The sheriff offered a $250 reward, while reporters criticized the undersheriff for sloppy security; Jacob Jarvis added even more locks to the jail despite the revelation that shackles clearly wouldn't stop Edward, who had weaponized his charm once again to influence two more people.

Soon, Jacob Jarvis was fired—and he angrily ordered his wife and their son to leave. The undersheriff had been suspicious of Jane and Edward, and Al had stopped listening to him as the teenager grew closer to the killer. Jane and Al were ruined, and they blamed Edward Rulloff. Edward was now an escaped murderer, but one with plenty of resources and a lot of charisma as he wandered around the New York countryside. The winter was particularly cold, and Edward lost one frostbitten toe as he traversed snowy hills. A cobbler designed a shoe just for his foot.

Edward ambled about until, in the winter of 1857, he found himself in Meadville, Pennsylvania, at the office door of A. B. Richmond, an inventor. Richmond surveyed the man, who seemed to be a farmer. Edward introduced himself as James Nelson, and he offered to help Richmond manufacture a machine mentioned in a local newspaper that the man had invented.

"I saw from the tone of his voice that he was evidently a gentleman of culture and education," said Richmond. "I took him into my laboratory to show him the machine. He seemed pleased with it and wished me to make him a proposition . . . I asked him if he could construct a model. 'Yes,' said he, 'I am a fine mechanic,' and with the science of which he seemed thoroughly conversant."

Richmond had a museum of sorts, a collection of insects, human skulls, and pieces of anatomy from numerous animals. Edward commented on all of them, no doubt to offer more proof of his intelligence to a skeptical stranger.

"By this time my surprise was unbounded, as I have had many learned men visit my collection," said Richmond, "but never found one that seemed to understand so well all the sciences connected with the objects in my museum."

But then Edward's countenance changed after Richmond's small, innocuous observation. Richmond had employed Edward for several weeks to work on his machine, when Edward asked for an emery wheel for polishing. When Richmond returned with a wheel, Edward suggested a different construction, one that Richmond knew was devised in the Auburn State Prison.

"I remarked to him, jocularly, 'Mr. Nelson, that is the way they polish cutlery in the penitentiary. Were you ever in there?'" asked Richmond with a grin. "He turned suddenly upon me, and his eyes fairly blazed with fire, with a look like a tiger ready to spring upon its victim, as he said, 'what do you mean?' and a more fiendish expression on a human countenance I think I never saw."

A few nights later, "James Nelson" was gone. Edward's youngest brother, Rulof, kindly offered to hide him in his large farm in Pennsylvania. Rulof had a knack for business; after leaving Canada as a young man, he moved to Maine, where he built America's first successful sawmill. He left for Pennsylvania, where he would spend the rest of his life as a lumber baron, the owner of numerous successful mills. Edward's other brother, William, was considered one of San Francisco's most talented photographers and presented his work at his high-profile studio in the city, Bradley & Rulofson.

Both of Edward's brothers seemed to have a penchant for success . . . and violence. Rulof claimed to have caught a deer by its horns and held it for a quite a while before it could be killed by another hunter. William had a terrible reputation for domestic violence, and after his first wife died, he married a woman eighteen years his junior. This union, and his abuse, caused such consternation among his five children from the previous marriage that many became estranged from him. In fact, his youngest daughter was murdered by her half brother. Edward Rulloff was apparently not the only troubled man in his family.

After spending a few quiet months with Rulof and his family, Edward grew restless. He still yearned for a respectable life in academia, even though he was a fugitive with a reward offered for his capture, so he crafted a new identity. Convict Edward Rulloff became Professor James Nelson as he roamed around Meadville. After nine months on the run, Edward introduced himself to faculty members of Allegheny College, a private liberal arts school in the Pennsylvania town. Edward feigned an English accent and claimed he was academically trained at Oxford University. He beguiled the president, Reverend John Barker, with his analysis of classical and modern languages, so much so that Barker issued Edward a certificate confirming that he was indeed an expert in those disciplines.*

---

* Barker was from Yorkshire, England, so Edward's English accent must have been remarkable.

As Professor Nelson, Edward began leading language classes. He seemed to have little sense of self-preservation and no concerns that he would be caught—at this point, his career ambitions were being fulfilled, his life's goal. He had no fear of being captured. Edward lived for every moment he spent teaching and thought of nothing else but his research. Near midterms, he brazenly requested a full-time position, usually earned as the reward for a lifetime of singular commitment to languages. The college had no permanent openings, but Barker was impressed with the new professor. He rummaged through his desk and discovered a request from the president of another university, this one in a southern state, who needed a professor of Greek language. After a short exchange of letters, Professor Nelson was offered a faculty position at the University of North Carolina at Chapel Hill. Edward would finally be surrounded by his intellectual peers at a prestigious school that might fund the completion of his manuscript. Even amongst some of the brightest minds in the world—his real identity would remain hidden.

Edward glanced over the railway schedule to Chapel Hill and noted the price, more money than he had. He lamented to the professors that he was penniless. They smiled and one of them loaned Edward twenty dollars for a railway ticket and food. Edward planned to ride the train to North Carolina the next day, so he graciously bid them goodbye and returned to his room. But first he stopped at the post office to retrieve his letters.

One letter had just arrived from Ithaca. It was from Jane Jarvis, the undersheriff's wife—the two had kept in touch. Edward had promised Jane that he would write often and update her on his location. Edward recognized potential in Jane's son, Al—he considered that the teenager might be useful later (yet another resource that the killer could leverage). He knew that Al was capable of being an apt criminal—but Edward didn't know just how determined Al was to do that.

Edward read Jane's letter carefully, including a note from Al. Edward quickly became alarmed by its intent—Al was in jail in Buffalo for burglary.

"I was about to start for the South, when I unfortunately received a letter from Jarvis saying that he and his mother were destitute," recalled Edward. "That his father had abandoned them, and that I just send him some money, or he would cut my throat."

Jacob Jarvis had fled to California in humiliation. Al Jarvis had apparently chosen a crooked path in life—a long string of unfortunate mistakes he would make throughout their relationship. The sweet teenager who had doted on Edward in Ithaca was now threatening to kill him if he didn't send $500 for bail.

"I have helped you once," Al wrote, "and now I want you to help me."

Edward could disappear to North Carolina and continue being Professor James Nelson, or he could honor his friendship with Albert and rescue the mother and son, he explained to Hamilton Freeman.

"I felt under obligations to him, and his mother," said Edward. "I could not desert them."

The decision might *seem* admirable, but Edward never honored obligations to anyone except himself. He watched Ham Freeman during this story. Edward sensed that the author admired his dedication to Al and Jane Jarvis; Edward relished feigning generosity, and Ham happily believed it, but it was simply more manipulation. Edward was gifted at reading his audience and providing appropriate feedback. As for his return to help Al Jarvis and abandon his career in North Carolina, Edward was likely frightened that Al would fulfill his threat to murder him on sight—it was self-preservation, not benevolence. Now that Edward faced a clear and present danger, his goal had switched to simply staying alive. Ham readily accepted his story of persecution and sacrifice.

"Eager to assist a woman whom he said he loved better than any other being on earth, he robbed a jewelry store nearby," wrote Ham, "and perhaps obtained the necessary funds therefrom."

Ham tended to romanticize Edward's plights as well as his relationships with others, including Jane Jarvis, whom Edward would later label "an old fool." The author prayed that within this wretched killer he would discover a kind soul—he could not know, of course, that Edward's lack of remorse and empathy was seemingly incurable because of his personality disorder. Edward would never place anyone else's needs above his own.

The sheriff of Tompkins County offered a $500 bounty for the killer's return, and the Schutts made a similar reward. Everyone in New York seemed motivated to find Edward Rulloff.

———

Edward never kept good company—after he brazenly robbed the jewelry store in Meadville, he rode out of town with a horse thief he knew from Auburn State Prison. After he threatened the man, Edward disappeared, and the horse thief was arrested. The thief told the sheriff that Edward had left for the West. When a constable traced Edward to a small town in Ohio, he denied his identity. He denial seemed ridiculous because they had a handbill with his description, so the constable and some volunteers put him in a wagon bound for the local train station. Edward hopped out, pulled out a three-barreled revolver (of his own invention), and shot at the men, clipping the whiskers of one while penetrating the jacket and vest of another. When the constable finally gained control of Edward, the killer smirked.

"After getting into the wagon, he ridiculed the constable for being so pale and scared," wrote Ham, "and apparently was the least excited one of the party."

The constable loaded Edward onto a train and promptly returned him to Ithaca to await word from the court of appeals. Edward had been convicted of murdering little Priscilla, but the judges were still deliberating whether his sentence was fair.

Professor James Nelson would not arrive in North Carolina for the fall semester.

———

Edward was sent back to Ithaca in mid-March 1859, to the jubilation of the country people in Tompkins County, particularly the Schutts. Finally, the New York Court of Appeals carefully read the document that Edward had written: *no body meant no crime.* It seemed like a simple decision, but it was an unprecedented argument in the United States—and it worked. Edward's conviction for killing his daughter was thrown out, and the judges ordered a third trial. Ithacans were enraged over the murders, the prison escape, Edward's affair with the undersheriff's wife, and the moral corruption of Jacob Jarvis's son. The locals had worked themselves into a mob frenzy once again—violence was inevitable.

"He did not have to put his ear to the ground to hear the murmurs of this on-coming mob," wrote Samuel Halliday. "For once in his life he was scared for a time before he was spirited away, he was in a state of terror."

That same month, town leaders distributed a handbill entitled: *Shall the Murderer Go Unpunished!* It ordered Ithacans to meet in the town center at noon. The notice read: "It will depend on the action you take that day whether Edward H. Rulloff walks forth a free man, or whether he dies the death he so richly deserves."

Harriet's father, John Schutt, gave an impassioned speech and prayed that the sheriff would release Edward to die at the hands of the mob.

"After a struggle of fifteen years they saw this monster they had vainly sought to throttle, slipping from their grasp," wrote Ed Crapsey for the *New York Times*, "and about to go free to work wickedness wherever he should choose. They knew him to be utterly without truth, and they sincerely believed that he was Satan incarnated upon earth."

The mob had built gallows and tied another noose while two thousand people crammed into the center of town, awaiting an execution.

"They decided to assemble on a certain day in Ithaca and organize a court which would be presided over . . . by a judge by the name of 'Lynch,'" wrote Halliday, "a court from which there would be no appeal; a court which did not indulge in technicalities and refined distinctions; a court in fact in which, according to David Crockett, there would be 'little larning', but a heap of justice.'"

Months before, the Schutt family had exhumed the body of William's wife, Amelia—they believed there was evidence of poisoning, but the toxicology test was inconclusive. Still, the mob was certain—Edward Rulloff had killed not just two but *four* members of his own family: his wife, Harriet; his child, Priscilla;

his sister-in-law, Amelia; and his infant niece, Amille. Edward needed to die, too.

The sheriff of Tompkins County disagreed and, despite a citizens' committee that stalked the jail, he told Edward that he would take him away to Auburn State Prison the next morning to save his life. Edward argued, saying he was safer in jail in Ithaca. Sheriff Smith Robertson replied firmly:

"Rulloff, you will go to Auburn tomorrow or to the devil the next day."

Edward must have preferred Auburn because he agreed to leave immediately. Edward was covered inside the bed of a wagon as he and Robertson drove the nearly forty miles to Auburn. Several times, Edward tried to convince the sheriff to take off his handcuffs because they were uncomfortable. Robertson had grown somewhat fond of Edward, despite his horrid reputation, because he had always treated the sheriff with respect, and he considered the request. But Robertson's common sense prevailed, and Edward remained shackled. When they arrived at the prison, the sheriff turned to his troubled friend.

"Rulloff," he said. "I have always been a friend of yours and kind to you. If you could escape by killing me, would you do it?"

Edward's eyes flashed anger as he snapped: "I would kill you like a dog."

The sheriff sat back—Edward Rulloff would no longer receive Robertson's respect, but the killer sensed the sheriff's fear and he was pleased.

"The charm with which he had enveloped that sheriff was broken by this incautious remark," said Halliday. "Generally, however, his methods were those of the persuader, the charmer and the snake."

Soon, the prosecutors would read over the court of appeals' long-delayed decision, which concluded that "Corpus delicti *had not been found*." Edward Rulloff had triumphed once again because prosecutors begrudgingly rescinded the indictment; they would not try him for murder. Then there were two other startling decisions. The district attorney decided against putting him on trial for the jailbreak—Edward would inevitably find a way to escape that penalty, too, was the reasoning. The prosecutor just wanted Edward to leave his county and never return. The owner of the jewelry store in Pennsylvania declined to press charges for the robbery because he had received back all the stolen merchandise (Edward didn't have time to sell it). There was no motivation for the owner to lose time and money on a trial.

Edward walked out of Auburn State Prison for the final time— a free man at last. He took little with him, but he was clutching his precious manuscript. His hopes for a legitimate life as a college professor had vanished. Edward could only see a downward spiral into hell for the remainder of his life.

"Every man is the architect of his own fortune or ruin," he lamented to Ham.

Edward had to make the best of it, and, perhaps, his manuscript would salvage his reputation. In January 1860, Edward Rulloff disappeared from Tompkins County, and he reappeared in New York City.

———

The years passed; New York City was an easy place to get lost in.

New York, the nation's largest metropolis, was by the late 1860s home to almost one million people. Almost half of them were born outside America, and many now found a home in Lower Manhattan in the notorious neighborhood of Five Points, an area bound by Canal Street to the north, Park Row to the south, the Bowery on its east side, and Centre Street on its west. Five Points was a cauldron of deadly diseases—tuberculosis, typhus, and the yellow fever all swirled through the air and water. The drinking water was polluted with garbage and excrement, and the air reeked of burning flesh and putrid entrails, thanks to the glut of nearby tanneries and slaughterhouses. The tenement buildings in Five Points, shoddy and mangled, were stuffed with people—some Black, but mostly Irish immigrants, former farmworkers desperately searching for a better life in America.

Manhattan could seem tantalizing . . . or threatening to a tourist from a countryside village, even before he stepped outside his quaint cottage. The recent reduction in crime didn't mean there weren't still threats in certain neighborhoods. The naïve visitor might tense up at provocative monikers like "Satan's Circus" and "Hell's Hundred Acres." But uptown, titans of industry and their families flitted around the white marbled mansions that lined Fifth Avenue and flirted with the southern tip of Central Park. Most of Manhattan's middle class never ventured to the parts of the city where the laboring class sometimes struggled to survive. New York's story was that of lives that rarely intersected.

Chic ladies strolled through Madison Square, at the intersection of Broadway and Fifth Avenue at Twenty-Third Street, the most fashionable neighborhood in Manhattan. This was also not far from the Theater District, where only the wealthiest patrons bought a ticket. The city's well-heeled politicians like kingmaker William "Boss" Tweed feasted on tenderloin steak, lobster Newburg, and

Baked Alaska at Delmonico's Restaurant in Lower Manhattan, on South William Street.

By the late 1860s, women were no longer forbidden from eating dinner in the restaurant, though they weren't allowed inside without a proper escort. Five months earlier, a fashionable reception greeted the city's first subway, meant to eventually help relieve Manhattan's streets crowded with horse cars and pedestrians, even though the first iteration would travel just one block. At a price of twenty-five cents per ride, only the elite could afford to sit in an ostentatious atmosphere complete with a grand piano and a goldfish tank.

Each day, Edward would complete his routine, one that he relished—the compulsive habits of a disciplined, consumed, and haunted scholar. Every evening, Edward glanced around his room— it was a dim, dreary space, even when the sun shone brightly during the day. Seated at a rickety desk chair, he rubbed his aching eyes— he refused spectacles, though a pair would have been helpful. Edward shunned alcohol and tobacco, but he was always hungry. When he looked in the mirror, he peered at the lines on his face, drawn there after years of squinting at ancient text. He saw the wrinkles caused by furrowing his brow during a vexing Greek passage. He used all his skills during his studies, and he had developed many new techniques by 1869, nine years after leaving upstate New York. Edward was now fluent in Latin, Greek, German, French, and English. He could understand Spanish, Portuguese, and Italian and knew a smattering of Hebrew and Sanskrit.

When he glanced at his manuscript, it frequently sparked a smile. Indeed, Edward would grin often at his landlady, Mrs. Jakob, and her fourteen-year-old daughter, Pauline—both of whom thought him a brilliant, if quiet, scholar.

"He was changing Greek, Latin, and German into English and French, or else English and French into Greek," said Pauline Jakob, the teenager. "I hardly know which. He would point with his finger, and say, 'See there; I have written so much today.'"

The Jakobs respected him: Edward played with the children outside on the stoop, tossing them pennies. They rented Edward two rooms above a dry goods store at 170 Third Avenue in Irving Place—a respectable section of Manhattan. And at twenty-five dollars a month, the rent was quite reasonable. Irving Place was the perfect location for Edward's studies; there were loads of book repositories nearby, such as the old Astor and Mercantile libraries.

"I would be perfectly content and happy to be shut up the rest of my life in one of these great libraries," Edward once said.

At eight o'clock most mornings, he would promptly leave his apartment, usually to haunt the Eclectic Library nearby. There he would dig through old volumes of lost learning, hoping to find more evidence to support his theory of language. He never brought women home or drank excessively, and he paid the rent promptly. He stirred only when his landlady nudged him awake on many mornings, just as his mother once did; he was oftentimes slumped over his desk, holding a black fountain pen.

"He lived a very quiet and sober life," said Pauline Jakob. "We called him a kind of steady old bachelor."

That "quiet and sober" exterior cloaked a much more devious inner life, however—one that would soon get Edward into trouble.

The Schutts, meanwhile, were mired in the past. They would never let go of their hatred—they couldn't. If the courts wouldn't grant them justice for Harriet and Priscilla's deaths until they found a body . . . well, then they'd find a body.

Using nets, workers dragged the southern end of Cayuga Lake, hoping to snare Harriet's skeleton, and perhaps Priscilla's, too. The enterprise cost more than $10,000, almost $400,000 in today's money. It was a huge sum for the modest family of farmers, yet somehow, they gathered the funds. But still, no evidence. The Schutts felt hopeless. Without the bodies of Harriet and Priscilla, Edward Rulloff remained hidden, the truth about his crimes shrouded in mystery. The whole case became a creepy, frustrating footnote in the legal archives of Tompkins County—the double murder that was never solved. If ever the rural countryside in New York had a bogeyman, it was Edward Rulloff.

Back in New York City, Edward pursued his double life with vigor. The last nine years had proven to be incredibly productive. He worked diligently on his manuscript on the origin of the human language, but Edward needed financing, a way to earn a living. First, he started off with some occasional burglaries. Those kept him afloat for a while, but he sometimes found himself in jail for his exploits, including a two-and-a-half-year stint in Sing Sing Prison in 1861, where inmates nicknamed him "Big Jim." Soon, Edward found some partners to assist. First, he recruited Al Jarvis, the teenager who had helped him escape from the Tompkins County Jail several years before. Edward had arrived in Buffalo in 1860 after his release from the Tompkins County Jail and arranged for Jarvis to be released from that jail for a burglary charge.

"He came to the hotel where I was, and we had a long talk," said Edward. "I told him that he had made a bad start . . . I said that I had a project in view whereby I could make money enough to keep us both."

After he settled with Jarvis in a different apartment, this one in Brooklyn, Edward tried to gain legitimate employment. He had worked for almost three years as a bookkeeper, but the job left little time for writing. Once again, he blamed his foul luck.

"It was constantly on my mind," Edward said, "and I could not help cursing the fatality which had led me into that condition, and the loss of two and a half years' time, which should have been employed in the sleepless study and research in the grandest field of thought into which the mind of man ever entered."

People with psychopathy lack remorse, so it's reasonable to assume that Edward rarely took responsibility for his poor decisions; that makes self-reflection and personal growth almost insurmountable for a psychopathic individual. They continue to make mistakes or harm others, and never learn a lesson that can change their actions in the future.

In 1862, William "Billy" Dexter, a criminal Edward met in Sing Sing, joined their group. Billy Dexter was an illiterate burglar with a desire for higher learning, so when they were both released, Dexter and Edward joined Al Jarvis in New York City.

Al and Billy were similar only in age—both men were in their mid-twenties while they lived in Manhattan. While Al was attractive, charming, and studious, Billy had none of those characteristics.

"Dexter, on the other hand, was not agreeable in person or manners, was rough, uncouth, almost without mind, lacking even rudimentary education, and a thief by nature," wrote reporter Ed Crapsey.

Even their personal styles were different: Albert sported a fashionable, thick moustache, while Billy preferred the traditional muttonchops style of facial hair that was popular in the Gilded Age.

Billy might have seemed dim-witted, but he was confident as

a burglar, and he admired Edward's enthusiasm for learning. Edward had convinced both Al and Billy that his manuscript, when completed, would be worth a fortune—a fantasy for two young men with little means. He warned Billy and Al that they needed to prepare themselves to become proper gentlemen in high society and that would require a lot of study.

By day, Edward would tutor the young men in modern and ancient languages, in classic poetry and writing. By night, the trio would rob silk merchants in Tompkins County, and then later sell their wares. They specialized in stealing sewing silk, an expensive item that was easy to conceal and difficult to identify. Few people knew the men's real names, and each landed in jail sporadically. Al Jarvis and Billy Dexter were certainly petty criminals, but they might have also been murderers. In 1866, robbers had stolen silk from a factory on Thirty-Fifth Street between Eighth and Ninth Avenues and beaten the security guard to death. The suspects resembled Dexter and Jarvis, but there wasn't definitive proof, so New York police were forced to close the case.

It was an uncertain, perilous life for two young men anxious for wealth and wishing to please their master. Edward saw in his young protégés something precious: freedom. Edward was forty-seven years old, and he just couldn't match Jarvis and Dexter's endurance and speed as they crisscrossed the New York State countryside late at night. It was more prudent to stay tucked away in his Manhattan apartment. He spent most of his waking hours that summer opening and closing hundreds of books—many he had hauled around for decades, relics from his old life in Lansing with Harriet. Edward retained a library of treasures that were crammed into every corner of his study. His focus never wavered from his manuscript, which was nearing completion.

"I was still ambitious of being a gentleman and of being respected by my fellow men," Edward insisted.

This might seem delusional, considering he had been in hiding from the Schutts *and* had been arrested sporadically for burglary. Could he really become a gentleman of high society? Oftentimes the goals of someone with psychopathy are too lofty to be achieved, but psychopaths will commit their lives to achieving those goals, even if they are unrealistic.

Life settled into a strange routine, as Edward Rulloff wandered through the great libraries of New York City by day, while committing just enough light felony work to keep his academic pursuits afloat. He soon picked up another member for the criminal ring: an Irish woman named Maggie Graham who sometimes cooked for them and would sell their stolen silks. She seemed loyal, an accomplice who constantly patrolled the apartment, discarding evidence like addresses of stores to potentially target and hiding burglary tools. But Edward trusted virtually no one, particularly in his circle of thieves (even Al), and he viewed Graham as yet another opportunist.

"She was not true to anyone," said Edward. "I never had any confidence in her, but the boys used to trust her to go about and sell some of the silks which they got hold of."

Still, she was helpful to Edward when she returned from selling their stolen wares and handed him money—but even more helpful were her contacts. Maggie's boyfriend, Tom, who was a boxer and a thief, joined Dexter and Jarvis on some of their robberies. A frequent caller was Jane Jarvis, Al's mother, and the former wife of Ithaca's undersheriff and Edward's former lover. This was surely Edward's longest sexually intimate relationship, but he wasn't sentimental about her, despite her many sacrifices. She had lost everything—her home, her husband, and her respect in Ithaca—but still—she seemed to covet Edward Rulloff. In return, Edward received her coldly, unsurprising for a self-serving psychopath who could no longer find a use for a resource.

"What made her come on here and slobber around so for?" Edward asked himself. "Why did she not keep away? I always used the woman well . . . she is a common sort of woman, and an old fool about some things."

In August 1866, Edward began consulting on legal cases on behalf of a gang of professional bank robbers. "They counseled with me in reference to getting some of their gang out of a scrape," said Edward, "and also with reference to cracking a bank in New Hampshire." He was diversifying his skills.

By 1868, Edward had remained ensconced for several years in the Irving Place apartment, surrounded by more than four hundred books. As he obsessively wrote and rewrote his precious manuscript, he knew the moment was drawing near to share it with the world.

The American Philological Association's annual conference was coming soon. It was a prestigious showcase for professional linguists, and Edward planned, at long last, to present his manuscript there. Or rather, Professor E. Leurio would.

———

Edward had dreamed for decades that he would impress the leading professors in the world of languages and linguistics with his innovative theory. What would happen next? Well, that's where it got a little fuzzy. Edward's plan seemed to be that he'd then sell his groundbreaking ideas to an esteemed university for a small fortune. Whether or not that was a realistic goal, it all hinged on getting the right people to read and accept his ideas . . . something that had proved tricky as a humble self-taught academic (not to mention a felon and murderer). Nevertheless, Edward was certain: if he could just finish his work in time, he would *finally* make his mark on the academic world.

Edward's room exuded a bookish sort of squalor. The flickering gas lamp revealed a stack of rare lexicons in the corner, and atop it was a small ad printed in the corner of a paper, one that newspaper subscribers throughout New York might read that day. Edward happily paid the fee for the advertisement (with funds acquired through numerous burglaries) and newspapers happily received the money.

"Great Discovery—Method in the Formation of Language!" read the headline. The advertisement promised a manuscript of "peculiar interest, disclosing a beautiful and unsuspected method in language spoken and read by millions of our race." The author offered it for the obscene price of $500,000, a notion absurd enough to attract the attention of a well-respected national magazine.

"*The Nation* has learned that for five hundred thousand Mr. E. Leurio, of New York City, will sell a manuscript which he cannot afford to give away . . . if Mr. Leurio describes it accurately."

Undeterred by the derision, Edward Rulloff set down his pen and admired his own writing.

"This manuscript will be formally brought to the notice of the Philological Convention to meet at Poughkeepsie on the 27th of July," it read.

That was in just a few weeks and this convention, he believed, was where his destiny would be fulfilled. Such fulfillment had been too long delayed, but Edward was sure the convention would prove the glorious apotheosis of his genius, following a long and altogether crooked path. Edward wept over his own brilliant words, and yet he worried that no one at the convention in Pough-keepsie, not even the world's most renowned philologists, would understand his discovery. The possibility tormented him, nearly drove him mad, because he yearned for little other than respect (though the half a million dollars wouldn't hurt). For much of his life, Edward Rulloff had dreamed of living the life of a country gentleman, a patrician who would be revered as a gifted academic and pioneer in his field of linguistics. Life hadn't worked out that way. But this manuscript—and this gathering of esteemed professionals—was his big hope.

At the linguistics conference in Poughkeepsie in July 1868, Edward dressed in a silly black frock coat and introduced himself as Professor E. Leurio, a pleasant academic. The other linguistics experts eyed him with suspicion. They had all heard about the ad, but it didn't matter if his theory was groundbreaking; its half-a-million-dollar price was laughable. Experts from Vassar College and Brown University gave Edward a courteous and serious hearing.

"They regarded the manuscript with great interest," wrote attorney Samuel Halliday. "It showed wonderful research, great knowledge, and was written in a hand as beautiful as copperplate."

As the committee began to question him more pointedly about weaknesses in his ideas, Professor Leurio's amiable facade began to crack. His face grew flush, as it often did when he became emotional. He snapped back at their questioning.

"They regarded him as a sort of a monomaniac or crank,"

concluded Halliday. "They simply reported that the convention had no money with which to publish the work."

The committee chairman later said, "The mild and gentle Mr. Leurio disappeared." In his place appeared the violent, abusive, and profane Edward Rulloff, whose mercurial attitude ran hot one minute, cold the next. Edward crowed to the committee about his own intellect, offering a diatribe peppered with curse words that seemed almost sadistic. The language experts stepped back and then walked away from Edward; they hoped he would retreat to Manhattan, and he did, in a storm of expletives that sealed his fate in academic circles as a serious scholar—at least for now.

"The convention was a sort of heterogeneous lot of literary men, the most pedantic and self-assuming," Edward recalled bitterly. This should have served as a self-reckoning for Edward Rulloff, but he was stubbornly unmoored from reality. "At any rate, I was treated very cavalierly, but I was not discouraged. I was resolved to make the learned men of the world appreciate and acknowledge the merit of my method, and with that end in view I returned to New York."

Despite public humiliation, Edward refused to abandon his theory, and the urgency he felt to finish his manuscript remained unabated. As he bellowed profanities and cursed the panel, he exhibited those types of "poor behavioral controls" that are a cardinal feature of psychopathy, a sign of someone who is incapable of reasoning with anyone, even themselves. Edward's facade of "country gentleman" crumbled abruptly at the convention, thanks to his grandiose, yet fragile sense of self. He was unraveling—unwilling to accept the dissonance between the image he wanted to project to the world as a misunderstood academic, and the reality he was starting to acknowledge. The determined academic was doing everything he could not to reveal the truth: he was a psychopathic criminal whose grip on reality was becoming ever more tenuous.

———

Inside the jail cell in 1871, Professor Richard Mather listened closely as Edward Rulloff concluded his summary of a life filled with strife. *He'd suffered such unfortunate luck at every turn, wouldn't the professor agree?* It was a feeble plea for understanding and sympathy, of the sort he didn't receive from the learned men at the philology convention.

"He complained that he had been laughed at by the public as a superficial scholar," said Mather.

Despite those pitiful appeals to Mather, Edward's focus during their lengthy discussion was his manuscript and his fear that it might not be completed if he were sentenced to death. Mather glanced down at his notes on a pad laying on his lap; they detailed Edward's analysis of the great works that Mather presented to him.

"In order to show his thoroughness, he criticized the common rendering of certain passages, and he did it with such subtlety and discrimination and elegance as to show that his critical study of these nicer points was more remarkable than his powers of memory," Mather noted.

And this was impressive because, Mather observed, his power of memory was remarkable.

"Subtlety of analysis and of reasoning was the marked characteristic of his mind," Mather said.

But the professor also observed something else—Edward's pre-occupation with his studies seemed deeper than just intellectual fervor, and it was troubling.

"Most persons think him a monomaniac, and certainly his enthusiasm is remarkable."

"Monomania" was an important term in the nineteenth century because it was a very specific diagnosis. French psychiatrist Jean-Étienne Dominique Esquirol explained: "[sufferers] do not rave and ramble . . . [their] reasoning is logical, whose speech is not only coherent but often lively and witty, but whose actions are opposed to their affects. However disordered their actions, these monomaniacs always have more or less plausible reasons to justify themselves, so that one can say they are reasoning madmen."

A patient inflicted with monomania suffered from a form of partial insanity provoked by one pathological preoccupation, such as an obsessed artist or a zealous inventor. By the early 1900s, monomania became an obsolete diagnosis, and modern psychiatrists would later use similar markers to describe other conditions, like obsessive-compulsive disorder or paranoid personality disorder. But using the lexicon of the time, Mather concluded that Edward's obsession with his manuscript had, quite literally, driven him insane.

Edward was unaware of Dr. Mather's assessment and pleaded with him to return, this time with several more learned men to evaluate his theory, to legitimize his decades of work.

"And you know that whatever is done must be done quickly," Edward said. The clock was ticking toward his seemingly inevitable execution.

Mather had no need to confer with colleagues; he had heard quite enough about Edward's (or Dr. Leurio's) theories. He'd talked with Edward at length, reviewed his manuscript, and ultimately deemed it—useless. Mather detailed Edward's idea that all languages had one central origin, that all words were spelled backward or altered by each culture's leaders in "some conventional manner," and found it utterly lacking in academic merit. Many revolutionary linguists in the mid-nineteenth century believed what we know now that the relationship between sound and meaning is arbitrary. Typically, the sound of a word gives *no* hint of its meaning, like "bird" or "dog."

"The reason why dog in English is dog and in German is hund and in French is chien and an Irish is madra has nothing to do with the innate meaning of dog, right?" Cornell University linguistics professor Michael Weiss told me. "Those sounds don't express that idea. They're arbitrary."

Weiss told me that Edward Rulloff was working with premodern philosophies—bad ideas that allowed him to convince lay people that he held a key to crack a code . . . that didn't exist.

"He very clearly didn't believe that the relationship between sound and meaning was arbitrary," said Weiss. "He thought that language was, in some sense, engineered, and that there were reasons why a particular word should have a particular sound. So, he was working in a long, long tradition going all the way back to Plato and beyond. But he hadn't basically kept up with the nineteenth century."

Mather insisted, however, that Edward's academic impulses were not without merit, even if his conclusions were flawed. "His illustrations show sound scholarship, patient investigation, and a wide range of reading," wrote Mather. "He can hardly be set down as a superficial thinker or scholar, though his conclusions are often far astray and absurd."

Perhaps with more time and a proper mentor, Edward's scholarship might have improved. And who knew—it might not be too late. Perhaps Edward could be redeemed, and some shred of his linguistic theories found to be solid. He was certainly very knowledgeable about languages, Mather thought. Could such a keen intellect perhaps be reformed?

But while the professor admired Edward's obvious intelligence, his ability to kill truly terrified Mather.

"Here is a profound and appreciative student of all that is beautiful and glorious in classical learning . . . and yet all the time living a life of crime," Mather said.

In short, Mather said: "The author was a much better murderer than philologist." It was a scathing, dismissive response to a lifetime of ultimately misguided academic study. When he returned to his home in Amherst later that week, Dr. Mather slid a chair out from his desk, flipped over a piece of paper, and wrote the title "A Learned Murderer."

"Here is a man of great philological pretensions, undeniably endowed with extraordinary abilities, possessed of varied acquirements . . ." wrote Mather, "yet a being heartless, soulless, a perfect Mephistopheles, who has gone through a long and checkered career of black and unredeemed villainy."

As Mather scribbled the last of his ideas about Edward Rulloff and his byzantine mind, he pondered Edward's character: "I do not believe the man has any tenderness save for language," wrote Mather. "In looking at him you would never imagine him as loving any human being, and you would be sure that his hatred would be implacable."

In short: Edward was brilliant . . . and perhaps that brilliance should save him from the gallows. After all, how many men with such an intellect were to be found in New York? In America? In the world? Could society really allow such brainpower to go to waste—even when it was found in such a horrid man?

Each of the professor's conclusions seeded a growing belief among intellectuals that Edward Rulloff's brain offered something unique, a facet of the human experience that had never been described accurately in literature. Edward's mind, Mather realized, represented the intersection of talent and what would one day be labeled psychopathy. What the twentieth century would come to call a "genius psychopath"* was as exciting a prospect as it was terrifying, for people like Edward are so uncommon and seemingly undetectable.

Until, perhaps, it is too late.

---

* Society's perception of a fiendishly clever psychopathic serial killer is frequently glamorized by movies like *Silence of the Lambs* and television series like *Dexter*, which feature intellectually gifted killers. Most psychopaths are not . . . and that's how they are usually caught and incarcerated. Researchers dubbed it the "Hannibal Lecter Myth" in a study printed in the *Journal of Psychopathology and Behavioral Assessment*.

5

The Educator

*With every day, and from both sides of my intelligence, the
moral and the intellectual, I thus drew steadily nearer to that
truth . . . that man is not truly one, but truly two.*
　　　　　—Robert Louis Stevenson,
　　　　　　　Strange Case of Dr. Jekyll and Mr. Hyde, 1886

George C. Sawyer scoffed as he read long pieces in the Manhattan newspapers that detailed Edward Rulloff's interview with Professor Richard Mather. He had not yet met the killer who was hailed as a genius, but Sawyer already disliked him. Sawyer tasked himself with evaluating whether Edward was a savant or a sham.

Sawyer was a career educator who had served as the principal of the Utica Free Academy, one of the country's first free secondary public schools, for thirteen years. Although it didn't require a fee to attend, the institute attracted families with means and, even more significantly, the pedigrees to become the next generation of American leaders. Sawyer insisted that the boys wear jackets and bows, formal attire illustrating their comfortable, respectable backgrounds. During the Civil War, the school had been destroyed by a fire; Sawyer supervised its resurrection, and he would go on to serve as its head for almost forty years. The academy was small, with only 143 students and 7 teachers by 1868, but a degree with Sawyer's signature was prestigious.

Sawyer was revered by his students for his expertise in languages, and his reputation as a scholar stretched beyond the walls of his institution. He traveled along a lecture circuit across the country, educating educators on the best methods to teach Greek and Latin to young students. Sawyer expected adulation from not just his pupils but also the fellow teachers he instructed, and he leveled biting, public judgment against any expert who contradicted him. He dressed down a fellow presenter at a conference when the man espoused a method of learning called the "natural method," where students simply mimicked the instructor's Greek or Latin without understanding the context and culture.

"Principal George C. Sawyer of Utica followed with a scholarly and exhaustive attack on the 'natural method' as a fraud and a sham," read a summary of the conference. "Dr. Sawyer claimed, that, under this method, all the work devolves upon the teacher, and the pupil picks up, with no disciplinary training, a parrot-like acquaintance with a limited vocabulary. Moreover, the main value from studying a language lies in learning to read it, to imbibe the thought and spirit and culture of another people, and not merely to hold a conversation in it."

Sawyer demanded context, serious scholarship with depth of understanding both the history of languages and their impact. He had earned a coveted degree from Harvard University—he thought highly of himself and his abilities to expose a humbug like Edward Rulloff, who had skillfully fooled a pair of naïve journalists and a gullible academic. As he reread the details of Mather's interview with the killer, Sawyer grew even more skeptical of the professor's effusive conclusions.

"Here is a profound and appreciative student of all that is beautiful and glorious in classical learning, working for years as a philologist, and with a zeal rarely equaled," read Mather's offering in a New York City newspaper, "and yet all the time living a life of crime as dark and terrible as any criminal in our land."

Poppycock. Sawyer was incredulous at the phrase "profound and appreciative" with regard to Edward's scholarship. The educator had already scanned the large excerpts of Edward's theory provided by Hamilton Freeman in his own local newspaper. Sawyer quickly concluded that Edward was nothing more than a fraud masquerading as a man of letters. He believed that Richard Mather was misguided in his generous assessment of the murderer as worthy of respect—if not admiration—and, worse, that Mather's attempts to sway public opinion toward Edward were careless at best, reckless at worst.

"Professor Mather, of Amherst College, who visited Rulloff in Binghamton, thinks there can be no doubt that his acquirements in the department of the classical languages were considerable," said Sawyer. "[W]e judged that the different result we attained from that of some other visitors, was to be ascribed to our setting before him what we wished him to do, instead of allowing him to discourse as he pleased."

Ask a leading question; get the answer you desire. Dr. Mather, Sawyer concluded, offered Edward Rulloff far too much guidance and coddling during their interview. Mather entered the jail cell hoping to find a language savant, and sure enough, that's what he had seen. Now, thanks to that interview and the resulting press, the public was convinced that the killer's life was valuable because of his immense scholastic potential—exactly what Edward had hoped for.

"He [Edward] took every opportunity of showing his knowledge, and claimed, and obtained with many the reputation of being a very learned man, of perfect scholarship," Sawyer concluded. Sawyer was far more skeptical than Mather about these claims of Edward's intellect and scholarship. He'd seen no such evidence of any research of note that had come from Edward's decades of research into languages—in fact, he saw the man as more a crank than a genius.

Weeks earlier, Sawyer had registered a similar reaction to a different interview, Oliver Dyer's report in *The Sun* titled "The Modern Eugene Aram": "The sheriff says he has written in all about two reams of law since his imprisonment," reporter Oliver Dyer wrote. "The articles for the press containing column after column of examples in small type are written entirely from memory. He says he can place his work in shape for practical use, provided his wants be cared for but, the world will not produce in the next two hundred and fifty years, one who can follow up his clue and substantiate his theory by examples as he proposed to do."

"The Modern Eugene Aram" referenced eighteenth-century English scholar Eugene Aram, a brilliant yet doomed sage in languages who had suspected that his wife was having an affair with his close friend. In 1745, Aram murdered Daniel Clarke, took his money to pay his own debts, and secretly buried his body before returning to his life as a philologist in London. Police had searched Aram's garden but could not locate Clarke's body, until the skeleton was discovered thirteen years later in Knaresborough in North Yorkshire, England. Aram confessed and was executed. George Sawyer knew this story well—Edward Rulloff and Eugene Aram seemed to share a common thread: linguistic genius that intersected violence and perhaps insanity. Sawyer noted that there was one glaring difference: unlike Edward, Aram had made unique, valuable discoveries in languages, while Sawyer dismissed Edward as a fraud.

Aram discovered that the Celtic language was connected to other languages of Europe; he also contended that Latin was not derived from Greek, a correct theory not yet published by other scholars. Edward Rulloff had proven to experts like Richard Mather that his own theory of a universal root of all languages was innovative, yes. But on further review, Sawyer claimed, it was also wholly misguided and unacceptable. Eugene Aram had been a gifted linguist with prolific, original ideas who murdered out of rage. Edward Rulloff, argued Sawyer, was a craven hack who schemed out of self-preservation and cowardice.

As Sawyer entered Edward's jail cell on Saturday, May 13, 1871, the killer sensed the educator's distaste. Standing beside the principal was Dr. Judson Boardman Andrews, an assistant physician at the New York State Lunatic Asylum in Utica. Boardman was there on a reconnaissance mission of sorts, on behalf of the head of the asylum, Dr. John Gray. Edward silently surveyed the men, particularly Sawyer, who presented to Edward as haughty, self-righteous, and slightly indignant.

Just as he'd done all his life, Edward started looking for an angle to exploit as he began talking with the two self-important scholars.

———

By 1870, five years after the conclusion of the Civil War, the physical damage and emotional trauma seemed irreparable in many parts of the country. More than 700,000 people had died in the battles, and much of the South was rebuilding, slowly, from almost incomprehensible destruction. America was still shaken by the assassination of President Abraham Lincoln in 1865. Radicals in Congress were determined to grind the former Confederacy into financial ruin. Meanwhile, Native Americans battled frontiersmen as the country expanded westward. Black people were given the right to vote, as tenuous as that would be in parts of the country, and the fight for women's suffrage would last another fifty years.

But despite the turmoil, the country was poised for growth. President Ulysses S. Grant declared to Congress that America was finally in a period "of peace and general prosperity" and enjoying its longest period of economic expansion in history. Immigrants flooded large cities to work inside factories built by the nation's wealthiest industrialists. The expansion of the country's railway system connected rural America with major cities, such as New York and Chicago.

Metropolises offered new, valuable opportunities in education, careers, and culture—but those opportunities weren't necessarily distributed evenly. John D. Rockefeller cofounded Standard Oil, a clever decision that anointed him one of the wealthiest men in America. The era heralded the rise of corporate titans, and New York City was their headquarters. As the city rapidly expanded, millions of dollars poured into its coffers, much of it siphoned by members of the Democratic Party political machine, Tammany Hall, led by William "Boss" Tweed. The "Grand Sachem" gained much of his power from the votes of Irish immigrants, poor men and women who stepped off boats in New York Harbor hoping to escape famine and political oppression in Europe. Immigrants from around the world made up half of New York City's population.

The city was torn by various factions trying to grasp power and wealth. The Irish mob continued to prowl the streets of Five Points, but the police patrolling that area were powerless and often corrupt. Racial tension had enveloped parts of the city since the 1863 Draft Riots, when predominately Irish immigrants attacked Blacks across the city, resulting in more than one hundred deaths. Cholera infested New York City's overcrowded slums, but immigrants also suffered from yellow fever, measles, and malaria. The city took notice only when the outbreaks reached more "respectable" areas uptown. Washington, DC, might have been America's hub for political power, but Manhattan was the epicenter of money and influence. Isolated rural communities that had once epitomized the country's landscape were now declining, usurped by a new urban, industrialized structure that offered Americana a new set of morals.

The decline of crime in Manhattan in 1870 didn't offer the city immunity from the violence that plagued other big cities. In many urban areas across America, domestic violence was prevalent, many authorities were crooked, and much of the time, mob rule governed the streets. People in those cities broke each of the Ten Commandments, several at a time, according to country people. Manhattan seemed to be filled with unscrupulous newspaper publishers, sanctimonious writers, haughty academics, and scheming politicians, all determined to challenge the edicts of the Bible.

In August 1870, Edward Rulloff's large wooden secretary desk sat near his apartment's window overlooking Third Avenue, its proper place during the sweltering summer months. Manhattan's weather would grow bitterly cold in just a few months; then Edward would drag it closer to the fireplace in his modest study—though most winter days, he couldn't afford any coal to burn. The months since his humiliation at the 1868 philological conference had been taxing on the aging academic, and his fortunes had declined further because Manhattan was more expensive than Brooklyn, where they were previously. Potatoes snatched from darkened farms outside of Brooklyn, itself a growing town in Kings County, served as the main course for many of his meals. Edward's clothes were tattered and filthy. When he purchased books from merchants in Irving Place, the copies were secondhand, battered from years of different owners. He had little money, but he was hopeful. He had concocted a way to earn extra income while he finished his manuscript—he would join Al Jarvis and Billy Dexter on their next heist.

As he prepared the robbery scheme, Edward shuffled his papers and picked up a copy of the *New York Times*, which a reader could buy for four cents. It had been printed just a few weeks before, on Monday, July 18, 1870. He skimmed a column on the front page's left-hand side with the headline "The War. A Battle Reported to Have Been Fought on the Frontier," a report detailing the beginning battles of the Franco-Prussian War, one of the most significant wars in the nineteenth century. The conflict between France and the German states would eventually result in France's loss of power in Europe, and New Yorkers were fascinated by the drama overseas. In fact, the *Times* dedicated its entire front page to its coverage. Edward was enamored of international news, as any contemporary gentleman would be.

With the newspaper clip tucked safely inside the drawer, he searched his secretary—the sturdy protector of his secrets. Edward stored his most important research there, along with his precious manuscript. But before he slid the lid down, he gently shoved some items to the rear. A visitor might find them to be curious tools, at least for a would-be professor: a slew of black masks, and a flat bar (known as a jimmy) used to pry open doors. There was even a curious ratchet drill set, along with some metal bits, a contraption Edward had invented himself. He admired his collection and then turned the key.

The summer of 1870 marked a juncture for Edward Rulloff. He sat for hours, jotting down phrases, and then crossing them out on his manuscript. At times Edward was sanguine, even gleeful, at the prospect that his theory might serve as his salvation from a lifetime of exclusion. Day and night, Edward leafed through his collection of prized books, the things he held most valuable. The yellowing pages crunched as he turned them. The gaslight was too dim to read some of the fading titles stamped on their spines, but Edward knew them by heart: *A Key to the Classical Pronunciation of Greek, Latin, and Scripture Names* read one title. *Letters of Junius*, a book of letters written in the late 1700s, criticizing King George III, was also in the stack. *The British Botanist* sat next to a volume about Roman antiquities. They were all vital to his theory.

Edward stroked the manuscript's pages like a devoted parishioner might caress the Bible during Sunday service. *This manuscript was precious*, he just knew it. But he also suffered through brief periods of doubt, cycles of anxiety that provoked bitterness and anger. He blamed so many people for his unfortunate luck.

So it was that in August 1870, Al Jarvis, Billy Dexter, and Edward Rulloff paced the study of the apartment in Irving Place, haggling over the details of their latest plan. Jarvis and Dexter would target a large dry goods store in the town of Binghamton, about fifty miles southeast of Ithaca. Their goal was to sneak inside the store at night, rob it of valuable items, and escape into the dark night. It was a ludicrous, tricky scheme for many reasons, not the least of which was its proximity to the town where Edward Rulloff had been tried for murder years before, and where Al Jarvis had broken him out of jail. Both men were known—and reviled—in that part of the state. In addition, stores selling expensive material, like silk, were most certainly guarded at night, even in sleepy Binghamton. The men knew they might need to disable any armed clerks, so Edward hunted inside his cabinet for a bottle of chloroform to bring on the mission.

―――――――

In the meantime, his in-laws, the Schutts, had spent the past decade both fretting about and despising Edward Rulloff. They feared that a man possessed by the devil would certainly seek revenge on the people who had sent him to prison. Much had happened to the family since Edward disappeared to New York City in 1860—there were numerous marriages, children, and deaths. The patriarch of the family, John Schutt, had died in 1868 at the age of eighty-two, still tortured over the assumed murders of his daughter and granddaughter. Sorrow over his passing spread through the Schutts, as Dryden mourned the loss of one of its most influential residents. One family member penned a long poem about John Schutt, an homage to a resilient figure who had guided his family through the trauma of several criminal trials with grace. The poem described Schutt's final days spent napping beneath a large tree on Brookfield Farm.

"He is leaning back in his old rush chair, and the light breeze tosses his snowy hair. His toil worn hands crossed beneath his breast, and near him his old dog watches his rest." John Schutt was a moral man with good character, his community agreed, but the tragedy of his life was the fact that he died believing that Edward Rulloff would never be punished for killing Amelia, Amille, Harriet, and Priscilla.

A local newspaper printed a long obituary that read: "Mr. Schutt was a man of far more than ordinary intellectual culture. He possessed a good memory and studious habits. He was well versed in the current news and of the literature of the day." If Edward had valued family as his father-in-law did, then his own obituary might have sounded similar; both men were educators, academically minded and diligent about things they cared for. But Edward Rulloff was destined for a very different type of legacy.

Why did Edward Rulloff join Al Jarvis and Billy Dexter on their robbery in Binghamton? He should have declined to participate and simply stayed in shadows, as he had many times before, but he was sure he could be helpful—and an extra pair of hands could help steal more items. As at other points in his life, Edward's self-destructive impulses overrode his inarguable intellect— he simply could not remain discreet and hidden in anonymous New York City. Edward wasn't delusional—he understood the risks. Those psychopathic individuals can appreciate that they might get caught, but the motivation for the reward is too great to ignore. Edward's desire to fund his research and then self-publish far outweighed the risk of going to prison. And now Billy, Al, and Edward turned to planning the heist.

"He [Jarvis] said that their store was very near the riverbank, and that it was easy to enter it and get away," explained Edward. "He said there was no danger; that he had everything fixed."

Al Jarvis promised Edward and Billy that the Chenango River was shallow . . . they would swim effortlessly across to freedom—what terrible judgment. Al cased the store and confirmed that all would be fine, and Edward acquiesced, hopping on a train on the Erie Railroad on Wednesday, August 17, 1870, from Manhattan to Binghamton. Once there, the men waited for nightfall and then squatted at the back doorway of Halbert Brothers dry goods store with a hand-cranked drill. Jarvis slowly, quietly, bored holes into the metal braces as the bolts securing the door released easily. It was between one and two o'clock in the morning as they stood with their backs to the rushing Chenango River. The men had determined that there were two clerks who were sleeping soundly inside the building, guarding its precious silk merchandise. Edward, Jarvis, and Dexter each unrolled their black face masks and pulled them over their heads. Edward's long gray beard peeked out through the bottom as his dark eyes darted back and forth over the store's ground floor.

The three men quietly slunk across the ground floor and stayed down, listening for any sign of stirring from the clerks asleep in beds on the top floor at the front of the store. Edward slipped off his patent leather Oxford shoes and walked quietly to the wooden staircase. He waited at the bottom as Jarvis and Dexter crept up the stairs and pulled out the bottle of chloroform. Jarvis poured a bit on a rag and hovered it close to the mouths of both clerks—they fell into a deeper sleep. Jarvis and Dexter silently wrapped up two or three packages of silk worth about $1,500 and left them at the door at the back of the store. The difficult part was done, so the men began feeling more brazen as they prowled around the building, collecting other items of value.

One of the clerks, Frederick Merrick, flipped over, spooking Edward. Edward quietly ordered Dexter and Jarvis to pour more chloroform on the rag, but as Dexter reached toward Merrick's face, Jarvis tripped over something, and both clerks suddenly roused, startled and alarmed, from their chemical slumber. Merrick and the other clerk, Gilbert Burrows, sat up on their cots and stared back at the thieves—no one moved for several moments, before Merrick suddenly sprang to his feet, yelling as he scrambled to find his pistol.

As Dexter tried to run down the stairs, Merrick fired the pistol twice, missing both times. The clerk snatched part of a wooden stool and threw it at the intruders as Jarvis and Dexter tried to escape down the staircase. Merrick chased Jarvis down the stairs, and Burrows snatched Dexter by the neck and hurled him to the ground. Burrows grabbed a heavy iron box opener and hurled it against Dexter's face; the burglar screamed out in pain, holding his eye as blood dripped through his fingers. In Merrick and Burrows, the burglars had encountered two strong, tenacious young clerks who were determined to stop their store from being plundered.

"Jarvis was a stout, athletic fellow," said Edward, "but Merrick had the strength of a maniac. He had been given just enough chloroform to make him crazy."

Somehow in the struggle, Merrick dropped the pistol, Edward found it, and he fired at his head. Merrick's slim body slumped on the floor. Burrows began calling for help as the trio of thieves ran toward the back of the store.

The Chenango River was just a few yards away from the building's exit, but both Dexter and Jarvis were stumbling from their injuries. Burrows left Merrick lying on the floor of the dry goods store; the clerk ran to the front, flung open the doors, and screamed, "Murder." His cries awoke the chief of police, who happened to be staying in a hotel across the street from the store.

Edward could hear the fire bells ring as he lugged Jarvis and Dexter toward the river. Dexter stammered that he couldn't swim. Edward surveyed Dexter's injuries—his eye was swollen shut, and blood was streaming down his cheek. He heard the police officers making their way toward them through the darkness. Their only hope was to slip away through the black water.

Al Jarvis turned to Billy Dexter and reminded him that this section was only a few inches deep, just shallow enough to walk across. Dexter was still unsure, but Edward was done negotiating; the police were approaching fast. He grabbed both men and they waded into the dark water as dogs barked at the back of the building.

In the blackness, it wasn't easy to determine the depth or the swiftness of the river—Jarvis had miscalculated. The river's current dragged them under, and they were submerged almost instantly. Dexter cried out and began to flail, reaching out for Edward, who pushed him away.

"He clutched hold of me and come near taking me down with him," said Edward. "He sank at once, and I do not think he came up again."

Then Jarvis screamed for help. Edward watched as his protégé sank, just feet away. Now he was alone, and Edward's skills at self-preservation took over; the police on the edge of the river hadn't seen him in the dark, so he quietly swam to the other shore. Someone near the dry goods store screamed for a surgeon to save Frederick Merrick's life. It was too late; Merrick had died almost immediately.

Edward dragged himself onto the shore and lay there for a moment. He was a mess—his clothes were disheveled and wet, his black and gray hair was matted, and he was missing his shoes, which were still inside the store. How might he explain his appearance to anyone he encountered?

Edward stumbled through a yard, searching for the tree where he had hidden his burglars' tools. He finally retrieved them and then stashed the pack underneath his jacket as he crept through Binghamton. Several people stopped him and asked about the fire bells—he pointed toward the dry goods store. No one suspected him of anything . . . he must have just seemed like a harmless old indigent.

Edward discovered an abandoned house in the woods, broke in, and sat there alone all night. For perhaps the first time in his life, Edward Rulloff was puzzled about what to do next.

The following morning, news of the botched robbery and the death of the young man, Frederick Merrick, had spread across Binghamton. The chief of police ordered a manhunt for the three burglars who were last seen swimming across the Chenango River. The surviving clerk, Gilbert Burrows, offered investigators detailed descriptions, and deputies collected evidence inside the store, including a curious clue—an odd pair of leather shoes that seemed to be crafted for someone with a malformed foot.

———

Two days later, several local men held an impromptu discussion on the bank of the river. They squinted in the sunlight at two large objects lodged against the piers of the Court Street Bridge as a fisherman climbed into his rowboat. The man cast out his line numerous times before snaring one of the objects. As he dragged it toward his boat, he stared at the swollen face.

Dead body, he yelled toward shore, and the fisherman soon hooked the second corpse. A newspaper photographer snapped photos of Al Jarvis and Billy Dexter lying side by side on wooden planks on the river's shore. Their clothes were disheveled; their faces were pale and bloated. One of the men was missing an eye, thanks to the fisherman's hook. Gilbert Burrows looked down at the smaller corpse and nodded. He recognized Billy Dexter, the robber that he scuffled with that night. He asked about the third burglar—*Where might he be?*

Nearly two hundred people had gathered on the shore to see the bodies. People in Binghamton began to cheer as Al Jarvis and Billy Dexter were searched, their personal items tossed onto the shore. New York City reporters appeared disgusted as townspeople stared at the corpses. One journalist wrote that nearly every citizen, woman, schoolboy, little girl, and small dog marched by the remains. Among the local reporters stood a young man who held a pencil and a notepad—Hamilton Freeman, the publisher of the local newspaper, the *Democratic Leader.* It would be six months before Ham would sit down with Edward Rulloff to write his biography. For now, the fledgling author was standing on the riverbank following a sensational story in Binghamton.

Ham silently watched the officers search Dexter and Jarvis and, as they turned out their pockets, he squinted at the contents spilling out. Lying on the ground were a glazier diamond used to cut glass and a metal bit used for boring holes, along with snippets of poetry. One of the men also carried a nautical journal as well as a copy of a popular fortune-telling book. *Who were these two? And where was the third man?*

This was big news, even down in New York City. The *New York Times* published sensational stories about the mystery of the dead burglars, along with newspapers around the country. Gilbert Burrows insisted to the police chief that there was a third suspect, a man with a dark beard who made it across the river alive. Details emerged about Merrick's death inside the store as investigators described to newspaper reporters how the clerk's blood and brains had been splattered across elegant reams of costly silk. Much of the town armed itself and prayed that police would find the third burglar, the man who had murdered Frederick Merrick.

———

Farmer Chauncey Livingston despised the thieves who were always poking around his orchard in Binghamton at night, hoping to steal some apples. During warm summer nights, neighbors knew that Livingston was likely rocking on his front porch late into the evening with a pipe in one hand and a pistol in the other, determined to protect his property from anyone who planned to trespass. Local investigators in nearby Binghamton had spent the last two nights hunting for the burglar, but everyone (including Livingston) figured he was likely long gone by now.

Livingston puffed on his pipe and surveyed his land as the wind blew the leaves on his apple trees. He glanced at his outhouse just on the other side of the front yard, but then he paused. The door to the small building was ajar, and there was a shadow cast by the light of the moon. Livingston stared at that shadow for a moment—it seemed too dark. And then he watched it move. Livingston slowly crept toward the outhouse door, cocked his pistol, and stepped inside the doorway. He glanced down and pointed his gun at an older man crouched in the corner, holding his breath.

It was an undignified hiding spot for the aspirant academic. Edward Rulloff hopped up, brushed off his clothes, raised his hands, and calmly introduced himself as Charles Augustus. Livingston surveyed the stranger, who was disheveled, harried, and suspicious.

The farmer dragged the man over to the chief of police, and Edward was quickly handcuffed and jailed, his name appearing in the blotter as Charles Augustus—one of many aliases that he offered investigators. Edward was just another ne'er-do-well on their interview list. There were no photographs of him, not even a drawing, and no way to connect Edward Rulloff, the murderer from Dryden, to this pitiful old man. But the police chief was immediately suspicious that Mr. Augustus might be linked to the mysterious burglar who had killed a clerk in Binghamton.

The chief engaged in an experiment. He retrieved each suspect from his cell, dragged him downstairs to the basement of the courthouse, and watched as he reacted to seeing the bloated corpses of Billy Dexter and Al Jarvis lying on the concrete. He escorted Edward down the wooden stairs and stood aside as Edward slowly circled Dexter and Jarvis. There lay the only two people who had committed their lives to Edward; despite poverty and prison, the young men had pledged loyalty to him in hopes of being proper gentlemen, of escaping their humble, troubled former lives. The police chief eyed Edward and then asked if he knew the men.

"No," he firmly replied. Edward asked to see their bodies from a different angle and stood near the top of their heads. *No.* He showed no nerves, just unwavering confidence—and excellent acting skills.

Now the chief fretted about his lack of evidence; he didn't have enough to hold "Augustus," or any of the other suspects he'd rounded up, much longer. In fact, Edward Rulloff wasn't the only man held on suspicion of the crime; the jail was full of all the vagrants and former prisoners the chief could rustle up, so great was the public pressure to solve this crime. The strain was stifling, almost unbearable. Hadn't Binghamton suffered enough? First the Civil War, now this. Justice must be served.

Despite a lack of physical evidence, prosecutors quickly convened a grand jury to indict each suspect. When he stood before the panel, Edward once again offered an alias and proclaimed his innocence. He smiled at the jurors—Edward was the most composed of the suspects, and the least suspicious of the lot. He spoke in a cultured, calm voice despite his unkempt appearance. *Surely, this could not be the killer.* The prosecutor nodded that he could go, and Edward prepared to walk away from a courthouse once again as a free man. Until he heard a familiar voice.

"You are Edward H. Rulloff," cried someone behind him.

Edward turned around to see an older man with wide eyes. He was wagging his finger and stuttering. Edward shrugged his shoulders as the prosecutor glanced from his suspect to the alarmed man.

"You murdered your wife and child in Lansing in 1845," the man yelled.

Edward might have denied the accusations—after all, why would they believe this man? But Edward seemed uneasy because he *had* recognized the accuser. He was Judge Ransom Balcom, a distinguished justice with the court of appeals in Ithaca. As one of the three judges who had ruled that there was not enough evidence to try Edward for the murder of his wife twelve years earlier, Balcom had always felt sickened by that decision. He understood the way Edward had used his legal knowledge to manipulate the trial and its aftermath. Edward was not ultimately convicted of his wife's murder, only of her kidnapping . . . but that did not mean he had been innocent. Balcom knew that better than most.

"This man understands his rights better than you do and will defend them to the last," Balcom warned the panel and the prosecutor. Edward glared at the judge and, undaunted, admitted to the jury that he was in fact Edward H. Rulloff—but he explained that he had good reason for denying his identity.

"There, gentlemen, you have an explanation of my strange conduct. Knowing of my misfortunes in this portion of New York, you can understand why I was anxious, being here accidentally when a murder was committed, to pass through the city without my identity being known," he told the jury.

Edward denied killing Frederick Merrick—he claimed that his appearance in Binghamton was simply coincidence. There was no physical evidence to place him inside the Halbert Brothers store that night. Edward had served his ten-year sentence for the kidnapping of Harriet, and now he was a free man. The prosecutor was powerless. He immediately released Edward as Judge Balcom fumed in the courtroom's gallery. Edward smirked, exited the front door, and began walking quickly toward the train tracks.

But as Edward traveled out of town, an investigator made a remarkable discovery. Police had searched Edward when he arrived at jail during the roundup of suspects. The chief discovered that Edward was missing the big toe on his left foot, thanks to a case of frostbite back when he was on the run in Pennsylvania in

1858. The investigator retrieved those curious patent leather Oxford shoes found by police inside the basement of the store.

One of them was oddly designed, specially made for someone missing a toe—this could be an important clue.

The chief sent a posse to recapture Edward, and he was tracked just east of the town that same day. The police shoved him into a cell, forced him to put on both shoes, and they fit perfectly. Edward Rulloff was now tied to a fifth murder, but this time, investigators would carefully gather a good deal of evidence against him.

By now, word had traveled to the Schutt farm about Edward Rulloff's arrest. The family quickly traveled to Binghamton. Edward was composed throughout his pretrial hearing in August 1870, with just one exception. As he sat on the stand answering basic questions, the prosecutor pointed to his former mother-in-law, Hannah Schutt. Now in her seventies, the family's matriarch had not seen Edward in almost fifteen years, at his last trial for murdering her grandchild. The prosecutor asked if Edward recognized Hannah, and after he squinted, he replied that he wasn't sure because she was sitting too far away. The district attorney offered Hannah his arm as he walked her to the stand. She stood in front of Edward and glared while he squirmed, gazing down at the wooden desk. His face went flush and he began breathing heavily.

"If I'm not mistaken," Edward replied quietly, "it is Mrs. Schutt."

Hannah stared at him after her testimony, and she quickly returned to her seat in the gallery. Edward shifted in the chair and looked down, trying to suppress the only emotion he had shown. People with psychopathy might have a difficult time controlling their panic when confronted with an accuser who has detected their deception. Edward had refused to be contrite, and Hannah Schutt had refused to allow him to remain comfortable at the defense table. She enjoyed watching him squirm.

Police were tasked with connecting the two dead burglars to their new suspect, Edward Rulloff, so the town's prosecutor requested help from the New York Police Department. The DA traveled from Binghamton to Manhattan to meet an eager young detective named Philip Reilley. The investigator studied the contents of the pockets of Dexter and Jarvis, some of which were scraps of paper with names, keys, and other bits of information. Detective Reilley spent days tracing Edward's life through New York, following his trail meticulously. He met some of his accomplices, including Maggie Graham, the Irish woman who fenced their stolen silks, after Reilley tracked down Billy Dexter's brother. Despite Edward's skepticism about Graham's loyalty, she refused to reveal anything incriminating about the crime ring—she remained loyal to Edward.

"During an interview with John Dexter, brother of the drowned burglar, forced upon that person at the tumbledown house at the dawn of an October morning, Reilley drew from him the address of a woman known as Maggie, living at No. 75 Carmine Street, who had been housekeeper for Rulloff, and knew where he lived," reported Crapsey.

When the detective finally located the apartment on Third Avenue in Irving Place, he uncovered evidence of the criminal conspiracy between Edward, Jarvis, and Dexter; the desk in Edward's apartment matched to a key found on one of the dead men. The prosecutor in Binghamton surveyed Reilley's evidence and charged Edward Rulloff with murder: the third murder charge of his life.

———

Christmas Day was glorious for much of New York City. At midnight, the bells of the old Trinity Church in Lower Manhattan chimed in celebration. The sweet tones echoed throughout the dark and otherwise silent streets of the city. During the day, New Yorkers packed outdoor markets down on Fulton Street in Lower Manhattan and in Washington Square to the north. Patrons elbowed each other to buy freshly killed deer, rabbit, poultry, and fish.

It was a special season for so many New Yorkers, but Edward Rulloff wasn't in town to enjoy it. He spent the day sitting on his lumpy bedroll inside the Binghamton jail, waiting for his trial. As usual for Edward, though, he was doing exactly what he would be doing as a free man—writing. He had always found prison conducive to doing his best work.

Edward's murder trial was set for January 1871. The date was quickly approaching, but instead of planning his defense, he frantically edited and re-edited his precious manuscript. The people in New York's countryside, particularly the Schutts, felt a bit more at ease this Christmas with Edward safely chained to the floor in the jail in Binghamton. Yet there was still a fear that once again he would escape justice.

Harriet's elderly mother, Hannah Schutt, died just a few weeks after she confronted Edward in court. Clearly, she had shaken him, but the emotional trial was too much for her fragile health. She passed away without seeing her son-in-law hanged for killing her two granddaughters, her daughter, and her daughter-in-law, but she died with hope that justice would finally be done.

In January 1871, buggies ringed the courthouse in Binghamton. The crowd angled for a look at the aged savant. Edward's younger brothers—Rulof in Pennsylvania and William in San Francisco—provided ample funds for a well-known defense attorney; they'd stuck by Edward, even after all these years and all his alleged misdeeds. The lawyer, George Becker, begged Edward to allow him to lead the questioning, but his client was determined to speak up and control his own fate. This isn't all that surprising; many bright, narcissistic, psychopathic criminals have been unable to sit quietly next to their attorneys over the years.

In 1982, an assistant district attorney in Georgia asked FBI agent John Douglas for help with a suspected serial killer. His name was Wayne B. Williams, and he was on trial for murdering two men in Atlanta the previous year. But Williams was suspected of at least twenty killings between 1979 and 1981, known as the Atlanta child murders. The ADA wondered aloud to Douglas if he thought Williams might take the stand. Douglas considered Williams's character.

"I said first that I thought there was a good chance Williams might take the stand because I had detected in him a fair amount of intellectual pretension and superiority and a feeling that the criminal justice system was a bunch of bumbling Keystone Kops," wrote Douglas. "He thought he could control the situation, even from the witness chair."

Douglas's assumption was correct; Williams did take the stand. At the agent's suggestion, ADA Jack Mallard placed his hand on Williams's arm during his testimony.

"'What was it like, Wayne? What was it like when you wrapped your fingers around the victim's throat? Did you panic?'" asked Mallard.

"No," responded Williams, before realizing his mistake and flying into a rage.

A convicted killer like Williams, contended Douglas, could be shaken by exploiting his weakness: insecurity cloaked in arrogance. The psychopath's desire to be the center of attention might eclipse all common sense, but there are other reasons that killers like Edward Rulloff might represent themselves.

"Some criminal defendants who act as their own lawyers want a stage to promote an ideology," wrote Richard Pérez-Peña in the *New York Times*. "Some apparently want the spotlight or think they can fare better than a real lawyer; some are too controlling to let anyone else be in charge; some are too paranoid to trust lawyers; and some are just delusional."

In 1871, Edward Rulloff registered a similar dose of bluster, or paranoia, or delusion. As he strutted around the courtroom, he demanded to question the first witness, the surviving clerk, Gilbert Burrow. He challenged Burrow's memory of that night and the identity of the man who shot Frederick Merrick.

"I saw him square in the face when he went downstairs after he shot Merrick and come towards me," said Burrow.

"By good light?" Edward asked.

"You know what the light was," Burrow replied, almost with a sneer.

The courtroom applauded, causing a jubilant uproar that was quickly quashed by the judge. Edward ignored the outburst and continued showing little emotion throughout the trial, despite the litany of witnesses who damned him to the gallows. But Edward's docile countenance crumbled after the prosecutor submitted a key piece of evidence—his hallowed manuscript. Witnesses in court reported that he held it with unusual emotion. One person said that he seemed to almost fondle it like a great treasure.

"There is the proof, your honor, that my occupation does not send me around the country breaking open stores," Edward declared to the judge. "There is a book that 500 men in 10 years cannot produce."

The manuscript was his alibi, he boldly claimed, because every moment of his life in New York City had been devoted to it. It was an interesting defense, one befitting a man obsessed with his own ideas.

The jury took hours debating behind a locked door. Townspeople feared that Edward would escape a death sentence by being convicted of a lesser charge, as happened in the trial for his wife's murder. Edward might even escape without jail time, and that was a thought that frightened just about everyone in upstate New York.

Rumor spread across Binghamton that a lynch mob was forming. In a repeat of the events of 1859, William Schutt boasted that he was prepared to unleash a group of two hundred men on the jail where Edward was being held. The minister of the First Presbyterian Church in Binghamton advocated for vengeance if secular justice didn't prevail.

Finally, after six hours, on January 11, 1871, the jurors reached a verdict: guilty of first-degree murder. Edward Rulloff was sentenced to hang on March 3, 1871.

Edward sat back in his chair for a moment, out of exhaustion. But soon afterward, he marched back to his cell. He lit his gas lamp, opened his manuscript, and began to write. Edward now had just two months to finish the book, to secure his legacy. Meanwhile, he could hear the men building the gallows just outside his cell.

After the verdict, the newspapers were laden with lurid stories of Rulloff the murderer, "a monster of unequalled monstrosity" read one headline. He was convicted of killing just one person,

Frederick Merrick, but by the end of the trial, Edward's reputation was that of a multiple murderer. The townspeople whispered about the deaths of his missing wife and daughter, as well as the deaths of his sister-in-law and her newborn. Reporters speculated that Edward had deliberately drowned Dexter and Jarvis to avoid leaving witnesses.

There was one journalist who had earned Edward's trust, his only confidant as he awaited execution. Edward shook Hamilton Freeman's hand for the first time inside the Binghamton jail in January 1871. Ham took notes as Edward sat with him retelling his life story, starting just one day after his conviction. As he flipped over his paper, the reporter grew uneasy when he heard chanting outside the jail cell: "Crucify him, crucify him."

Edward Rulloff had exercised little patience in life, and even less modesty. His interview in May 1871 with Drs. George Sawyer and Judson Boardman Andrews would challenge him to embrace both, as they sat in wooden chairs across from him in the tiny, fetid cell. Edward refused to offer his customary affable greeting to the pair as they fidgeted with their pencils. Edward was quiet while he evaluated Sawyer; mistrust grew between the men. Edward, for his part, had never received such an inhospitable guest.

He eyed a packet of written material that Sawyer was cradling. *A test of languages*, the killer suspected. He braced himself for several hours of passive judgment, recorded on notepads that then might be passed on to newspapermen. Edward quickly realized that Sawyer's opinion of his theory might doom his chances of saving his own life or, even worse, spoil his legacy. Edward might die on the gallows if someone didn't intervene.

Sawyer pulled out some sections of Edward's manuscript, those excerpts printed in both Hamilton Freeman's newspaper and Oliver Dyer's interview with him in *The Sun*. As Andrews scribbled notes, Sawyer read aloud, line by line, Edward's theory and questioned each of his assertions about the origin of Greek, which was the language he considered superior to all.

"What is the origin of the Greek language?" asked Sawyer.

"A superior Greek mind at some former period of time," replied Edward, with a faint smile. "Yes, they were philologists with aforethought and prepense."

Sawyer smirked subtly. No expert had been as well-versed in languages as George Sawyer, including Richard Mather. Sawyer began to point out inconsistencies with the methods, including the idea that just one group of people "invented" a language, such as Greek. And other parts of Edward's theory didn't jibe with the contemporary understanding of linguistics, that the connection between a word's meaning and its sound or form is arbitrary, not a pattern that can be traced. Arbitrariness is one of the characteristics shared among all languages. In fact, it was Edward's rules, to Sawyer, that appeared to be arbitrary. Edward's face reddened.

"You must remember my system is not perfected, and must pardon any little inaccuracies of mine," Edward stammered.

Edward was growing hesitant with each query, as his evaluator seemed to press him on details he had not yet worked out. Edward gave Sawyer another example: how the word "jubar" is derived from "umbra." Edward smiled.

"How significant that the word meaning 'shade of the night' should be transformed into a word meaning 'the morning twilight,' yet how plain!" said Edward.

Edward explained that both "jubar" and "umbra" already shared a *u* and a *b*.

"Then transpose ra and you have ar, while the j and m are readily seen to be interchangeable," he explained.

Sawyer seemed confused. "By what law were these seemingly arbitrary changes made?" he asked.

"It depended," was Edward's vague reply.

Now, Sawyer was perplexed. Did a linguist, even a self-educated one, really believe that all language was coded, and for thousands of years, only one man had broken that code? Yes, this was Edward's belief.

But Sawyer's criticisms of Edward's intellect weren't focused solely on his theory—perhaps Edward wasn't as bright as he claimed to be. The killer, Sawyer claimed, had trouble translating a simple section of Greek, though this happened at the beginning of the interview, when Edward had been reticent to answer any of the principal's questions fully. Then, Sawyer asked him a question about the concept of onomatopoeia—a word that phonetically imitates, resembles, or evokes the sound that it describes, such as "clap," "hiss," or "crackle." Any competent linguist in the 1800s would have been familiar with this concept and the theory that these words arrive organically and independently in each language.

"When asked to what origin might be assigned to the words 'clap,' 'hiss,' 'crackle' . . . examples of onomatopoeia," said Sawyer, "the principle of onomatopoeia was scouted as silly." Simply put, the so-called scholar of languages didn't believe in one of the most fundamental principles of linguistics. It was like a physicist not believing in gravity, or a mathematician who didn't believe in pi. To Sawyer, Edward's lack of understanding of this basic linguistic concept undercut his entire understanding of what language was—and exposed him as a fraud.

Next, Sawyer turned to a different language, one Edward wasn't as directly familiar with as Greek but which, according to his "universal theory" of languages, should have some relevance to his work. When asked how the language of Sanskrit had figured into his philosophy, Edward dismissed it. But the scholar could only ignore offering context for so long—Edward was clearly losing control of this interview.

"[H]e said he had nothing to do with Sanscrit [sic], that he meant, with a smile, no disrespect to that language, but it had nothing to do with his method," said Sawyer.

Sawyer begrudgingly admitted that Edward's memory of Greek was remarkable, as were his intellect and his ability to use Greek to create a unique theory. But Edward's comprehensive understanding of linguistics seemed fragmented and ultimately useless, according to Sawyer. Edward's anxiety increased, though he presented as indifferent to Sawyer.

"As children use blocks to build houses of any form, according to fancy," concluded Sawyer, "so Rulloff seems to have determined in the exercise of his will to make a universal language, for no one principle of which he should be indebted to anyone else." Sawyer's final determination: Edward was a fraudulent academic peddling a ludicrous theory. He mused that the attention Edward drew was a reminder that "a little learning is a dangerous thing." He could easily fool a gullible public, an eager biographer, an ambitious newspaperman, even a hopeful professor. But under the close questioning of a learned linguist, Edward's ideas crumbled to dust.

"The only wonder to us, after our interview, was that his elucubrations have attracted so much attention," said Sawyer.

Sawyer blamed Hamilton Freeman, Oliver Dyer, and Richard Mather for entertaining a fraud and duping all Americans. The educator was incredulous that an academic with no formal education, like Edward, would hold the public's fascination. *He was a charlatan, not a serious scholar!* Sawyer argued that the most erudite minds in linguistics had achieved their knowledge through training and "the most patient investigation of the principles of the science." Edward brought none of that scientific rigor or work to these flimsy ideas.

Edward's most damning attribute, according to Sawyer, was his criminal mind. Perhaps he had used that to manipulate and guide the way he was portrayed in the press for months—and to influence others who had crossed his path over the previous years and decades. He most certainly was not like most other people. But, insisted Sawyer, Edward Rulloff was most certainly *not* insane. And he wasn't stupid, either. He was intelligent—just completely amoral.

Sawyer's final assessment of their more than two-hour interview was ruinous for Edward's tenuous grasp on the public's sympathy, calling him "a conspicuous example of the utter worthlessness of high intellectual endowments, severed from moral culture." Sawyer continued: "Someone has speculated as to how much evil a man perfectly developed intellectually, and thoroughly unscrupulous, might accomplish. Rulloff approaches to the type of such a moral monster."

George Sawyer refused to relieve Edward of any responsibility for his crimes. Edward Rulloff's magnetism and manipulation proved to be ineffective when faced with a skeptic who matched him intellectually. But the killer did offer him some valuable insight.

Three years after their interview, in 1874, Sawyer appealed to the public to infuse more culture, more moral learning in schools. He insisted that moral and biblical teaching *must be* taught in tandem with standard academic achievements, to avoid rearing brilliant, brutal killers like Edward Rulloff. In this approach, Sawyer was in fact quite forward-thinking. Moral teaching might have helped redirect some young criminals, but there was little in the Bible that would sway a psychopath who embraced a fixation.

There is no cure for psychopathy—no drug can inject empathy, no vaccine can prevent murder in cold blood, and no amount of talk therapy can change an uncaring mind, because as we've learned, psychopathy is not a mental illness but a personality disorder. Many psychopaths are lost to the normal social world, even if they can function, but researchers believe that the destructive behavior of some young patients can be modified through positive reinforcement.

"These kids are more aggressive. These kids are more likely to be delinquents as they grow up. [They are] more likely to offend as they grow up now," said psychopathy expert Craig Neumann. "The key with psychopathology or with medical disorders is the earlier you find some form of pathology, the earlier identify it, the more likely you can provide some sort of treatment and be of help."

Neumann pointed to a program run by Dr. Michael Caldwell

in Madison, Wisconsin, called the Mendota Juvenile Treatment Center. Caldwell treats young men under eighteen who have failed out of the justice system because they're so violent and so aggressive; Caldwell brings them in and does a complete treatment that includes psychiatrists and therapists.

"Everyone's involved to try and move these kids towards motivational changes in that they can get what they want in life through pro-social means as opposed to antisocial," said Neumann. "So, the more you show pro-social behavior in today's context, the more likely you are to have privileges down the line. You can decrease psychopathic traits in these young adults and there's some evidence that suggests that the treatment effect is holding."

Neumann said that many of these research projects suffer because of a lack of federal government funding, which is frustrating because the data from research in psychopathy could be life-changing . . . and lifesaving.

"One of the things these kids show is a relative absence of eye contact with their parents. When you look at someone's face and make eye contact there's a part of the brain that lights up; it has to do with motion, emotion, and motivation and these areas of the amygdala," said Neumann. "By teaching kids to make more eye contact with their parents to potentially increase the attachment connection, you are potentially altering the course of these kids from a psychological point of view, by showing them how to become less calloused and potentially more empathic."

If only Edward Rulloff had experienced such thoughtful intervention at a young age.

Back in 1871, George Sawyer's fifty-two-page assessment of Edward was soon printed in the esteemed *American Journal of Insanity*. It was an account so thorough and so damning that it sounded the death knell on Edward's theory of languages—and the defense championed by Dyer and others that Rulloff was "too smart to be executed"—in newspapers across America.

"We think the world will not suffer seriously through being deprived of his work," read one editorial, based on Sawyer's conclusions.

But word had also spread that a local reporter, Ham Freeman, was writing a biography; Edward's defense attorney sensed a shift in public opinion and Hamilton Freeman wanted to help. As the time grew closer to Edward's execution, Ham felt immense guilt for not doing more, for not saving the man he now considered a friend.

Ham and Edward's defense attorney asked the killer to write a petition to New York's governor that might delay his own execution long enough for Edward to finish his precious manuscript. Instead of a rational argument, the page was filled with ramblings centered on Edward's theory, an overwhelming array of jargon that any language expert might find confounding.

"The modes of formation were various; sometimes by making other words directly from the original root," read the petition, "sometimes by the interposition of subsidiary or of collateral forms, from which other words were more immediately derived."

Edward invited scholars who had tested his knowledge in languages, including Professor Richard Mather, to sign the petition so his life might be spared. He didn't bother with Dr. George Sawyer, who had all but accused him of duping everyone he had ever encountered. And despite Dr. Mather's earlier curiosity about Edward's theory on languages, even Mather refused to add his signature to the rambling screed. Edward's former allies were dropping away.

Edward Rulloff was reaching the end of his options. Or perhaps not.

Hamilton Freeman sat at his wooden desk in his home in Binghamton in mid-April 1871, transcribing notes from his journal to loose-leaf pages that described the macabre spectacle instigated by the town's sheriff several weeks earlier. Edward's formal legal appeals, each written in his own hand, had failed in the New York Court of Appeals. The justices were indifferent to Edward's legal pleas.

"Notwithstanding that Rulloff had many fine-spun, hairsplitting theories in his favor," wrote Ham, "the court did not deem it worthwhile or expedient to interfere with the course of justice. . . . It is said one of the judges proposed, after the case was argued, *to hang Rulloff first and examine his case afterwards.*"

The court of appeals ordered that Edward be sentenced to death (once again) by the General Term of the Supreme Court in Elmira, a sixty-mile train trip west. Hamilton felt sorrow for the killer.

"It was indeed a pitiable sight to see this man of learning, of talents, capable of adorning any high station in life, a convicted murderer," wrote Ham, "carried about the country by the officers of the law, manacled."

Edward was handcuffed to a large policeman as he was marched on foot from the jail in Binghamton to the nearby Erie Railroad depot. The manacled pair was followed by a "vast and eager crowd, who were up early in the morning to see this distinguished victim of his own self and the law." The train lurched forward and, in less than an hour, rolled to a stop at the next station. It had been telegraphed ahead that Edward was traveling to receive his death sentence, so as the train arrived at each stop, throngs of gleeful gawkers met its arrival. Ham recalled this scene with bitterness.

"Arriving at Elmira, the streets and passages about the depot, and from the depot to the Court House, were densely packed," remembered Ham, "and it required the united force of the stalwart Sheriff Martin and his deputies . . . to push their way through the surging crowd." He was grim, sarcastic: "It was a proud day for Elmira!"

Observers commented that it seemed more like a perp walk than a press conference, all theatrics and showmanship for the press offered by a gloating sheriff who seemed pleased with himself. The jubilant mobs fueled by bloodlust appalled Hamilton, though the author believed that there were some who walked within the hordes who were decent and maybe even concerned for Edward.

"Men searched their hearts that day to find, if possible, some bright palliating shade in the character of this wretched old man," wrote Ham, "that they might at least heave a sigh of pity as he passed on, but his offenses were too rank and smelt to high Heaven."

Edward slunk to his pallet inside his jail cell as the iron doors locked. He sat down, cross-legged, flipped open a law book, and began writing. His legal mind had saved him from countless crises in the past, and now he could lean on his knowledge of the law once again. In mid-April, one month before his scheduled execution, an anxious Edward summoned Hamilton Freeman to his cell. Edward pointed to a stack of law books. Inside one, he believed, he had uncovered a legal argument concerning the testimony of the surviving clerk, Gilbert Burrows, who claimed that Edward had shot and killed Frederick Merrick. The prosecutor offered little direct evidence that Edward was the murderer and had relied solely on Burrows's hazy memories that night, which were complicated by confusion and violence.

Edward excitedly insisted to Ham that the clerk's testimony should be dismissed as unsound; the jury was offered misleading information during the trial, so its deliberation should be voided. Edward gave Ham a handwritten petition, one he had spent all night crafting, and then he made a special request. He asked that the author confront all twelve jurors and implore them to add their signatures, then Ham would present the petition to Governor John T. Hoffman. The legal document requested that Governor Hoffman commute his sentence—Edward demanded to be released or at least saved from the gallows.

Ham reluctantly slipped the petition into his bag and began approaching the jurors, based on a list supplied to him by the court. The journalist rapped on each door, explained Edward's argument—and each man shook his head. They were still unanimously convinced that Edward was guilty. Despite the killer's glibness, charm, and intelligence, it was Gilbert Burrows's sincerity and courage in the witness box that swayed the jurors. Once again, Edward Rulloff was demoralized by biting, truthful criticism.

6

The Alienist

I declare, at least, before God, no man morally sane could
have been guilty of that crime upon so pitiful a provocation.
—Robert Louis Stevenson,
Strange Case of Dr. Jekyll and Mr. Hyde, 1886

Despite the seemingly overwhelming evidence of his guilt, the
question of what to do with Edward Rulloff—and, crucially,
how to understand such a brilliant, perverse mind—was still being
debated at the highest levels across the country. The arguments
were passionate on both sides, and boiled down to this: Was Edward too evil to live . . . or too exceptional to kill?

Some influential scholars believed the latter. They were convinced that the prosecutor in Binghamton, New York, had failed
to prove his case beyond a reasonable doubt—and that the clerk's
murder had been a crime of circumstance rather than one of cold-
blooded calculation. One of those was Tayler Lewis, a respected
American scholar, orator, and author, who once held a seat as a
professor of Greek at the University of New York. Lewis and Edward were exchanging letters while the killer was jailed, and

Lewis became convinced of Edward's innocence. Lewis was alarmed as Edward's execution drew near, so he wrote the *New York Times* explaining that Merrick's death was not premeditated and therefore Edward should *not* be executed.

"I had been led to feel a deep sympathy for the condemned Rulloff," wrote Lewis. "I still think that the lack of evidence of any intent to kill, and the peculiar aspects of the case, which Rulloff so clearly and ably states in his published petition, confirmed, as they are, by the bearing of some of the testimony, ought to weigh strongly on his behalf."

Others believed that his work—the glorious manuscript that Edward and many others still believed in, despite George Sawyer's dismissal—might still warrant a delay in the hanging. An editorial in the respected *Christian Union* newspaper recounted all of Edward's crimes, yet still defended his academic merit . . . and his penchant for producing drama: "We hope that Rulloff will be permitted to finish the manuscript on comparative philology which it is said he has in preparation," concluded the editors, "and if he writes a confession, as it is hoped he will, we may look for something almost unprecedented in that unusually dreary line of literary enterprise."

A Presbyterian church service in Binghamton, where Edward was jailed, featured a usual sermon; its minister had reviewed the sinner's many crimes and then mourned the inevitable doom of a brilliant mind. "He paid an eloquent tribute to the prisoner's erudition, making a comparison between the man as he was and what he might have been," read the summary in the *Herald*, "possessing those rare gifts of the mind as he does, and deprecating the use he has made of his literary attainments."

Soon, Edward's theory was gifted with a powerful endorsement from a bellwether in American politics. An editorial from Republican Horace Greeley arrived in the pages of the newspaper he had founded thirty years earlier, the *New York Tribune:* "In the prison at Binghamton there is a man waiting death who is too curious an intellectual problem to be wasted on the gallows," Greeley wrote on the editorial page. "He is one of the most industrious and devoted scholars our busy generation has given birth to."

Greeley's stance on Edward's impending execution wasn't unforeseen by the American public, despite the domination of pro-death-penalty sentiment. By 1871, Greeley was considered a radical within the Republican party, so much so that he led the pathway to a new offshoot the following year, called the Liberal Republican Party. For decades, Greeley was a staunch abolitionist and a passionate orator of the North's antislavery sentiments. When he'd originally founded the *New York Tribune*, it was a daily paper dedicated to espousing society reforms; Greeley's writers were outstanding journalists who wrote with moral zeal.

Greeley spoke out fervently against those issues he considered to be the ills of society, particularly liquor, sex work, tobacco, gambling, and capital punishment. Greeley's support of a multiple murderer like Edward Rulloff might have seemed curious, but Greeley was a smart businessman as well as an astute politician. Inserting himself into a controversial case like Edward's would certainly sell more newspapers and perhaps even bolster his political ambitions—he had hoped to run for public office (he would be nominated to run against Ulysses S. Grant for the presidency the following year but lost, and then died shortly after).

In the editorial, Greeley effused over Edward's intelligence and his right to life. Edward, according to Greeley, was clearly a rightful member of the upper class; the newspaper editor, like most Americans, adhered to the nineteenth-century belief that an insane man would present as a clichéd lunatic.

"He does not attire himself in motley, with straw in his hair and a reed in his hand, in mockery of royalty," read the editorial. "He does not go howling and shrieking through the towns in the noisy rage of the commonplace maniac."

Greeley suggested that the Democratic governor, John Hoffman, delay Edward's execution for three months so he could finish the treatise. "With his great power of application and method, he might be made of great use in the administration of a prison or an insane asylum," wrote Greeley, "and a liberal portion of his time should be allowed him to develop his scheme of universal philology."

Greeley admitted that Edward was likely insane and seemed to be fatally consumed with his own manuscript, but that offered Greeley even more proof that the state should *not* execute him. "He murdered the shopkeeper in the interest in philology," concluded Greeley. "A man in this disordered state of mind is dangerous to the public peace, and should not be permitted to remain at large. But nothing is to be gained by killing him."

Greeley found other literati to support Edward. Respected author and humorist Mark Twain submitted a satirical piece to the *Tribune* under his given name, Samuel Langhorne Clemens; it requested that someone else take Edward's place on the gallows because the linguist was *too intelligent* to kill. The editorial, approved by Horace Greeley, was titled "A Substitute for Rulloff. Have We a Sydney Carton Among Us?"

Twain referenced one of the main characters in the 1859 novel

A Tale of Two Cities by author Charles Dickens. Carton was a young Englishman who held an unrequited love for Lucie Manette, a woman whose husband is scheduled for execution in France. As one final act of love for Manette, Carton switched places with the doomed man. Twain wrote: "I am not sorry that Rulloff is to be hanged, but I am sincerely sorry that he himself has made it necessary that his vast capabilities for usefulness should be lost to the world," wrote Twain. "For it is plain that in the person of Rulloff one of the most marvelous intellects that any age has produced is about to be sacrificed."

Twain went on to request a surrogate for Edward on the gallows. "If a life be offered up on the gallows to atone for the murder Rulloff did," wrote Twain, "will that suffice? . . . I will instantly bring forward a man who, in the interests of learning and science, will take Rulloff's crime upon himself, and submit to be hanged in Rulloff's place."

The thirty-five-year-old author was a master at the satirical essay, and to scholars, this would later be received as a droll tongue-in-cheek response to Hoffman's intent to proceed with Edward Rulloff's execution. But despite his sarcastic tone, Twain felt strongly that Edward's proficiencies with languages, writing, law, and medicine could still be used to serve his community. Twain included a short explanation with the letter he submitted to Whitelaw Reid, the editor of the *Tribune*.

"Sir: I believe in capital punishment," wrote Twain. "I believe that when a murder has been done it should be answered for with blood. It is plain that in the person of Rulloff one of the most marvelous intellects that any age has produced is about to be sacrificed, & that, too, while half the mystery of its strange powers is yet a secret. I have written this thing for an object—which is, to make people talk about & look at, & presently ENTERTAIN the idea of commuting Rulloff's penalty."

Contemporary observers were bewildered and infuriated by the prominent support that Edward had collected, particularly those who had spent any time with the killer.

"Among the supporters of this petition was no less a person than Horace Greeley, always kindhearted and singularly susceptible at times to the claims of fakirs and frauds," wrote attorney Samuel Halliday, who had once met Edward decades earlier. "Horace Greeley started at one time to go and see Rulloff in the jail at Binghamton but, on the contrary, he asked a friend to go in his place, saying frankly that his sympathy for Rulloff was so great that he could not control his emotions. If the great Greeley had at that time been governor of the State of New York, Edward H. Rulloff would have died a natural death. Fortunately, he was not."

Greeley's friend handed Edward the proof sheets of a translation in German that seemed to interest the killer. When Edward finished reading them, he passed them back and said: "I want to get a copy of that work when it is published."

When Greeley's friend reminded him that he could be dead by that time unless the governor intervened, Edward laughed.

"He either acted superbly on this occasion or else he was so absorbed in the new translation of 'Faust' as to forget his surroundings," wrote Halliday. "It may be he had the power of will to enable him to dismiss for the time being all thought of his then predicament."

Edward Rulloff seemed doomed to die, but his defense attorney and Ham Freeman had another trick up their sleeves.

———

Edward Rulloff despised being undermined. He seethed, sitting cross-legged on his cot, as the rotund man in the three-piece suit—his lawyer, Hamilton Freeman—strolled toward his cell. Edward's academic legacy was ruined, thanks to the lack of interest in his petitions and the damning report from George Sawyer. Edward had felt hopeless for days, shifting quickly between quietly sulking and boorishly cursing. He directed the worst of his anxiety toward his long-suffering champion, Ham.

Ham felt Edward's frustration keenly. He watched his friend and became pained by the thought that he might be dead soon. The author had developed a devotion to the killer, equal parts empathy, respect, and fear.

Each of Edward's efforts to stay the execution had failed. He rarely listened to the advice of his attorney, George Becker, much to the lawyer's dismay. Becker had an impressive academic pedigree with degrees from Brown University and Yale College. Eleven years earlier, Becker had received his first murder case, the trial of a woman suspected of murdering her child in Worcester; later he would defend a man accused of arson. So, he had been experienced in capital crimes and was clearly qualified to defend a now-feckless academic turned killer.

"He tries a case with boldness, and skill, and tact," reported Hamilton. "Addresses a court and jury with great ease and eloquence, and is a rapid thinker, and versatile and graceful writer."

Becker was primed intellectually to sort out a solution, but Edward was reticent to depend on anyone's instincts but his own. He requested a visit from Becker, and the defense attorney braced for more of his client's rude retorts to his suggestions.

"He [Becker] found him in a very unhappy frame of mind," remembered Ham, "sour, cross, and fault-finding." Edward accused Becker of not working hard enough to secure his freedom. Becker had grown weary of these visits and unexpectantly snapped at his mercurial client.

"You chose to take your own course against my advice," Becker retorted, "and you see what has come of it, but I do not wish to criticize a man in your situation and shall not . . . anything I can do for you I will do, as I have always been ready and willing to. If there is anyone else who you think can do any better, name the man, and I will get him if possible."

Hamilton stood near Edward during this rebuke—he watched the killer slink back to his mattress, like a whipped dog. Ham was impressed with George Becker, a man constantly abused by his client but who remained committed to freeing him, or at least to saving his life.

"It seems that the meanest feature in the character of this man was that in the end he would always abuse, and turn traitor to his counsel, and his best friends," said Ham. Edward's true character seemed *finally* obvious to Hamilton Freeman, and it was as confounding as it was grotesque. "His manner towards those he chose to receive, or to treat well were very bland, cordial and conciliatory," said Ham, "but to those for whom he had conceived a dislike, and who intruded themselves upon him, he was cross and even brutal. The man had a dual character."

Despite his reservations about Edward's growing contempt toward everyone around him, Ham remained faithful. He had an idea, one last volley to save Edward Rulloff's life. Ham was certain it would prove to be unpopular with Edward, so he pulled aside Edward's defense attorney.

"At the suggestion of myself and others," said Ham, "Mr. Becker drew up and had numerously signed a petition to the Governor praying that a Commission of Lunacy be appointed to examine Rulloff under the recent act of the Legislature."

Without telling Edward, his attorney appealed to Governor John Hoffman to appoint psychiatric experts to determine Edward's sanity. It was the only way to save his life.

"Lunacy commissions" had been ordered by New York State for decades, but in the 1870s, they were largely political (rather than medical) bodies. Decades later, New York State senator Thomas C. Desmond outlined how corrupt these commissions had been for many years: "Defying public opinion, judges appointed their relatives, political district leaders and followers to lucrative positions on these commissions," Desmond wrote in 1940. "Political appointments to the commissions inevitably brought rumors that decisions of the commissions could be bought. Murderers and other criminals successfully faked insanity before lunacy commissions, and thereby escaped punishment." It was a crooked system, but in 1871, it was Becker's only hope to stay the planned execution. Would his petition on behalf of Edward Rulloff sway the commission's members?

On Friday, April 28, less than three weeks before Edward's scheduled execution, Becker traveled to Albany and shook the hand of New York State's governor. John Hoffman listened to Becker's pleas for consideration—Edward Rulloff was gifted, Becker argued, but also insane. He should be sent to a state asylum, not the gallows.

Hoffman seemed to listen carefully to Becker's argument. After some consideration, the governor scribbled a name on a piece of paper and handed it to the lawyer: "Dr. John Gray, Utica Lunatic Asylum." Hope remained alive; the governor would assign

Dr. Gray and another colleague to examine Edward Rulloff and advise Hoffman on an appropriate fate.

"This was the dernier resort of counsel, really the forlorn hope of the defense," wrote Ham. The commission took a few weeks to be finalized, and on the tenth of May, Dr. John Gray and Dr. S. Vanderpoel of Albany traveled to Binghamton.

"Governor Hoffman has requested Dr. Gray, of the Utica Asylum for the Insane and Dr. Vanderpoel, of Albany, to see Rulloff, and to communicate to the Executive the results of their observations," read one local newspaper. "It is to be presumed that if they think there is probable cause, a commission will be appointed to decide whether or not the law in the case of Rulloff should take its course."

This one final examination was Edward Rulloff's last chance. If he could convince the revered Dr. Gray that he was truly insane, then he would be transferred to an asylum and avoid the noose. He might even be allowed to finish his theory and have it published. If not, his execution would proceed as scheduled.

The townspeople in upstate New York were horrified.

What if Edward Rulloff were freed again?

———

Dr. John Gray was America's most respected alienist, a Gilded-Age term for what would today be called a forensic psychiatrist. The odd word evolved from the phrase "mental alienation"— alienists were those who treated sufferers of mental illness. Dr. Gray had testified at some of the country's most pivotal, complicated criminal cases—assessing suspects and demystifying on the stand their sanity. His judgment might save a man's life, doom him to the gallows, or, perhaps even worse, dispatch him to one of the country's controversial lunatic asylums, like the one Gray headed. Dr. Gray's legacy was as the superintendent of New York's Utica Lunatic Asylum.

This was not an easy assignment—by the late 1800s, asylum superintendents were in a very public war with America's revered neurologists, each side trying to wrest control over the mentally ill. Neurologists crusaded to abolish the proven abuses in the asylums, while superintendents like Gray argued that they were more qualified to treat insanity—their methods might seem cruel, but they were effective.

John Gray's reputation was exemplary on the witness stand and within his cadre of contemporaries in charge of the country's asylums. But Gray was under constant scrutiny from the press. In the 1800s, the media homed in on social inequities, particularly those inflicted on the insane. Over his thirty-four-year career at the Utica Lunatic Asylum, Gray was the subject of numerous investigations involving abuse of patients, including using physical force, false imprisonment, and forcing medicine on patients. He was also accused of withholding contact between patients and their families. Gray enjoyed immense power at the asylum—he ruled his fiefdom with a free hand and fired those who disagreed with him. His reputation also was influential outside the asylum's walls; he was the editor of the prestigious *American Journal of Insanity*, and competitors accused him of omitting their articles if the subject matter was in opposition to his own philosophy on psychiatry. Gray was a potent, polarizing figure in the field of insanity assessment . . . and Edward Rulloff's life was now in Dr. John Gray's hands.

The killer sat among his books, flipping through a tome as the psychiatrist stood at his iron door. Dr. Gray stepped inside the cell as the men quietly evaluated each other. Edward surveyed Dr. Gray, noticing what others had. The alienist weighed around three hundred pounds and he had a powerful, physical presence on the stand during a criminal trial.

Gray examined Edward's appearance, too. The killer seemed calm, with no signs of anxiety as he adjusted his white shirt and light pants. This visit was unexpected, and while Edward was determined to remain courteous because his guests were gentlemen, he was taken aback. Gray greeted Edward and explained their purpose. Edward's attorney and his biographer had requested an official assessment of his sanity in hopes of commuting his death sentence. Edward's face flushed with anger. He would prefer to die rather than be declared insane, which would discredit his manuscript and nullify his life's work. *Who would believe the rantings of a batty, failed academic?* Edward was also aware of just how horrible state asylums could be—force fed, compelled to take unwanted medications while strapped to a bed. Edward would prefer to die rather than be institutionalized, particularly in Gray's facility. He quietly planned to avoid offering Dr. Gray any fodder—he was determined to remain in control of his own destiny. Rather than leveraging a meeting with Gray to fight for his life, Edward switched gears—he would battle the alienist for his right to die with dignity. This might seem bewildering—don't all people with psychopathy prioritize self-preservation over everything else, even other people's lives? No. Psychopathy selects a goal and makes it surmountable, even self-destruction. Edward's goal was now to preserve his reputation as a scholar after his death. It was a sorrowful conclusion to a man who once had promise as a studious boy in Canada under his mother's tutelage.

"Gentlemen, this is no work of mine," Edward said firmly to Dr. Gray. "I don't pretend to be either insane or an idiot. I am feeble in body, as you may see, but this has not affected my mind. The proposal of a commission is no work of mine."*

Dr. Gray noted Edward's reaction—another example of the level of self-defeating narcissism now so often associated with psychopathy—and swiftly dismissed it. He had no choice in the matter. The evaluation wasn't a request; it was an order from the highest levels of government.

"After a little preliminary conversation, he was informed that the Governor had ordered the examination, and that it was no idle curiosity that brought the commission there, but simply a duty," Gray explained. "That they desired to make a thorough examination and, first, of his physical condition."

Gray reached into his medical bag and retrieved a measuring tape; he determined that Edward was about five foot eight inches in height. His head was large and broad, his jaw was square, a large mouth and compressed lips. Edward's eyes were dark gray, and his pupils were dilated (probably thanks to his heightened emotions).

"He wrote and read . . . without spectacles, and only having a single lamp in his cell; as there was no disease, the dimness of vision probably came from age," noted Gray. "Appetite good; craved no particular food; could eat anything; digestion perfect; slept well, and the body was well nourished."

---

* Other psychopaths have registered a similar reaction to an insanity assessment, including Ted Bundy, who was furious with his attorneys for requesting a psychiatric evaluation. "I said I wouldn't have anything to do with an insanity defense," Bundy told journalist Hugh Aynesworth. "I know I'm not crazy! And I was insulted by even the suggestion by my attorneys that we should consider the defense. They knew damn well I wasn't crazy."

This might seem like an unorthodox examination for sanity. But as a leader of the biological psychiatric theory in the 1800s, Gray believed that mental illness was connected to physical causes, and it should be treated as a bodily illness—like measles. Dr. Gray believed that insanity was caused by a physical lesion on the brain created by, in some cases, irregular or overuse of the brain— Edward's decades of intense research would certainly qualify.

"Insanity, a physical disease due strictly to physical causes, was one of the distinctive features of his belief and teachings," read the *American Journal of Insanity*. "This was deemed a most important step, as it gave the first place in treatment to therapeutic measures and divorced the subject more fully under the influence of the metaphysical theory that insanity was a disease of the mind."

Gray contended that "rest, nutrition, medication—could then be presented in truth, as the relief of the sorrow." The superintendent had recently added a pathologist to his medical staff, a man assigned to treat the physical diseases that evidently plagued the minds of his patients.

The biological theory of mental illness—that you could heal a broken brain in the same way you could heal, say, a broken leg— was controversial with some of Dr. Gray's contemporaries in forensic psychiatry. Many experts in the 1800s dismissed this theory, pointing out that there were patients who were diagnosed with insanity but found to be of sound physical health, as well as strong and able-bodied. Gray dismissed these criticisms, claiming that those patients were incorrectly diagnosed. He was stubbornly unconvinced that it was possible for the mind to be diseased while the body stayed healthy.

In 1870, Gray established the first pathological laboratory in Utica related to an institution for mental illnesses; the goal was to study the physical brain with the same rigor physicians used to understand the anatomy of the rest of the body but with the purpose of curing mental illness. Alienists in the 1800s were specifically trained to assess criminals for insanity before trial; later at the turn of the century, alienists would evolve into studying the origin of criminal behavior, rather than focusing on neurology or physiology. But John Gray was preoccupied, as were other experts in the 1800s, with how biology influenced mental disturbances— he was not concerned with childhood traumas or past experiences, which might have offered context for a criminal's behavior, as modern forensic psychiatrists are.

Gray's goal to cure mental illness was a worthy one, and a necessary one. There were varied theories about those afflictions in the late 1800s. At the time, scientists were just beginning to understand the structure of the brain (a study that continues to this day), and he and his colleagues were fascinated to investigate how physical anomalies or injuries like tumors or concussion could affect the body.

But Gray's theories faced skepticism and cynicism from several different groups in 1871, including those whose beliefs were rooted in religion. Delusions of sin and unworthiness were often present in the mentally ill, so for centuries the care and aid of those suffering from extreme mental illness had often fallen to the church. Curing these patients' physical illness, some argued, was often useless without also tending to their souls.

"Care of the insane was clearly the function of the clergy," contended some psychiatrists, "and their position was supported by the fact that notions of demoniacal possession had not wholly disappeared."

Forensic psychiatrists now know that a myriad of factors may cause or exacerbate mental illness, including genetics, psychological triggers (like a divorce or a death or abuse), or medical conditions (like postpartum depression), as well as substance abuse.

But in 1871, Dr. John Gray believed that, if Edward Rulloff seemed physically healthy, then he was also mentally sound. Edward quickly realized, based on Gray's line of inquiry, that the physician before him truly believed that physical health and mental health were inextricably linked. Just as he had throughout his life, the intelligent Edward sized up his adversary and swiftly leveraged that knowledge to try and convince the alienist of his sanity—despite his awareness that it would likely lead to his death.

Gray asked about Edward's time in the Auburn State Prison, the institution that forbade convicts to communicate with each other. Auburn's motto, "industry, obedience, and silence," resonated with Edward. A Boston clergyman who visited the prison in 1826 was impressed.

"The whole establishment, from the gate to the sewer, is a specimen of neatness," he wrote.

He mentioned the "subdued feelings of the convicts."

Edward had produced more physical labor during that decade than he would for the remainder of his life. Gray insinuated that, perhaps, Auburn was responsible for Edward's poor physical health while he was imprisoned there.

"How long since your constitution was thus broken down?" asked Dr. Gray.

"I don't say that my constitution was broken down," Edward retorted. "I was appointed cook in the hospital for twenty or twenty-five persons. I was then so sick that I could not stand up and do the work, but had to sit with my elbows on the table to handle the things in cooking."

Edward told Gray that his developing theory of languages had saved his life in prison.

"I wanted to complete my book; that was the only reason that I cared to live," explained Edward. "One night, when sick and feverish, having eaten nothing through the day, I got up, cooked a pig's cheek and ate it all, went to bed, and woke up in the morning as well as usual."

Edward stayed in surprisingly good shape for a middle-aged man who had spent equal time in and out of prison. A journalist once asked him why he preferred to stroll around his cell without clothes—did he not want exercise?

"He was accustomed to prison life, he said, and knew how to keep his muscles in good condition when lying idle and unemployed," read one paper. "At the same time he exhibited the strong, hard muscles of his arms. From the time he was sent to jail he bathed himself in cold water every morning before breakfast, and he took exercise by walking across the floor of the prison."

Edward watched Dr. Gray pull out some equipment from his bag—a sphygmograph. Developed less than twenty years earlier, the mechanical device was used to measure blood pressure. Gray strapped it to the underside of Edward's wrist atop his radial artery; a scale-pan, attached to series of levels, held small weights that determined the amount of external pressure needed to stop blood flow through the artery. The measurements, recorded on smoke paper, were frequently inaccurate, but the sphygmograph was the predecessor to the modern-day blood pressure cuff.

Edward watched the needle scratch the paper and looked over at Dr. Gray. The alienist took down the measurement: "pulse, taken under the sphygmograph, 90 per minute, the sphygmographic trace showing an entirely sound condition of the heart." Gray asked Edward to open his mouth: "tongue clean." Gray flashed a light in Edward's eye.

"When the pupil was tested by a light applied directly to the eye, the dilation and contraction were rapid," recorded Gray, "and demonstrated that the largeness of the pupil was natural, and not due simply to confinement in a dark room."

The psychiatrist asked the killer a series of questions about his appetite (which was strong), his digestion (he had no known food allergies), and his sleeping habits (he slept well and his body was well nourished). Soon the examination had concluded—Gray had determined that the killer was healthy and physically sound. It was settled—one of America's most influential alienists had labeled the country's most controversial killer as sane. This denouement pleased Edward, but confounded Hamilton Freeman. The author considered his own effort to save Edward's life as a fool's errand.

"He was almost crazy in his hopes and efforts to be saved," wrote Ham, "and when the only chance he had to save himself was offered, he threw it away in scorn, and cursed those who had made the attempt. Such was another of this man's idiosyncrasies."

Edward's fine physical health might have convinced Dr. Gray that the prisoner's sanity was intact, but the alienist was also curious about Edward's intellectual capacity, considering the attention it had garnered in the press; Gray hoped to glean more about a man who had labored on a canal decades earlier, and had since been transformed into one of America's most polarizing intellectual figures. Edward smiled—he guessed that Dr. Gray's directive to determine his sanity had been satisfied, but the psychiatrist continued to persistently press for more data—he was an asset to Gray.

"In answer to questions, he said that he would prefer not to be asked where he was born, but it was in the North; his parents were of sound and vigorous health; his father died when he was five years old, and an uncle took care of him," wrote Gray.

Hamilton stood near the cell and listened closely. He watched how the two men interacted, each eyeing the other. Criminals with psychopathy are frequently skeptical of psychiatrists or psychologists. Traditionally, psychiatrists have been tasked with determining sanity or mental illness by asking series of invasive questions. After some reluctance, Edward offered Gray a brief sketch of his life story—his family's modest income, his education in law and botanical medicine, as well as his fascination with languages. Edward avoided all details about his past crimes, including the murders of at least five people.

"He married, and at twenty-five years of age his career was interfered with by what he denominated a difficulty that sent him to Auburn Prison," reported Dr. Gray.

The alienist was polite enough to avoid the details of Edward's past violence against four family members. Dr. Gray even neglected to summarize the murder of clerk Frederick Merrick.

"Did you originally select the Greek language from which to develop your system?" Dr. Gray asked.

"No, I was gradually led up to that," replied Edward. "My first purpose was vague."

The interview then shifted to Edward's philosophy on moral responsibility.

"Would the fact of another existence make any difference to you in regard to your acts?"

"No," Edward replied curtly. "I should do as I intended, without regard to the existence of a God or a devil, a heaven or a hell; I have felt this pride during my whole life."

Edward Rulloff was unsure about the afterlife—he only believed in himself.

"Rulloff then went on to argue and answer various questions with the commissioners and attempted in every way to show off how smart he was," said Ham, who watched his friend's sabotage of the interview with growing frustration. He'd hoped his friend would take this lifeline—an insanity defense—and run with it. Ham knew it was likely Edward's last hope to avoid execution. "It seems he would rather die than be considered a fool," Ham said bitterly.

Hamilton began to feel misled, even tricked. His feelings for Edward Rulloff were cooling. Edward confronted the author after Dr. Gray had left—*How dare you set me up for an insanity defense!*—and demanded to know what *he* thought should be Edward's fate. Ham considered his reply carefully.

"I don't think you ought to be hung," replied Ham slowly. "I never have. . . . I think, and always have, that you are crazy; that you are insane on some subjects, and that you are not legally accountable for your crimes."

Edward stayed silent for a moment.

"Well, I am not half so big a fool as you are," he plainly replied, with a sneer.

"Well, if you are sane, you ought to be hung a dozen times for what you have told me, and you know it," Ham snapped. "The only way that I could ever excuse you, was on the hypothesis that you are, and always have been, of unsound mind; as some call it, a 'little cracked.'"

The conversation was growing hostile, so the men opted to end the discussion and reconvene soon. Edward offered Ham his hand and the author reluctantly obliged, then he was left wondering why the killer had decided to be cordial. It was because Edward was in good spirits—he would soon need Ham's help.

"If we saw Rulloff a dozen times a day, he would always wish to shake hands every time we met him and when we came away," recalled Ham. "We used to think it was because he liked us, and appreciated our efforts and sacrifices on his behalf, but we now, in the light of subsequent events, think that this apparent cordiality was only the disguise of his false heart."

When Dr. Gray returned to his home that night, he reflected on their interview as he transcribed his notes. The beginning read:

"Dear Sir: In accordance with the request of your Excellency, we proceeded to Binghamton on the 9th day of May, and on the 10th of May made a careful and thorough examination of Edward H. Rulloff."

Gray labeled each question and answer with Q and A. He looked over the six-page document. Edward was intelligent, cruel, and arrogant, but his body was in fine health and his mind appeared to be so, as well. The alienist filled out his report and sent it to the governor.

"Edward H. Rulloff is in sound physical health, and entirely sane."

Hamilton Freeman was utterly incredulous as he reviewed the report.

"Of course, the commission reported him sane," he said. "How could they do otherwise . . . so ended this farce."

What did Dr. Gray reveal to the public about Edward Rulloff's byzantine mind? Nothing.

The biological theory and its tests were a wasted effort, offering no illumination on a diseased mind. If only Edward could have been studied in the twentieth century, when so much progress was made with our knowledge of mental illness, personality disorders . . . and the litany of reasons why people kill. In contrast to Gray's methods, modern forensic psychiatrists are constantly revising the list of potential causes of criminality as science advances. We now know that the criminal mind is abstract and far from transparent.

But there was some interesting news from Gray. Once again, a nineteenth-century behavioral analyst was *partially* right. Edward *was* sane because psychopathy is not a mental illness. But it is a personality disorder . . . an affliction that science and psychiatry at the time were not equipped to measure. After his examination of Edward, Gray's reputation continued to grow, though not always in a positive direction. Gray was continually investigated by the press and state officials for mistreating patients in his asylum. He was sued by an angry neurologist for libel, and the complaints of his former patients plagued him. Eleven years after his interview with Edward Rulloff, Gray was shot and wounded in the face by a former charge named Henry Remshaw on March 16, 1882. The sixty-two-year-old slowly recovered, but never fully. Gray resumed work at the asylum four years later, but he died shortly after his return of Bright's disease (an inflammation of the kidneys).

In 1871, Dr. John Gray might have offered his blessing to the state to execute Edward Rulloff, but not everyone agreed. No journal was more influential than the *American Journal of Psychology*, edited by esteemed neurologist Dr. William Hammond. Hammond was a bitter enemy of Dr. John Gray, and their differing opinion over Edward Rulloff would illustrate how divided the world of psychiatric health really was.

7

The Phrenologists

*All things therefore seemed to point to this: that I was slowly
losing hold of my original and better self, and becoming
slowly incorporated with my second and worse.*
—Robert Louis Stevenson,
Strange Case of Dr. Jekyll and Mr. Hyde, 1886

hree days before his execution date of May 18, 1871, Edward
Rulloff reflected on his life. He was utterly despondent. The
sheriff of Broome County, New York, sent prominent citizens
around the county another round of cordial invitations to Edward's execution; the first set had arrived at homes three months
earlier, just ahead of his original date with the gallows. The initial
summons had read:

> Sir: You are hereby invited to be present at the Execu-
> tion of EDWARD H. RULLOFF, at the Jail of said
> County, on the 3d day of March, 1871, at 12 o'clock M.
> Or in case of postponement, of which you will doubt-
> less learn by the public prints, on the day then fixed.
> F.W. Martin, Sheriff

Edward's manuscript was still not complete, a big disappointment, and after months of enthusiasm and intrigue, the academics, the press, and the public ultimately ridiculed him. The killer's scholarship was labeled as valueless, his life deemed worthless. Edward continued to write, still obsessively, but now he penned long missives to family and friends whom he hoped to see soon. Over the past few days, he had vacillated between being furiously productive, then bemused, and finally hopelessly despondent.

"One of his watchers tells the story that RULLOFF had been busily writing far into the night, and saying that he would write a letter, and then go to bed, began the missive," reported one paper. "But stopping at the commencement, he turned to his guardian and asked to be told the day of month, as if he, with only a few hours of life before him, took no note of time."

For months Edward refused to allow journalists inside his jail cell, other than Hamilton Freeman, but that would change as he grew more nervous about how his life would be perceived after his death. One of Edward's most vehement critics, *New York Times* journalist Ed Crapsey, stepped inside his jail cell just two days before his scheduled execution, May 16, 1871.

Unlike the novice writer Hamilton Freeman, Ed Crapsey was a veteran journalist who had served as a war correspondent with the Union during the Civil War. This turned out to be an unfortunate assignment for Crapsey. In 1863, eight years before he met Edward Rulloff, in a widely read story, Crapsey implied that General George Meade didn't pursue General Robert E. Lee with enough vigor after the Battle of Gettysburg. The article infuriated Meade, who ordered Crapsey to be tied to a mule and walked around the camp with a sign reading LIBELER OF THE PRESS. Crapsey appreciated humility in others, and he hoped to recognize some of it during his observations of Edward in 1871. He watched the prisoner fidget as he flipped through a plethora of books inside the cell, including a medical dictionary, along with a guide to Homeric lexicon.

"On the pillow, at the head of the bed, lay a Bible," wrote Crapsey. "But the centre of attraction, both to visitors and to the prisoner, was a chair that stood directly in front of the cot, and on which lay the last completed page of the philological work that has created so much talk and speculation."

Crapsey was incorrect—Edward still had some more work to do. And the newspaper reporter seemed impressed with the immense volume of the manuscript and marveled at Edward's claim that one city bank held some 1,500 pages of his theory—a decision that typified how valuable Edward considered his work. The reporter wondered if these final visits with curious spectators might serve as a reckoning for Edward; would a moral monster attempt salvation by means of confessing in his waning days? No—only Ham Freeman would hear the truth and even that was suspect considering the unreliable source.

Surrounded by ogling guests, Edward refused to settle on a mood—his thoughts became tangential as he veered away from discussing his inevitable fate, even dismissing it. At times, Edward appeared nervous, unable to control hysteria, but then he would quickly recover; his patience was not broken no matter who questioned him. Occasionally, he would apologize because months of incarceration had apparently dulled his conversational skills.

"I am unused to much talking and get nervous," explained Edward, "please excuse me for a moment."

Crapsey watched Edward as he quickly composed himself, shifting from agitation to poise.

"[T]here sat the man, as quiet and calm as ever," observed

Crapsey, "going on with the conversation in the monotonous tone of a college professor in the quiet of the class-room. This peculiarity appals [sic] the spectator, and you are only too glad to escape from his presence."

One hundred years later, the sheriff of Leon County, Florida, showed Ted Bundy a warrant to have an impression taken of his teeth and had him escorted to a room; the serial killer became enraged when confronted by three dentists, their equipment, and a dental chair.

"He lost it," said former sheriff Ken Katsaris. "He didn't know that what I had was a bite mark from the crime scene, which I believed at the time, was Ted Bundy's signature."

"You can't do this without my attorney," Bundy screamed.

"Then on a dime, his mindset changed like he was a different person," recalled Katsaris. "He looked at me, he turned around, he sat in the dental chair, he leaned back, put a smile on and said 'Ken, you know you don't need all that stuff. I'm not a violent person.'"

When Ted Bundy realized that he had appeared briefly disorderly, he retrained himself—criminals with psychopathy like Edward Rulloff and Ted Bundy do their best to prevent their emotions from derailing their goals. Forensic psychologists say that psychopaths *do* have emotions, like sadness and rage; they just lack the emotions that prevent most of society from killing, like empathy or remorse.

On Tuesday, Ed Crapsey lamented that the forthcoming execution on Thursday seemed too distant because the people of Broome County demanded biblical punishment for a butcher *now*. Edward, always defiant, seemed oblivious to the public's disgust.

"The prisoner awaits his doom with no perceptive tremors, and he will probably suffer death in as cool a mood as when he heard the verdict of the jury who convicted him," recalled Crapsey. "In that first moment of suspense RULLOFF startled his counsel by saying: 'Bastard, your jurymen didn't hold water, did they!'"

Edward's only hope was a final reprieve from New York's governor, but it seemed an untenable goal. On Wednesday, the day before the scheduled execution, Ham Freeman discovered that John Hoffman was staying at the Clarendon Hotel in Manhattan, almost two hundred miles away. The author was emotionally depleted because his friend, Edward, would soon die, but Ham had vowed that he would exhaust all options, even at Ham's own financial expense.

Edward's defense attorney George Becker agreed to remain with his agitated client in Binghamton while Ham traveled by rail to Manhattan. Becker had hoped to greet one of Edward's brothers, Rulof, at the train station so the siblings could meet perhaps for the last time. Edward hadn't seen his other brother, William, the famous photographer in California, for years, and they rarely communicated. Edward yearned to see Rulof again; he was the younger brother Edward had once protected from a cruel teacher.

As Hamilton hurried into the hotel's lobby, the journalist presented Edward's petitions to commute his sentence to Hoffman's executive clerk with a hopeful smile—the pressure from anti-death-penalty social groups might have convinced the governor to change his mind. But Ham's optimism swiftly waned as he listened to the clerk's solemn response.

"I saw Mr. Apgar and he informed me that it was too late," said Ham, "that the Governor had decided upon the papers presented by Counsel, and others, to neither grant a commutation nor respite."

Ham was distraught—his long trip had resulted in nothing for

Edward Rulloff's case. There was no need to hear the news from the governor himself, so Ham composed a note to be wired to Binghamton immediately.

"I telegraphed the sad news to Mr. Becker on Wednesday morning," said Ham, "who was at the prison when he received the telegram and read it to Rulloff."

George Becker steadied himself as he read over the short telegram detailing what was certainly the most difficult news that Ham had ever delivered.

"All hope is gone, all is lost," Becker read aloud, sadly.

Becker explained to Edward that his most recent request was rejected. There were no more appeals available, nothing left to be done. Edward Rulloff would die tomorrow, on Thursday, May 18, 1871, to the delight of just about everyone in New York's countryside. Edward listened to Becker quietly.

"Up to that moment we thought that Rulloff still had some hope," recalled Ham.

The author arrived at the jail in Binghamton from Manhattan that morning, exhausted to find Edward raging inside his cell, flinging papers and writing supplies against the stone walls.

"It was then that he really broke down, and became almost a maniac, and denounced, in his ravings, Mr. Becker, the clerks, the governor, and even his own brother," remembered Ham.

Edward's brother, Rulof, reneged on his promised visit, leaving the killer feeling incensed and abandoned by the only family he had valued. The shadow of the gallows, still in production, darkened his prison door through the small, barred window. Ham watched Becker frantically pace outside the cell as Edward bellowed madly, peppering each accusation with horrid curse words.

"He denounced everyone who had been his friend in the vein hope that the world should always remain in ignorance of his black crimes," recalled Ham. "It was characteristic of the man."

The *Times* reporter Ed Crapsey viewed Edward as a fraud, sharing George Sawyer's stern assessment of the killer. In a series of stories for the *Times*, Crapsey disclosed details from sources inside the jail, men who claimed to have never witnessed that level of anger from a sane man; much of his vitriol was aimed at Governor Hoffman.

"He indulged in abusive behavior language so grossly profane as to be unfit for publication," wrote Crapsey. "The course of the Governor, he said, had been dictated by his political ambition, as he was afraid he would lose a few votes when he next ran for office if he interfered."

Edward then snapped at George Becker with a snide comment about the man's large frame.

"'Well, Becker, you and I are the two greatest men living—I in philology, you in weight avoirdupois.'"

Becker stayed silent as Edward snickered, snatched up an oil lamp, and began lighting his notes on fire. While the documents burned, Edward castigated the attorney for failing him in court; Ham felt little else but reverence as well as sorrow for the killer's dedicated defense attorney.

"Throughout every embarrassment, every deceit, every disappointment and defeat," said Ham, "and amid all the prejudices with which his client was surrounded, and through every sort of difficulty, betrayal treachery and abuse, from friend, client, and enemies, after he once undertook the case, he never left a step untaken, by way of appeals . . ."

Becker often used his own funds to supplement expenses, like multiple excursions to meet with the governor to argue Edward's many appeals. Ham admired Becker, describing him as faithful "when nearly all others had deserted him, and *even after Rulloff had abused him* without any cause or provocation whatever."

Becker had taken on Edward's case reluctantly with the promise of funding from Edward's brothers, Rulof and William, but they rarely offered him compensation. Even more troubling was that Becker's client had hamstrung him in court seemingly from the start.

"Rulloff at first misled him as to the material facts of the case," said Ham, "that he concealed from him the place of his abode, in New York, until the officers of the law had smelt it out, and gobbled everything there of value to them and injury to Rulloff."

After Edward had exhausted items to hurl inside his cell, he resumed cursing and bellowing loud, obscene stories to the guards— the genteel gentleman facade was stripped away as Ham Freeman stood in the corridor, shocked, and disillusioned with the sudden change. Edward Rulloff had finally discarded his mask, and Hamilton Freeman was repelled.

"In the glare of that eye, there was an unearthly expression, such as I had never witnessed, and which indicated to my mind that this man was not all himself," said Ham, "that he was insane, or else the very incarnation of all that is devilish and wicked."

Edward glanced at Ham, and the author shuddered. The rattle of the chain around Edward's ankle clanked as the yellow light of the gas lamp highlighted the deep creases of his aged face. There were dark circles around his eyes—a macabre portrait of a ghoul in the final hours of life.

"His habitual expression is thoughtful and cynical," wrote one reporter.

Edward, calmly, listened to George Becker's query.

"Shall I continue the appeal to the governor?" the attorney asked.

"No, let her rip," replied Edward with a cackle. "I shall be remembered long after Governor Hoffman is forgotten."

The citizens of upstate New York were giddy with the prospect of witnessing a just end to a devil holding a writing pen. "Rulloff Swings Tomorrow," read one newspaper headline. "Morbid Curiosity Gratified."

"The sayings and doings of this man have an almost dramatic interest as he confronts the gallows after thirty years of warfare upon mankind," wrote Ed Crapsey in the *Times*, "and it is not singular, therefore, that they constitute the sole topic of public talk."

Crapsey intended to convince his readers that the killer was not a legendary murderer that deserved their attention. The newspapers had sketched a killer that rivaled any fabled monster with unequaled selfish brutality. Crapsey opined that the man who leapt up from his shabby pallet to greet visitors, the authentic Edward Rulloff, was a disappointment to most who met him.

"There is no hardened look here, no indication of animal passions," recalled Crapsey, "nothing but a pale, stout man, with an abashed look, divided between bashfulness and sullenness, both born of a nervous temperament."

Ed Crapsey couldn't resist analyzing Edward's physical features, as many people did in the nineteenth century, by presenting readers with an amateur phrenological assessment.

"The head is not high, but is very broad, and the ears are placed so far back that the practical eye easily sees the vast preponderance of brain in front," wrote Crapsey. "The eyes are dark gray, and restless when talking, but at times they are eager and fierce."

There were two other men acutely interested in Edward Rulloff's facial and cranial structure because they would always betray his integrity. Dr. Daniel Swift Burr, an anatomist in Binghamton, had followed Edward's case since he had seen Billy Dexter's and Al Jarvis's bodies pulled from the Chenango River the previous August—Dan Burr had embalmed both men. He had also confronted Edward in court about medical evidence. Dr. Burr hoped to seize an opportunity to apply his skills and Edward's head for a scientific investigation.

The twenty-five-year-old physician spoke with his father, Dr. George Burr, a professor with the Geneva Medical College. Dan Burr discussed Edward's scheduled execution and he had an interesting idea: If no one in Edward's family claimed the killer's body after he died, then might they purchase the corpse for research purposes? The father and son aimed to use the killer to explore the nature of evil using science, not biblical teachings, or an elementary physical exam. Dr. George Burr drafted a contract for George Becker in case Edward's body were available for sale.

"For the privilege [sic] of making certain anatomical examinations and experiments upon the body of Rulloff, I will, after making such examinations decently inter his remains in a lot which I own in the old cemetery grounds—George Burr."

If they were given Edward's body, presuming the execution would go forward, the Burrs would examine his skull and then his brain, all to hypothesize *why* Edward was both brilliant and wicked. They would then present their findings at phrenology conferences.

When modern psychologists attempt to denigrate unscientific approaches to analyzing the mind, they often compare those failed disciplines to phrenology, now considered a racist, bigoted type of pseudoscience. But that contention ignores the immense contribution phrenology made to criminal psychology.

Phrenology was developed in 1796 by German physician Franz Joseph Gall after he believed he had discovered a pattern that connected anatomy to the mind; Gall observed that his classmates who had the best memories also tended to have large, protruding eyes. Gall believed that the brain could be divided into parts and those parts governed different character traits. Later, Gall determined that the shape of the skull matched its brain's shape, so an assessment need not be delayed until the patient died—a phrenologist would simply examine his skull and it would reveal the sections of the brain.

Phrenologists were trained to draw lines on the skull and mark dozens of different regions, like the "instinct to love," "secretiveness," "benevolence," and "destructiveness." These phrases were not in any medical dictionary, even in the nineteenth century. A phrenologist would declare that if a patient's "destructiveness" area had been large, then he was certainly violent.

Phrenology could lead to worrisome outcomes. A man might be labeled a deviant simply because of the bumps on his head; it was used to justify racism and sexism, boosting the sense of superiority in the upper classes because phrenology was highly interpretive.

In the mid to late 1800s, phrenology was seen as an advancement in the study of the mind despite its dubious, even dangerous, uses. The prevailing theory at the time about the brain, known as the dualism theory, was that the mind and body were inherently separate—one did not control the other.

"The mind is about mental processes, thought and consciousness. The body is about the physical aspects of the brain-neurons and how the brain is structured," explained researcher Dr. Saul McLeod. "Is the mind part of the body, or the body part of the mind? If they are distinct, then how do they interact? And which of the two is in charge?"

This is still being debated today—most psychologists dismiss the rigid dualist theory because data suggests that the mind and body are deeply connected; phrenology helped lead future researchers to that theory, even though modern scientists applied scientific methods and phrenologists used bunk. In the history of studying the criminal mind, phrenology helped contribute to the belief that criminality was a mental illness and therefore criminals were not responsible for their behavior, which later became the basis for the insanity defense. It also sparked debates over nature versus nurture—can criminality be inherited?

In the early 1870s, Italian criminologist Cesare Lombroso (known as the "father of criminology") developed a theory which contended that criminals were born, not made. Lombroso examined a skull of a criminal and noticed an indentation on the back that he thought resembled a marking found on the back of ape skulls.

"At the sight of that skull, I seemed to see all of a sudden . . . the problem of the nature of the criminal—an atavistic being who reproduces in his person the ferocious instincts of primitive humanity and the inferior animals," wrote Lombroso in his book *Criminal Man*.

Like Dr. John Gray, Lombroso believed that there was a connection between criminal psychopathology and bodily defects. He concluded that there were hereditary causes of crime, men and women who were regressing to a more primitive stage of human evolution proven by certain markings—a theory laden with racism. Despite the theory's popularity in Europe, most criminal psychiatrists eventually disagreed and endorsed the idea that environmental factors influenced criminals more than genetics. But in 1871, the Burrs suspected that Edward Rulloff's skull and his brain might provide them with some crucial answers about the criminal mind.

For centuries, behavioral experts have arrived at jail cells with various job titles, including phrenologists, psychologists, and therapists. Many were well received by their subjects; serial killer Dennis Rader sent to forensic psychologist Dr. Katherine Ramsland letters, drawings, and even secret codes to offer her information for her research. Forensic psychologist Kerry Daynes interviewed British serial killer Dennis Nilsen, who murdered at least fifteen men and boys in London between 1978 and 1983. Soon, Nilsen started phoning Daynes just to chat.

"I used to get telephone calls from Dennis Nilsen, who I've met in prison," said Daynes in *Cosmopolitan* magazine, "and he'd just drone on and on about himself."

But some forensic psychologists have found hostile patients as subjects. Ted Bundy was resentful of Al Carlisle, the psychologist assigned to evaluate him at the Utah State Prison. A judge in Salt Lake City had found Bundy guilty of murder and Carlisle was tasked with determining whether Bundy was violent and should be sent to prison or if he should receive parole. Bundy received Carlisle very cordially, extending his hand and greeting him with a smile, but the serial killer reacted differently to the psychologist's invasive questions about his childhood.

"The psychologist, well, he was an asshole, but there must be, some better words to describe that kind of mentality," Bundy said later. "The prison psychologist hoped so much that he himself would be responsible for opening Ted Bundy up for the world to see what was ticking inside Bundy's obviously devious mind."

Despite the positive portrait that Bundy offered Carlisle about his mental health, the psychologist wasn't swayed. Carlisle noted that Bundy, who had a degree in psychology, was extremely passive aggressive as well as secretive.

"I felt there was a good deal of hostility directed toward me and other personnel," Carlisle wrote in his report to the judge in Bundy's case. "I feel Mr. Bundy has not allowed me to get to know him and I believe there are many significant things about him that remain hidden."

Ted Bundy had prevented the psychologist from gleaning any substantive information about motives or personality—psychopaths are excellent at subterfuge, but it didn't always serve Bundy well; his glib charm was useless when confronted by a professional behavioral expert who refused to be duped.

"The above personality profile is consistent with the possibility of violence and is consistent with the nature of the crime for which he is convicted," concluded Carlisle. "Therefore, I cannot comfortably say he would be a good risk if placed on probation."

Perhaps Drs. Daniel and George Burr could discover more about the psychology that shaped Edward Rulloff's mind in 1871. But the day before Edward's walk to the gallows, Ham Freeman was as close to a psychologist as there would be inside his cell. The author was underequipped to provide an accurate assessment, stymied by the intersection of temerity, evasiveness, and sagacity he found in Edward Rulloff's personality.

"I could not reconcile this enigma of mankind, with the rest of the human family, upon any other hypothesis than that he had a deranged intellect, or disordered brain," thought Ham, "that though he might do say some smart things; that though he was undoubtably a great scholar . . . still there was a species of insanity or monomania which affected all his intellectual faculties, pervaded his whole soul and irresistibly controlled all his actions."

Hamilton still couldn't believe that Edward, the brilliant scholar, had control over his emotions. Ham seemed to dismiss any notion that his friend could be *intentionally* cruel, heartless . . . someone we now recognize as a psychopath with an abnormal brain that would soon be studied by some of the brightest minds in the world. Ham concluded that Edward Rulloff was afflicted with uncontrollable impulses that resulted in violence and death— a casualty himself who still deserved a measure of sympathy.

"And that being the truth," concluded Ham, "he was not morally or legally accountable for his deeds. I could not divest my mind of this impression."

Hamilton was a victim himself of Edward Rulloff for almost six months, though the author never seemed to realize the extent of the killer's manipulation. To secure the initial interviews with Edward in January, Ham had to establish a level of trust that involved offering Edward unprecedented access to the public via Ham's newspaper. At Edward's urging, Ham immediately began publishing large sections of his theory in Ham's paper, the *Democratic Leader,* and much of the time, Edward wrote the copy himself—Ham's journalistic integrity was in jeopardy from the start. The following months, Ham was converted from a biographer into a common errand boy.

"I frequently went to the jail and carried with him books and papers, received copy, and compared proof with him," said Ham. "He would sometimes be very confidential [when they were alone in the cell] . . . always first giving me his hand, and requiring either a pledge or oath of secrecy."

Most behavioral experts in 1871 labeled Edward a monomaniac with a fixation on his manuscript, but when it was dismissed by language experts, Edward erupted at their ignorance and refused to regret the crimes he had committed.

"[They believe] that there was no merit in them whatever," said Ham, "he was so wrapped up in the belief that he had made a discovery that was going to revolutionize the whole Republic of letters that he had come to believe that any means were justifiable to accomplish his end."

But Ham still wasn't quite convinced that Edward wasn't worthy of his help. He was still seduced by the killer's charms, still vulnerable. Ham's relationship with Edward should have served as a cautionary tale for future journalists about cultivating relationships with psychopaths. As journalists Stephen G. Michaud and Hugh Aynesworth concluded their interviews with murderer Ted Bundy before his execution in 1989, their conversation with the serial killer ended in an almost wistful tone.

"I've enjoyed visiting with you more today than ever before," Aynesworth told Bundy. "I hope to see you again, but I don't know if I ever will or not."

"Yeah . . . that element of pressure always separated us because *you* always felt you had to get something from me and I felt that your interests were not *my* interests," replied Bundy, "so we floundered a bit all the way."

"Well," said Aynesworth, "we both learned some things."

Experts say that psychopaths constantly aim to manipulate—and even a seasoned journalist can become a victim. Hamilton was wary of Edward's influence as their relationship grew deeper over the spring because the author believed, after decades of criminality, that Edward thought sacrificing others was worth it to accomplish his scholarly work.

"He would not hesitate to commit the crime of burglary or even murder, so long as the fruit of it was going to assist him in benefitting the world," said Ham.

Yet Edward Rulloff was charming, friendly, and engaging. It was all a trick, Ham realized—a charade to reach a goal that only the killer understood. Ted Bundy admitted to the authors of his biography that he became an expert at modifying his behavior in early adulthood.

"At the University of Washington, I was a nice, presentable, affable young person," Bundy told the journalists. "I compensated a lot for what I consider to be my more vulnerable aspect, my introversion by being seemingly aloof and arrogant and intellectual but nice and tolerant and that kind of stuff. I had to sit down one night and say, 'this is what I want to be.'"

Edward frantically struggled for control, even the night before his scheduled execution. He begged attorney George Becker to refute George Sawyer's negative public comments about his theory—Becker responded that it seemed too late for that. That evening, a respected local Catholic man, John Guilfoyle, approached Edward in his cell, hoping to convince the killer to repent, but in the past, Edward had wanted "no such damn nonsense." Guilfoyle begged Edward to consider the fate of his soul as he gripped a crucifix and cried, imploring the killer to atone for each of his crimes. Edward squirmed as Ham eyed him.

"Rulloff listened in an uneasy manner for some time," remembered Ham, "but finally said he had no desire to talk on the subject, and was not inclined to accept any religious consolation."

The next day, Hamilton arrived at the jail in Binghamton; it was the morning of Edward's scheduled execution, May 18, 1871.

"I had been up for two nights in succession," said Hamilton.

Hamilton looked toward the edifice that had finally been transformed into the gallows. It was built near the northeast corner of the jail yard the afternoon before. The heavy timber aperture held an iron pulley over which the silk rope was passed. On the other end was a weight of 250 pounds scheduled to fall about two feet. The sheriff of Broome County was charged with the construction of the gallows—men had worked day and night as the execution approached.

"The method adopted is that used in the Tombs [the municipal jail in Lower Manhattan], of hoisting instead of dropping the condemned," wrote Ed Crapsey. "His cell opens directly upon the yard, as do all the others, and it would be impossible to keep him in any one of them without his being aware of what was going on."

The apparatus made Ham Freeman queasy—so did the giddy people who milled around him, mostly wearing grins as they examined the gallows.

"Quite a number of persons were admitted to the jail yard on Wednesday to witness experiments, a bag of sand being fastened to the end designed for the condemned man," said Ham.

Thursday morning, Ham reflected on what he knew about his friend, Edward Rulloff—the killer whose mind was both sage and malevolent.

"No one could become acquainted with Rulloff in a day, or a

week," mused Ham. "I cannot say that I really knew the man, or fully understood all the devious ways of his singular mind."

———

The day of the scheduled execution was one of the most beautiful of the spring season. Starting early in the morning, women placed blankets on the grass, which would serve to hold their places for the violent spectacle in Binghamton's town square.

"The streets were crowded with eager, excited people, all wending their way towards the jail in hopes of getting a glance at the doomed man, and satisfying a morbid appetite," wrote Ham. "The hotels were crowded for two or three days previous, with reporters and others, from all sections of the country, anxious to elicit every fact of interest they possibly could, concerning Rulloff."

Ham was disgusted with the whole spectacle, the worst representation of bloodlust and depravity that was distinct from Edward's own violence, he thought.

"The streets at the time of the execution looked more like a festal day of celebration," said Ham, "and one unknown to the facts, would little think it was occasioned by the fact that a fellow man was to be launched from the gallows into eternity."

Several thousand people surrounded the jail, challenging the militia and police to prevent them from forcing their way into the building. This enthusiasm for executions wasn't unique—it was biblical, an eye for an eye.

In June 2001, about 1,400 members of the media arrived to Terre Haute, Indiana, to report on Timothy McVeigh's execution for the 1995 bombing of the Alfred P. Murrah Federal Building in Oklahoma, killing 168 people, including 19 children. When McVeigh received the lethal injection, the public had received no invitations, but ten representatives of his victims did.

McVeigh offered no apology, except "I am the master of my fate, I am the captain of my soul," which seemed to infuriate some of the family members.

"It was a totally expressionless, blank stare," said Larry Whicher, the brother of a U.S. Secret Service agent who died. "He had a look of defiance, and that if he could, he'd do it all over again."

Other family members, some watching on closed-circuit television, believed that McVeigh's execution was just.

"I think I did see the face of evil today," said Kathy Wilburn, who lost two young grandsons in the bombing.

Some families valued witnessing the execution, citing a need for closure, but recent studies show that very few families and friends of murder victims (called co-victims) report achieving closure because of capital punishment—just 2.5 percent of those surveyed in a study by University of Minnesota sociology-anthropology professor Scott Vollum said they achieved "real closure" and expressed feeling empty after the murderer's death.

"The long judicial process between conviction and execution, which can span many years in some cases, also prolongs grief and pain for co-victims," wrote Dr. Robert T. Muller in *Psychology Today*. "Some co-victims in the Vollum study voiced that the death penalty was not harsh enough, while others communicated a wish to personally inflict harm on the condemned. In many cases though, executions were not sufficient to satisfy these desires."

Psychologists say that might be because healing comes with time, not one event like an execution—the Schutts would discover that later. In 1871, *New York Times* reporter Ed Crapsey surveyed some of those in Binghamton who began gathering in the square the night before. Crapsey claimed that none said a positive thing about the condemned man.

"I doubt if there will be a single witness of his execution unable to endure the spectacle with equanimity, unless, as many fear, his seeming stoicism should prove to be mere surface bravado, and he be utterly unnerved when the awful moment actually arrives," wrote Crapsey. "As yet, however, it must be said that he gives no sign of weakening, and stoutly declares that he will die as he has lived, without whining."

But Edward *was* weakening, or at least he grew more anxious the night before. With less than twelve hours before his scheduled execution a guard noticed that Edward seemed . . . distracted.

"He turned to his dictionaries, but Thomas Johnson, one of his keepers, saw that his attention to them was mere pretense," wrote Crapsey, "as he observed that Rulloff had a book wrong side up, which he had seemed to be carefully examining for some time."

Johnson asked Edward if "his business in this world had all been closed." Edward replied "yes." The manuscript was done. And after that conversation, the killer no longer looked at it. He spent the remainder of the night bellowing obscenities and regaling the guards with vile anecdotes, determined to make everyone around him uncomfortable for just a bit longer. But Edward also fretted as each hour passed—and it showed. The feelings of fear and insecurity, a loss of control, were so unexpected to him. He tried to distract himself with games like an old puzzle that challenged the player to arrange figures so that they added up to fifteen in all directions.

"He made several failures at this," wrote Crapsey, but finally succeeded with this example:

$$2\ 94$$
$$7\ 53$$
$$6\ 18$$

At one point, Edward turned to his guard and began recounting the story of the deadly robbery at Halbert Brothers dry goods store, the murder that resulted in his death sentence.

"[A]nd with terrible emphasis again declared that Jarvis," said Crapsey, "not himself, fired the shot which killed Mirrick [Merrick]."

Facing death, Edward turned on the person he claimed to be most fond of in life. The psychopathic person is committed only to himself, despite any fleeting actions to the contrary. Edward paced. In fact, he paced so vigorously that the sheriff allowed him to walk back and forth along the corridor of the row of cells. The morning of his execution, the clock in the parlor struck the hour— Edward stopped short and listened before turning to the guard and asking for the time. He had tried to count the strokes of the clock, but it was too maddening.

"Five o'clock" was the response.

Edward gasped.

"My time is getting short," he replied quickly before snatching up a dictionary and skimming it. The guard suspected this was all for show because Edward Rulloff, for perhaps the first time in a long time, was at a loss. Another guard picked up a book lying in Edward's cell, titled *The Cross in the Cell: Or, The Way of Salva-*

tion Explained to a Prisoner Awaiting Execution written in 1866 by minister Nehemiah Adams, concerning conversations between clergy and prisoners. The guard approached Edward, handed it to him, and boldly requested his autograph, a memento of his time guarding a vile killer. Edward glanced at the religious book and curtly replied:

"I don't buy, or read, or believe such damned stuff, and don't want my name in it."

At seven o'clock, the sheriff escorted Edward upstairs to the second floor as the gallows were being finished. He stayed silent as he ascended the stairs and seemed to understand the significance of this change.

"[He] stepped lightly and firmly from the corridor which he knew he would never enter again except to pass through it on his way to his doom," wrote Ed Crapsey.

Edward gazed through the large glass window in his new holding room and seemed to marvel at the vision of the countryside he once strolled around anonymously, hands always shoved into his pockets. With no throng of gawkers peering up at him, he seemed at peace with what was expected to happen in just four hours.

"He stood for some minutes looking steadfastly at the broad expanse of country smiling beneath the morning sun, and glorious with the fresh glad greenness of the Spring," observed Crapsey.

But then Edward Rulloff seemed frightened once again, as was Ted Bundy in the days approaching his own execution. The serial killer told FBI profiler Bill Hagmaier in 1989 that he would refuse to sit in the electric chair when it was time.

"I said, 'Well, what are you going to do,'" Hagmaier asked.

"I'm going to die right here," Bundy replied.

He held a pen in his hand as he told Hagmaier that he could stab himself in the artery and he would bleed to death before help arrived.

"Is that what you want to do?" asked Hagmaier.

"I'm not going to let them kill me," retorted Bundy.

Eventually, Hagmaier convinced Bundy, who had been reading scripture, that suicide was not a good choice, even as the chant "burn, Bundy, burn" grew louder outside the prison.

In 1871, reporters chronicled Edward Rulloff's every movement as families with cold drinks and food continued to crowd outside. Edward angrily declared that one day the academic world would respect him—he envisioned (correctly) that theories on linguistics would evolve over generations. The issue was, of course, that his theory would be no more accepted in 2022 than it was two hundred years ago.

Edward had finally determined that his manuscript's acceptance among scholars in 1871 was not to be fulfilled. He would die at the gallows, just as the Schutts had wished. Edward seethed at the vision of his wife's family glaring at him from below the noose, smirking because they would *finally* see him swing after almost thirty years. *No.* He refused to gift them with a view of his death, or an executioner with the opportunity to boast about pulling the level that ended Edward Rulloff's life. He whispered to Hamilton.

"He had requested me to provide him with a lancet, and with fifteen grains of sulplate [sic] of morphia, so that he would be prepared to commit suicide in case his counsel were not successful in saving his life."

Ham stayed silent while Edward quietly repeated the details.

"He had several plans for me to give it to him," said Ham. "One was, to procure the lancet, take off the handle and place the blade in a book; the other was to put the morphia into one of the two capsules."

Ham had remained a steadfast confidant of Edward Rulloff for six months, his only friend and more loyal than Edward's own family. Now his fidelity to a multiple murderer would be tested one final time. Would Hamilton Freeman help Edward Rulloff die?

8

The Neurologists

*I knew myself, at the first breath of this new life, to be more
wicked, tenfold more wicked, sold a slave to my original evil;
and the thought, in that moment, braced and delighted me
like wine.*

—Robert Louis Stevenson,
Strange Case of Dr. Jekyll and Mr. Hyde, 1886

Ephraim and Aaron Schutt examined the gallows on a beautiful
spring morning. This surely would be a gratifying day for the
two of them, the day that their loathsome, murderous brother-in-
law would finally swing from the gallows. Just two hours earlier,
Aaron Schutt had approached the county's sheriff with a request:
he and his brother Ephraim wanted to talk with Edward Rulloff,
offering the killer a day of reckoning before he died. They would
implore him to reveal the fate of little Priscilla, whom Edward had
always denied killing. Aaron and Ephraim needed to know about
his motives for poisoning William's wife and daughter. They
hoped to discover *why* all this happened—what had caused Edward to turn so vile and violent? The Schutts prayed he would
agree, but Hamilton Freeman was doubtful because after three
decades of troubles, Edward's venom and disdain for the Schutts

had only deepened. The sheriff presented Aaron Schutt's offer of a meeting to Edward.

"The condemned man would not see him," reported Ham.

Even at the end of his life, Edward was still determined to tuck away his secrets—the Schutts would receive no gratification from a final encounter with the villain from their family's dark history. Resolution meant nothing to Edward unless it benefited him. Aaron was crestfallen by Edward's curt response, but the brothers felt some solace because they would soon see him die in humiliation. The Schutts watched the sheriff's deputies as they adjusted the rope. The sun cast a glow on the jail's yard, and the brothers could feel the rumble of the crowd behind the fence; so many people had traveled on crowded trains for long distances to see the spectacle. But none seemed more pleased than the spectators from Dryden and Ithaca, New York.

"People from Tompkins County, where Ruloff [sic] first began his murderous depredations, came in large numbers, and indicated by speech and gesture their joy at the coming fate of the murderer," Ham told the writer of a pamphlet about the trial and execution.

The Schutt brothers seemed pleased with their vantage point. Secular justice might finally be offered to their suffering family and then biblical justice would commence . . . they would finally have closure. But while Thursday, May 18, 1871, was a notable day for the Schutt family, author Hamilton Freeman was mired with misery.

"At 10:30 o'clock of the morning of the execution, I visited the doomed man," said Ham, "where he received me very affectionately."

Edward did not sleep the night before, instead settling on

pacing the room. He eventually sat on the couch, watched for daylight, and waited for a final visit from his biographer. The loud crowing of roosters startled Edward, and he jokingly wondered aloud about their early-morning schedule. During breakfast time, he refused all food and settled on coffee, which likely only worsened his anxiety—the noose terrified him, but so did the public shaming that was sure to precede it. Edward feared that the sheriff would escort him to the stage and brandish him for the mob amid its cheers, like a fattened pig on display during an auction. Even more upsetting to Edward was that his scholarship was sure to be lost to time and prejudice.

Ham stammered as he looked at Edward, the murderer he had once championed in public and private; the author's bereavement seemed to make the killer skittish.

"Stand firm, Ham," said Edward as he nibbled on a pine stick that he picked up from his small side table. "Do not give way; you feel much more affected than I do."

They chatted for about ten minutes as Edward once again railed at the governor for not recognizing the merits of his work. There was no hope of a stay of execution—Governor Hoffman was now traveling to Virginia with no time to aid a failed academic.

"Nothing more can be done for me," said Edward. "I shall go satisfied, though. I have nothing to regret. I have done a great work.

"A work of beauty—a triumph of genius must have educated recognition," he told Ham. "Learned idiots make ridicule of it, while ignorant alike of its fundamental truths and the beautiful and symmetrical principle involved. It is a shame to deprive me of life just now, when I might confer such a lasting blessing on mankind."

Hamilton wondered aloud about the current location of Edward's manuscript, the sacred grail that seemed to be the provenance of many terrible things.

"My great work, carefully arranged and ready for publication, is in the hands of my brother, who, though no scholar, will, I trust, see to it that the result of my life is not lost to the world that rejects me in my hour of need," replied Edward. "I have sent beside some interesting manuscript to the local press, which will appear after—a—Friday."

Ham sensed tremor in the killer's voice as Edward envisaged things to come after his death, which was just a few hours away. Then Edward turned to Ham, grinned, and offered a coarse joke about polishing his manuscript, perfecting it.

"'If I could have had time'—absently looking about the cell and clasping his neck with significant anguish," recalled Ham, "'you know.'"

Edward ended the sentence with a choking sound, a lewd and insensitive joke that made Hamilton shudder. Defense attorney George Becker also visited Edward's cell that morning, despite suffering an abusive tirade from his ungrateful client the day before. Becker, usually positive and supportive, seemed subdued.

"I am sorry, George, to see you feel bad," said Edward. "I guess you feel worse than I do."

Becker was quiet and then asked Edward curtly:

"Did you tell anyone anything about this thing?"

"No," replied Edward.

"I wouldn't advise you to either," cautioned Becker.

In one final benevolent act to protect his client's reputation, the defense attorney requested that Edward stay quiet about Frederick Merrick's murder—he seemed unconcerned about the fate of the killer's soul. As Edward watched Becker and Hamilton examine the holding room, Edward reflected on his time in the jail in Binghamton. He seemed pleased with the duration, at least, because it was likely his briefest stint behind bars.

"I was arrested on the 18th of August; this is the 18th of May," he commented to Becker. "Just nine months in prison."

Edward was reminded of the visit from Dr. George Sawyer, the principal at the nearby Utica Free Academy. He was still livid that Sawyer had denounced his theory along with his intellect, and Edward wanted everyone to understand why. The school principal had duped him.

"In the first place, they gave me no notice that they were coming, what they were coming for, or what the results would be upon my fate," Edward complained.

He insisted that he had purposely misled Sawyer because Edward mistrusted all visitors, particularly so-called "experts," and Edward labeled Sawyer's examination of his scholarship "a damned unjust trick." Ham listened as Edward finally soothed himself with self-assurance that he would be vindicated. As Edward's defense attorney, Becker had been tasked with asking his client a morbid question. The sheriff needed to know where Edward wished his remains to be placed.

"I simply wish it decently buried," replied Edward quickly.

It must have been a dismaying answer for a man who faced death with a rising level of fear. Edward then requested that his brother, Rulof, claim his body and then oversee his burial in a safe, secretive place; Edward worried that grave robbers would disinter his body and sell it to an anatomist. He couldn't stand the thought of being on display yet again—this time as the prop during a medical lecture. Rulof, his kind brother, would surely grant him this final wish. But Edward's other defense attorney issued dire news that was just sent to him in a letter from Rulof. He read it aloud to Edward.

"Is there any hope?" it said.

The note mentioned that $100 was enclosed in the envelope for legal expenses, but there was no money inside. Edward appeared deflated, while Ham felt disgusted because it seemed that he cared more for the killer than his own family.

"The family of Ruloff [sic] kept entirely aloof from the hapless monster," said Ham. "[H]is brother kept up a passing interest, sending careless notes of enquiry occasionally, but manifesting so little concern that even this day found him absent, and, informed of the contents of his brother's note, Ruloff [sic] manifested the only emotion observed during the day."

Hamilton noticed a small shift in Edward's mood after that news—the killer seemed woeful after the desertion of his entire family.

"With the hope of a personal communication with his relative, some of the bravado that had heretofore sustained him seemed to die out," the writer noticed, "and he seemed for the first time to mark with apprehension the narrowing span between him and eternity."

When the sheriff asked Edward once again about the fate of his remains, he snapped that they could do whatever they "god damned pleased." Despite feeling defeated by the lack of support, Edward spent a portion of his final hours receiving welcomed visitors from the town, including a few police officers. This might have seemed unorthodox, but Edward was a curiosity to just about everyone—his intelligence and gentlemanly habits were a respite for the officers from the miscreants they typically encountered. Edward crassly joked to one of them:

"Sears, I've a mind to take that club of yours and knock you on the head with it."

After the menagerie of visitors left the cell, Hamilton watched Edward dress himself with clean clothes provided by the sheriff. He stepped over to the mirror, combing his black and silver hair. Edward carefully slipped on his old frayed black frock coat and smoothed it with as much dignity as a king adjusting the crown atop his head. But Ham noted that Edward certainly didn't address his audience in the jail with the decency of monarch.

"He continued his repulsive jesting, thoroughly bearing out his defiant cynicism," said Ham, now even more dismayed.

To one deputy, Edward joked that he hoped to be hanged before noon because he expected to "take his dinner in Hell." This didn't surprise Ham, and it seemed consistent with Edward's mood.

"Outside the prison the crowd by ten o'clock numbered thousands," said Ham. "There were a great many ladies and children among them, but since nothing could be seen, there was more harm in the intent than in fact."

At 11:15, a deputy sheriff approached him with the strap for pinioning his arms, a warning that Edward's walk to the gallows was imminent.

"As our interview drew to a close he earnestly thanked me for the interest I had taken in his case and efforts in his behalf," said Ham, "and he hoped I never would have occasion to regret my course towards him."

Ham felt no contrition, the author promised, and he assured Edward that his life's story would provide the public with a full profile of a complicated, confounding man. That might have been a comfort to Edward because Ham had offered him little reason to mistrust him. Edward had one last wish—he hoped that Ham had granted him his request for a knife or poison. It would be a gift to die by his own hand and not outside amid the hordes of gleeful onlookers.

"He then took me by the hand and gave it a hearty shake," remembered Ham.

As guards led Edward toward the gallows, the killer pulled him forward and offered Ham a passionate, open-mouth kiss. The author was stunned, but Edward was strategic.

"I sometimes think that the reason why he embraced me on the morning of his execution was so that I could slip a capsule, containing poison, from my mouth into his," said Ham, sadly.

Despite months of acute manipulation and parasitic overtures, despite Hamilton's many financial and emotional sacrifices, the author was steadfast with this request. He refused to help Edward. He would have to die on the gallows, stripped of all dignity.

Edward, not finding the poison after the kiss, stepped back and surveyed Ham—the author had finally revealed his strength of character. Edward's course was now set. He could hear the wave of noise from the crowd outside, as if they were awaiting a much-anticipated dramatic play. Ham watched Edward's color change.

Edward "implored the writer to stand firm, as he certainly should on the gallows," said Ham.

The sentiment seemed sincere, but the killer was rarely authentic. Edward quickly turned terse as he continued to dictate what terms he still could control.

"You won't have any clergymen bellowing down there, nor

prayers, nor any of that damned bosh, will you, Mr. Sheriff?" Edward asked.

"No, sir," replied the sheriff.

It was another affront to Christianity that served as a theme in his life. The night before, the sheriff sent a Roman Catholic priest to visit Edward in jail, perhaps to offer last rites. As the priest presented him with a crucifix, Edward cried angrily, "Take away that damned thing."

All during that day, Edward seemed to be spiraling into madness, dismissing any past preservation of his image as a regal scholar. He had subverted his own bluff.

"All day Wednesday he conducted himself with the greatest recklessness, shouting and singing so that he could be plainly heard outside his prison walls," said Ham, exasperated.

But by midnight, Edward seemed calmed, apparently resolved to his fate. Just minutes before he walked toward the gallows that morning, Edward asked Ham to join him near the noose for support.

"[G]oing down the stairs he was cool and collected, exhibiting no nervousness as he took his place on the gallows," said Ham. "When the straps were placed around his ankles and knees, he stood perfectly quiet, seeming inclined to aid the officers."

"The Sheriff then asked him if he had anything to say," said Ham. "He hesitated some minutes."

The crowd tried to remain quiet, hoping to hear one last comment from Edward H. Rulloff. These final words would have cemented his image to the throng of thousands who stood on the other side of the fence. The people inside the jail yard, including the Schutts, strained to listen. Edward rarely missed an opportunity to speak publicly—but not at the end of his life.

"Nothing, I believe," Edward replied.

An officer placed the silk noose rope around his neck and tightened it.

"The chief deputy will now read the warrant," said the sheriff as he stood nearby Edward.

The document detailing Edward's crime took ten minutes to read aloud, which must have been torturous to a man who just wanted to die quickly, but Edward tried to stay calm.

"The small, half-closed eyes, apparently more stupefied and daunted, gave him a fearfully repulsive appearance," remembered Ham. "The irony of a man within a minute or two of a shameful death, standing with his hands in his pockets, added to the strange surroundings of the man. An expression of horror spread overall."

The execution was apparently ahead of schedule, so the sheriff asked Edward if they should proceed early. The killer nodded and then began to panic.

"I cannot stand still!" he whispered to the deputy closest to him.

As Ham had noted, Edward kept his hands in his pockets, a habit he picked up as he strolled the banks of Cayuga Lake years earlier—the same lake where Edward discarded his wife's and child's bodies into the dark water. Edward stayed silent but continued to act jittery.

"Is it your desire to say anything?" asked the sheriff. Edward shook his head.

"You do not desire any delay?" the sheriff asked. Edward shook his head again. He felt more restless as the crowd grew louder.

The sheriff nodded to the deputy, who pulled a white cap over Edward's face. He yanked the noose tight and gave a tug on the cord, signaling to another deputy sitting in a nearby barn that it was time to the cut the large weight at the other end of the pulley with an axe; the weight dropped to the ground and Edward was violently jerked upward three feet in the air, dislocating his neck. He began to gasp for breath. The jolt forced Edward's right hand from his pocket, but then something distressing happened.

"[A]s if the stubborn will of the dying murderer was resolved to assert itself in every defiance of the gate of eternity, after a few efforts to find the pocket the hand slipped in again and remained there," reported Ham.

The crowd watched, horrified. Edward's death was so troubling that some of the bloodthirsty townspeople turned away.

"There was no struggling or twitching of the limbs, (a movement of the shoulders once or twice being all that was perceptible)," wrote Ham.

At 11:51 a.m., Dr. Daniel Burr and his colleague walked over to Edward as he hung extended from the rope, still swaying from the jerk. Burr placed his fingers on Edward's radial artery in his wrist and felt for a pulse, expecting to find nothing. But after several minutes of searching, there were signs of life, which caused murmurs amongst the crowd. How could this man *still* be alive after fifteen minutes? Some in the throng in Binghamton's town square had witnessed public executions before, but this was terrible. Perhaps it was because Edward Rulloff had terrified much of upstate New York for decades that some worried that he *might* be able to fool the doctors.

Dr. Daniel Burr stood by Edward Rulloff's body, glancing at his pocket watch and determined to check again only if the man were certainly dead. He walked over to the killer, placed his hand on his wrist once again and felt . . . nothing. Edward H. Rulofson was pronounced dead on May 18, 1871, at one minute past noon. The crowd in the jail yard grew quiet, staring up at the corpse of a multiple murderer. After another twelve minutes of the crowd's gawking, Edward's body was lowered and carried over to a wooden coffin nearby.

Edward was immediately examined by Daniel Burr, and the physician came to a swift conclusion: his thick neck wasn't broken, only dislocated. He was strangled and died after more than fifteen minutes of choking and gasping for breath beneath the hood. Hamilton Freeman offered his book readers some contradictory observations of Edward's death, including deference to the local sheriff.

"His death seemed to be very calm and easy, and the face was not in the least distorted," he wrote. "The execution was conducted in the most humane manner possible, and reflects great credit on Sheriff Martin, who, by the duties of his office was required to prepare for this terrible tragedy."

Hamilton Freeman's belief that the hanging was largely successful was inconsistent with what medical science tells us about strangulation.

"The noose would squeeze on the carotid arteries that ferry blood to the brain and press down on the trachea, which brings oxygen to the lungs," writes Vasudevan Mukunth for *The Wire*. "As its supply of blood drops, the brain begins to swell, so much so that at one point it presses on the top of the spinal column and pinches on the vagal nerve. This action stops the heart. By this time, the person will have been unconscious thanks to the lack of oxygen in the lungs. In all, they'd be unconscious within 20 seconds and dead within 20 minutes."

Ham might have hoped to mitigate any public backlash from

readers who opposed capital punishment, or he hoped to pacify his own fears that his friend died an excruciating death. Despite his realizations that he had been deceived by a killer, Ham prayed that his execution was peaceful at the end even though it certainly was not.

Edward Rulloff's hanging was the last public execution in New York State. Some thought it was a fitting end to a life of brutality, but it also illustrated the inhumanity of capital punishment. The day before Ted Bundy's scheduled execution in January 1989, people gathered outside the Florida State Prison, chanting "burn, Bundy, burn" and holding signs reading ROSES ARE RED, VIOLETS ARE BLUE, GOOD MORNING TED, WE'RE GOING TO KILL YOU. TV crews from across the country set up tripods on the grass just outside the gates, angling for space amid the thousands of spectators chanting and holding up paper signs that read TUESDAY IS FRY DAY. Vendors sold commemorative T-shirts and metal "Old Sparky" pins depicting Florida's electric chair—businesses posted signs that said SEE TED BUNDY DIE. The crowd was so boisterous that Bundy could hear them inside the prison as he sat waiting to be escorted from his cell. Television reporters detailed his final moments, including his last meal of medium rare steak, over-easy eggs, buttered toast with jelly, milk, coffee, juice, and hash browns. Bundy ignored the food tray, just as Edward Rulloff did. As fireworks exploded outside, a display rivaled only by those at an Independence Day celebration, Bundy seemed bemused.

"They're crazy, they think I'm crazy, listen to them," he told journalist Hugh Aynesworth.

Bundy didn't seem surprised by the public reaction—the death penalty is biblical vengeance, he said, an "eye for an eye." Investigators who worked on his cases, exhausted and disgusted, said they were happy to see him go, like a bad virus that could only be treated with time.

After Edward Rulloff's execution, the Schutts seemed more disturbed than relieved—it was not the closure they had prayed for.

"I was present at the execution, not with any taste or wish of my own," wrote Ephraim to Dr. George Sawyer. "But the people hereabouts would have me see the man dead. I can assure you it was a sorry sight to see a man die so wicked and depraved, defying both God and man."

Edward Rulloff's death seemed horrendous, painful, and much deserved to many in the horde who watched the man struggle to place his hand back inside his pocket. The placement of Edward's body in a coffin soon triggered one of the most macabre traditions in America.

"[T]he coffin containing the remains was placed outside the jail, guarded by two companies of the 44th Reigment, N.Y.S.N.G., and were viewed by over five thousand persons," said Ham, disgusted.

The author rushed over to Edward's defense attorney, George Becker, and described the chaotic scene.

"He immediately called upon the Sheriff and requested that the remains be removed into the jail, and the horrid exhibition closed, which request was soon after complied with," recalled Ham.

Now there was the matter of what to do with the body. Edward had worried about experiencing humiliation, even in death, by being spirited away by ghouls with shovels and sold to a medical school. He refused to accept the fate of lying on an anatomist's table and Ham Freeman believed that Edward had a valid reason to fret over his own remains.

"There were at least twenty-five medical men and students in

Binghamton, who were walking around like a lot of hyenas, prepared to *snatch* the remains soon as they were deposited in a vault or grave," said Ham. "Large sums were offered to counsel for the remains, and to the Sheriff, which were declined."

As the killer's remains lay in the jail cell he once occupied, Becker made a crucial decision, one that would place Edward Rulloff in the annals of the history detailing criminal psychology. His relatives never arrived to claim his body, so Becker read Dr. Daniel Burr's proposal: the pathologist hoped to take possession of Edward's corpse and study it in the interest of discovering some anomaly using phrenology that revealed why Edward's mind seemed cursed with an undercurrent of evil. His head would be removed, and the remainder of his body would be buried in a secret location, owned by the Burrs, at a cemetery in Binghamton. Edward hoped to be recognized by future scholars—that would be the case, but not in the way he had hoped.

———

The elder Dr. Burr, George, struggled in his lab as he maneuvered the saw. It was laborious to remove Edward Rulloff's head because his neck cords were so thick—the work quickly became tedious. Once Edward's head was detached, his skull wouldn't crack easily—it was twice the thickness of ordinary skulls.

"The head was opening in the usual way, by parting the scalp over the top of the head. From one ear to the other," read Burr's report, "and sawing off the top."

The surgeon labored for almost an hour before turning the remains over to the sheriff and preserving the head. Before the funeral, Hamilton marked the finale of Edward Rulloff's execution with a glum observation as he described how the body was loaded onto a cart that served as a hearse.

"The few fond mourners followed in a single buggy, drawn by an old, solemn looking horse," remembered Ham.

A well-known poem from 1817, "The Burial of Sir John Moore after Corunna" by Irish poet and priest Charles Wolfe, was read aloud at the burial ground.

"Slowly and sadly we laid him down, from the field of his fame fresh and gory; we carved not a line, and we raised not a stone, but left him alone with his glory."

Hamilton lamented the final line of Wolfe's piece because Edward Rulloff's soul was unlikely to rest in peace.

"But poor Rulloff was not left alone in his glory, for as soon as the shades of night closed over the scene, the harpies were at work," the author wrote. "Medical students from St. Louis, Albany and other places, that night invaded his grave and dug up what was left of him, in the vain hope of finding the head. In this they were of course disappointed, and had only their pains for their trouble."

Dr. Burr was methodical as he examined Edward's brain and one thing was clear: it was the largest and heaviest he had ever seen, at fifty-nine ounces. In fact, neurologists now place it in the top 1 percent for both categories. *But what did that mean?* Burr wasn't sure as he measured the length and depth of every fissure and fold. He searched for abnormalities, like pools of blood or obvious physical damage. The surgeon's final report was full of data, but it was also peppered with odd statements about a warped mind—brain-imaging analysis from the nineteenth century. Burr's goal was to determine the evil nature of human beings using scientific means, but he approached the brain from a psychological point of view.

"The lower, brute portion of Rulloff's brain and the mechanical powers were unusually large," read Burr's report. "The upper portion of the brain, which directs the higher moral and religious sentiments, was very deficient in Rulloff."

According to the pathologist, Edward's brutish nature far outweighed his innate morals, despite his intensive study of the Bible. Modern pathologists now know several things that contradict phrenology and Dr. Burr's report.

The cerebellum, which is located at the back of the brain, doesn't dictate a penchant for violence; it controls motor commands and cognitive functions, like language. The cerebrum, the largest part of the brain, doesn't regulate morality—it controls movement but also judgment, thinking, and reasoning, along with problem solving. Hamilton Freeman glanced over Burr's assessment and provided his own phrenological interpretation of Edward's brain. The author concluded that the sections of the brain that indicated egotism and adoration were large and of course, Ham wasn't surprised.

"His was the veneration for ancient temples, languages, books, mythology and places, and not of a religious character," said Ham. "His egotism and vanity all who knew him will certify, was inordinate—it was with him a weakness."

Phrenology was mostly confined to studying the bumps on a skull, but Burr was homing in on Edward's brain using techniques that were the precursor to neuropsychology. Burr decided that the wiring of Edward's brain had doomed him from birth.

"This distortion of his mind prevented Ruloff [sic] from

cultivating the higher moral sentiments, or developing his finer emotional nature," Burr wrote. "Burglary, arson, and murder, would all be resorted to, to carry on his operations, and to remove all obstacles to his success."

Burr believed that Edward wasn't responsible for his crimes, despite the alienist's conclusion. Life in an asylum was appropriate.

"In the formation of his brain, Rulloff was a ferocious animal, and so far as disposition could relieve him from responsibility," concluded Burr, "he was not strictly responsible for his acts."

Experts in 1871 couldn't agree—Should his abnormal brain have saved him? And there's *still* debate over that idea. The brain scan has since crept into American criminal courts through a phenomenon called "the brain defense." A Duke University study found that between 2005 and 2012, roughly 25 percent of death penalty trials used neurobiological data to argue for life in prison. Over that past decade, that number has likely increased. In one example provided by researchers, a PET scan of a murder suspect's brain showed abnormally low neuron activity in his frontal lobe. Scientists say that often causes an increased risk of aggressive, even violent behavior. But prosecutors argue that others suffering from that same condition are nonviolent—environmental factors likely distinguish between a murderer and a nonviolent but potentially disturbed person.

Dr. Burr was troubled by Edward's lack of remorse and empathy; he labeled him a "personal devil." The physician's report, printed in several prestigious scientific journals, was read widely. But no journal was likely more influential in years to come than the *Journal of Psychological Medicine,* edited by esteemed neurologist Dr. William Hammond. Hammond was a professional enemy of Dr. John Gray—and the men were avatars for the very public struggle between alienists and neurologists over the treatment of the insane.

As William Hammond flipped through the newspaper articles, he surveyed the array of resources he might use to solve the puzzle of Edward Rulloff's mind. By this time, Dr. George Burr had sold Edward's dissected brain to a neurologist at Cornell University, but Hammond studied Dr. Burr's phrenological report on Edward Rulloff's brain, and he noted the conclusion of the anatomist that Edward was not responsible because the "animal" section of his brain was unusually large. Hammond also paid special attention to Oliver Dyer's narrative of Edward Rulloff's life story in *The Sun*. He noted Greek scholar Richard Mather's positive assessment of Edward's work. Dr. Hammond concluded that each article would complement his journal and each piece would allow him to create a larger profile of Edward Rulloff.

Dr. Hammond was an authority among forward-thinking, scientific researchers—and he's now known as America's "father of neurology." He was the first American physician to devote himself entirely to neurology. Hammond was a sought-after expert witness regarding sanity at some of America's most celebrated (and controversial) trials. He had an outstanding reputation, but one that was not unblemished. He served as President Lincoln's Surgeon General of the United States Army during the Civil War, but it was a tumultuous appointment. Hammond had banned the use of a mercury compound by the military to treat a host of ailments, including cancer and bronchitis. Hammond believed the treatment wasn't effective and hurt the health of soldiers—and he was right. But his obstinance irked the secretary of war and Hammond was court-martialed for disobeying orders.

Hammond also had professional enemies in science—competing experts who were threatened by the neurologist's international reputation—but his hostile rivalry with Dr. John Purdue Gray was the most acrimonious. Gray was the alienist who had determined that Edward Rulloff was perfectly sane based on his good physical health and remarkable acumen in academia. Hammond and Gray accused each other of being charlatans, imposters that applied a black mark to other expert witnesses. They bitterly disagreed over the assessment of just about every criminal they had in common.

Their arguments were indicative of the well-publicized debates between alienists and neurologists, a feud based on big brains and even bigger egos. Gray claimed that during his tenure as head of the asylums, patients received unparalleled treatment. But neurologists accused psychiatrists of quackery because they failed to research psychiatric disorders and insisted on using antiquated methods, like treating physical diseases or leaning on religion. Neurologists believed they were the authority on all brain disorders, including insanity.

Hammond and Gray had a dustup earlier that year during the murder trial of David Montgomery. Gray testified that Montgomery, who had epilepsy, was insane when he killed his wife. Hammond argued that he was "perfectly sane" and that Gray's testimony represented a lack of professional experience. Hammond won the case and the intellectual battle, and he was right, because we now know that neurological disorders *don't* compel someone to kill.

Edward Rulloff offered them both more fodder for their unique theories about the criminal mind. Dr. Hammond believed that science, not morality, drove criminals—insanity arose from a diseased brain. Therefore, he cracked open skulls (after death, of course) and searched a criminal's brain for physical inconsistencies. Gray leaned on a killer's bodily health and intellect for clues—an examination of the mind. His work happened while the subject was still alive (even if his conclusion often led to their deaths).

Edward Rulloff provided Dr. Hammond with valuable data. The neurologist believed that the size of the brain was indicative of a man's morality, the prevailing (and racist) theory in the 1800s. Hammond and most other scientists assumed that elite, white men would certainly have the largest brains and were, therefore, more intelligent, and more principled. There had been few comparative anatomy experiments contrasting the brains of different races, the absence of which benefited white men.

But the measurements of Edward Rulloff's brain, found in Burr's reports, would prove Hammond and other neurologists wrong. *How could such a large brain govern such a wicked man?*

After studying the data about Edward's enormous brain, Hammond was forced to correct himself in national newspapers.

"[Rulloff] is an argument in favor of the theory that, however much the brain may be the organ of intelligence, we cannot judge a man's morality from the weight of his brain or the size of his skull," Hammond wrote.

Hammond had admitted that the size of a man's brain did not reveal his virtue—and soon another neurologist would take that discovery a step further.

Dr. Hammond was partially right, because we now know that brain size is no indication of intellect or morality, or of belonging to a privileged group with claims of superior intelligence—it's the *quality* of the brain, not the quantity. But we also now know that the brain of a psychopath is likely to have less gray matter in areas that control empathy and remorse, two emotions that stop us from killing. Hammond's theory about Edward was certainly more accurate (and more modern) than Gray's assessment.

Hammond believed that the motives of criminals, whether sane or insane, are more nuanced than a postmortem examination could reveal. Hammond wondered if one day we would know *why* someone kills—*What was their true intention?*

"A person who aims a gun at a bird, and kills a man concealed in the shrubbery, is guilty of no crime whatever, because there was no intention to kill the man," wrote Hammond. "Such unintentional acts may be committed by the insane as well as the sane."

And Dr. Hammond believed, ultimately, that a case like that of Edward Rulloff showed that all victims, like Harriet, Priscilla, Ameila, Amille, and Frederick Merrick, deserved justice, no matter their station in life.

"Neither is the existence or the extent of a crime to be determined by the position in the society of the individual injured," wrote Hammond. "Before the law all should stand alike. To rob the chief justice is no greater crime against society than to steal forcibly from the humblest citizen."

In 1871, Dr. Hammond was compelled to also include Dr. Gray's examination of Edward in his widely read psychological journal. His decision wasn't out of professional courtesy but of necessity—his journal would be expected to publish the high-profile report. But Hammond added a short introduction, a warning for readers about the abilities of the alienist to accurately evaluate Edward and stating that "comment upon the character of the examination would be superfluous." Hammond wrote that while Gray's findings would be of interest, they were wholly inaccurate, even derelict. It was a stark condemnation of Gray's professional skills. Ten years later, Gray and Hammond would clash again, this time during the trial of the man who killed President Garfield.

"I see no evidence of insanity but simply a life swayed by his own passions," concluded Gray.

But Hammond determined Guiteau was in fact insane and a "reasoning maniac," just moderately delusional. It was their final duel in court because Gray would die just six months later. William Hammond continued to develop his reputation as one of the most respected, influential neurologists in history. His conclusion about the size of Edward's brain in relation to his morality was a judgment against other "scientists" who leaned on theories steeped in nineteenth-century bigotry. But the final expert to examine Edward Rulloff was perhaps the most important, the most influential of those who dissected Edward's brain and his character. That scientist was determined to discover whether nature or nurture creates a killer—and if all brains are created equal.

In 1909, the first conference of what would later become the NAACP in New York City featured an energetic scientist in his late sixties attacking scientific racism in front of hundreds of luminaries in literature, religion, and social reform. Racialist brain science was the specific target of the conference, and neurologist Burt Green Wilder was the weapon. Wilder pointed to a photograph of a massive brain belonging to white murderer Edward Rulloff.

Edward's brain was Wilder's first purchase in his new brain

collection, one he began just a few years after Edward Rulloff's execution. Dr. George Burr had kept Edward's brain preserved until he finally found a buyer in Dr. Wilder. In fact, it was the first brain collection in the country—Edward's brain marked the start of comparative anatomy and neuroscience. Cornell University psychology professor Barbara Finlay compared Burt Wilder's brains to Charles Darwin's finches.

"Darwin was giving structure to the biological world through natural selection," said Finlay. "And brain collections were a similarly momentous step for recognizing cognition of any kind, for starting things like artificial intelligence and computers. This was just a world-changing difference in point of view about how we think about brains."

Wilder acquired Edward's brain to study the neurobiological underpinnings of criminal behavior, but he wanted to expand his studies to other areas, too. By the time he retired in 1910, Wilder had collected about 1,600 brains of both animals and people— about 430 of those brains were human.

———

At the 1909 conference, Wilder asked the audience to compare Edward's brain to the image of the brain of a Black janitor. He produced a photo of the brain of a person of mixed race and another photo of the brain of a brilliant white philosopher. He lined them up next to each other. They all looked the same, he declared, despite their various sizes. None was more impressive than the other—their fissures and folds were almost identical. He was the first scientist to make that statement publicly, and other scientists were aghast—it disputed scientific racism, including the study of phrenology.

Newspapers around the world reported on Wilder's evidence, which included Edward Rulloff's brain: "Phrenology now discredited," wrote one paper. "Theories as to depth of convolutions, amount of gray matter, relative weight not proved."

Wilder spent the next decade making paradigm-shifting public declarations at a time when few neurologists dared to speak out; he was perhaps the first key whistleblower in history to publicly dismantle the widely accepted defense of scientific racism.

As part of his comparative anatomy research, Wilder was determined to learn why people commit crimes. He studied the brains of dozens of criminals, including that of Edward Rulloff. Wilder wanted to know if the brains of killers differed from those of "moral" people and, if they did, were they born with "evil" brains or did their immorality develop later? When he first created the brain collection in 1875, Wilder really wasn't sure. He thought he had detected some similar abnormalities in the brains of criminals—a particular organization.

Other scientists believed that criminals had a specific fissural pattern, but Wilder didn't see it in the brains of his criminals. Burt Wilder tried to dispel some disturbing ideas that all criminals were born evil but some could be reprogrammed, and the theory that crime had a physical origin, like the theories of Dr. John Gray and Cesare Lombroso. These theories opened a long list of possibilities in the treatment of crime: physicians instead of jailers and surgical operations instead of execution. We know now that people who habitually commit crimes do it for various reasons, including mental illness and abusive childhoods.

By 1897, Wilder did believe that there were marks on the brains of criminals, yet once again he defied conventional wisdom, because he thought that all criminals had normal brains at birth, but when they chose to commit a crime, then a mark would be left behind. Newspapers reported widely on Wilder's discovery.

"His investigations seem to indicate that a criminal life leaves its mark upon the brain rather than that the peculiar brain formations are the cause of crime," a story at the time read.

Now we know that brains do change structurally as we age, but a mark isn't left when someone chooses to make an amoral decision. By the early 1900s, Wilder had learned enough about the criminal mind—and he had dismissed his theory about impressions left on the brains of criminals. Wilder declared that Edward Rulloff's brain had not made him a murderer—it was his own choice to kill.

Rulloff's brain "is large and richly fissured," wrote Wilder, "and presents no feature now recognizable as indicating criminality."

Biology is not destiny, Wilder concluded, and he was partially right; indeed, current neuroscience shows that most people who commit crimes are unlikely to have a brain defect. People who are multiple murderers tend to be sociopathic or psychopathic; psychopaths may be born with brains that are structured abnormally, while a sociopathic mindset is something that society has brought on—something happens to sociopaths to change their psyche.

New studies show that psychopaths tend to have brains that are structured differently. Perhaps Edward Rulloff, a nineteenth-century psychopath, was predestined to lead a troubling life because of the structure of his brain. Dr. Nigel Blackwood, an expert in forensic psychiatry, and his team at King's College London have studied the MRI brain scans of forty-four violent criminals diagnosed with antisocial personality disorder—men convicted of crimes like murder and rape. Blackwood compared those scans to twenty-two healthy non-offenders without psychopathy and he concluded that psychopaths have reduced gray matter volume in the anterior and rostral prefrontal cortex and the temporal pole. Dr. Blackwood said that both those areas help process several important things in healthy people: remorse, social stigma, and a lack of empathy. Psychopaths might also use aggression in a planned way to get what they want.

"Classically the psychopath will struggle to have a sense of remorse, to have a sense of embarrassment for some of the things that they've done in the past," said Dr. Blackwood in our interview. "They're more likely to use violence in an instrumental way to get what they want."

Dr. Blackwood said that remorse and embarrassment help prevent most people from killing—but not people with psychopathy. He said that his brain study proves that psychopaths have structurally different brains from everyone else and psychopathy is engrained in their brains from birth. There are larger studies that arrived at the same conclusion—the brain scans of many killers show reduced gray matter. Blackwood hopes that new medicines might help, but there's still so much more to explore, including behavioral therapy.

Reliable medicine and modern rehabilitation were not available in the 1870s for a criminal like Edward Rulloff, but despite his brain's likely abnormal structure, his circumstances certainly played a role in his decision to repeatedly kill. Edward was offered little guidance, but that's also the case with many people who don't commit crimes, even when their brains are underdeveloped in their youth. While some people with psychopathy do commit violent crimes, many do not, and yet Blackwood's study was certain about the brain's influence of some patients with ASPD.

"Most violent crimes are committed by a small group of life-course-persistent male offenders, who meet diagnostic criteria for conduct disorder as children and antisocial personality disorder as adults," his study confirmed.

Researchers continue to explore why and how the violent offenders cross that line, but one thing is clear—the psychopath has only self-interest and self-preservation in mind.

In 1989, Ted Bundy's defense team hired Dr. Dorothy Lewis, a clinical psychiatrist, to evaluate his mental state. Lewis specialized in understanding the brain chemistry of violent men. After a series of tests, she determined that Bundy was not psychotic, like previous psychiatrists had concluded. Lewis believed that Bundy was bipolar, based on his mood swings. The psychiatrist said it was during the down phase during depression when he didn't feel love or empathy. But she was also convinced that something was wrong with the structure of his brain, like a tumor that blocked his empathy. Ultimately, there was no satisfying answer.

Dr. Wilder's conclusions about criminal brains were crucial to his greater goal of defying scientific racism. Neurologists in the 1800s placed criminals in a subhuman class which included mentally ill people, people of lower intelligence, people of color, and women. Wilder guessed that if he could find no correlation between Edward's brain and the brains of people from those other categories, then it would disprove those racist theories. Step one was dispelling the myth that all criminals were born with unique brains, and he had done it.

But Wilder lacked the modern tools, like MRIs, to properly analyze the brain—the methods he used are now archaic. He died in 1925, wishing he could have looked deeper into gray matter. But the public conversation he began by using Edward Rulloff's brain in the country's first brain collection reverberates today as modern scientists continue to counter that same scientific racism, despite being offered definitive answers.

In 2003, researchers mapped the human genome, which showed that humans have 99.9 percent of their genes in common—no one is biologically superior. But in the Trump era, it still isn't enough evidence for racists who continue to advocate for eugenics, those bigots who believe that anyone who is not white or "normal" should be purged. In this chapter, we can trace the history of scientific racism from Wilder's death in 1925 (when IQ tests were gaining popularity) to more recent trends like racist theories offered in *The Bell Curve* and other current scientific research that contends that racial differences are genetic and not a social construct.

Without Edward Rulloff's brain and Burt Green Wilder's analysis, we might not have explored so deeply, so early into the criminal mind, and scientists continue to do that today, exploring why psychopaths like Edward kill and if their brains are structurally different. Wilder created a life-changing collection that sparked neuroscience, the first scientific evidence that everyone deserves the same rights—and Edward Rulloff was a crucial piece to that puzzle. As neuroimaging technology began to develop, brain collections began to wane. Wilder's collection at Cornell University dwindled, thanks to years of neglect and poor storage in the university basement. There are now just eight on display on the second floor of Uris Hall. What remains of Edward Rulloff, with his complex, contorted mind—a man who frightened

America and haunted a family—has been relegated to a dusty glass jar. One note: Edward is in illustrious company because Burt Green Wilder's brain is to his left.

———

Did anyone know the *real* Edward Rulloff, even Ham Freeman? Was he simply an evil genius, as the myth of his life became, or was his brain wired differently? Was he not in complete control of his decisions? Edward could have done something positive with his life, perhaps even groundbreaking in academia, but he charted a much different, erratic, and destructive path for himself—an outlier in the history of killers and psychopaths.

Journalists who spent years with Ted Bundy say they still think about him in the middle of the night after spending years delving into the mind of a serial killer; they are left with a taint they couldn't seem to remove. Edward Rulloff wasn't a product of the devil, despite the label of "moral monster" assigned to him by George Sawyer and others. He was simply a man and that's what seemed so terrifying to the people in the 1800s. It would have been easier to accept if Edward appeared unkempt, almost brutish, because his murderous spree might have been predictable. But somewhere inside the killer's brain was the same humanity that we all share—the loathed criminal Edward Rulloff and the revered educator John Schutt were cast in the same mold.

EPILOGUE

A Cautionary Tale

Whatever he had done, Edward Hyde would pass away like the stain of breath upon a mirror; and there in his stead, quietly at home, trimming the midnight lamp in his study, a man who could afford to laugh at suspicion, would be Henry Jekyll.

—Robert Louis Stevenson,
Strange Case of Dr. Jekyll and Mr. Hyde, 1886

Edward Rulloff was the type of killer who was unable to be categorized in his lifetime because he belonged in a classification that wouldn't exist for decades. Despite being examined by more than a dozen experts from a litany of fields, none of his contemporaries would have been able to analyze his characteristics to create a profile of a psychopath—and warn people that he was dangerous.

Edward's story became the news event of Gilded-Age America with details that seemed plucked from the same penny papers that eulogized him: dead children, murdered women, a lurid affair with an undersheriff's wife, the violent end of a brave clerk, culminating in the execution of a genius criminal. At the conclusion of his series on Edward Rulloff in *The Sun*, journalist Oliver Dyer considered each group's assessment of the killer—and he began with America's eternal question about him.

"Is Rulloff a fiend, lunatic, humbug, villain, lawyer, burglar, simpleton, or what?" asked Dyer. "The sheriff who has had Rulloff in charge and is present at all interviews held with the prisoner, considers him the most hardened wretch he has ever had to deal with."

Dyer said that the district attorney who prosecuted Edward labeled him a "bag of wind, a bundle of insolent pretensions from beginning to end." Sheriff Brown had arrested him and discovered Edward's deformed foot, matching it to the shoe found in Halbert Brothers dry goods store. Dyer noted that the sheriff called Edward "smarter and wickeder" than any of the lawyers, judges, sheriffs, and anyone else with a legal opinion on his case. Dyer also summarized the assessment of the bevy of educators who had ventured into his jail cell.

"An impression prevails among educated people who have examined his articles on language that he is a monomaniac," wrote Dyer. "Rulloff's past history redress him a character to be shunned and though all are of the opinion that he ought to be got out of the way, many are doubtful as to whether hanging is just the thing in this instance."

But most of the people in Broome and Tompkins Counties, where his crimes were committed, agreed with the punishment; they relished the drama of the trial, and celebrated his long-awaited execution. Edward's story was titillating fodder to people in the Gilded Age, a time that prided itself on high morality and Spartan denial of problems. Edward's case sparked a crucial debate over the death penalty, starring high-profile intellectual observers in New York City, who railed on the barbaric nature of small-town justice.

But Edward Rulloff's story has deeper meaning—he was the

first high-profile killer to inspire neuroscientists to dig deeper into the criminal mind. Neuroscience is still young, and the images on a brain scan are not yet definitive when interpreted in a criminal court. But as the data mounts and the instruments become more precise, we'll have to come to terms with the possibility of changes we'll need to make as we deal with the most dangerous people in our society. Biology is not destiny, but those nineteenth-century mindhunters who made a grab for criminal brains had the right idea.

Edward Rulloff both defined brain science and defied it. His case was used to subvert what scientists knew about brains at the time, and it overturned received wisdom about equal rights. The string of experts who sat in his jail cell, analyzed him, and then mined his brain all believed that they could characterize him based on their own beliefs and biases, but in the end, none was successful. Edward was an enigma to each observer who viewed him through his own lens. But the experts all compiled details that added up to one profile, that of a criminal psychopath. Edward Rulloff's intellect almost saved his life because his mind and his brain were fascinating. More than a century later, we are still just beginning to scratch the surface of brain science, neurology, and how someone becomes a murderer.

The brains of killers have been scanned and studied for years since Edward Rulloff's brain first lay on Burt Green Wilder's lab table. Henry Lee Lucas was found to have brain damage, likely from childhood abuse. Arthur Shawcross, known as the Genesee River Killer, also had significant brain damage. Charles Whitman, who killed his mother and wife before fatally shooting fourteen people as he stood in the University of Texas tower in 1966, had a pecan-size tumor in his brain. NFL football star Aaron

Hernandez had the worst chronic traumatic encephalopathy ever discovered in a person his age, according to researchers at Boston University.

One of America's most prolific killers, Ted Bundy, warned journalists and FBI that gathering data on psychopaths would be crucial to preventing crime because there were criminals out there who were brighter than him.

"We want to be able to say we can identify these dangerous people," Bundy told journalist Hugh Aynesworth before his execution. "And the really scary thing is you can't identify them . . . the really scary thing is that there are a lot of people who are not in prison, a *lot of* people who are not in prison, who are *far* more successful than I."

The results of research into the criminal brain do have real-world repercussions. The Brain Defense, now effectively leveraged in criminal courts, can be extremely dangerous—the punishment for bad behavior can be mitigated as the result of an MRI. Experts I've spoken with say that juries are swayed simply by using the word "neuroscience." We know so little about the brain and we're constantly being presumptuous about its capabilities, and that's frightening. Misleading science propagates scientific racism, eugenics, and bad plea deals. Judges must not allow untested neuroscience into criminal cases—the techniques (just like forensics) must be vigorously tested and peer-reviewed.

We must fund more research to combat scientific racism. Former president Trump says that Mexican immigrants are predisposed to be criminals. White supremacists point to rising, inaccurate research that Anglos have superior brains. Unreliable science justifies incredible biases. Real scientists must contest those bigoted modern researchers who are published in renowned journals. Those journals must vet the biased theories more closely. Just like climate change denial, bad neuroscience must be exposed and discredited.

Meanwhile, the notorious Gilded-Age killer who helped ignite the interest in these issues on a larger scale now has his brain in a glass jar, moldering away behind a glass display at Cornell University; it was perhaps a fitting end for a failed academic who hoped to become famous. In 1871, journalist Hamilton Freeman struggled to define Edward Rulloff, the friend he admired and feared, the killer with psychopathy who used him as a conduit to craft an often inaccurate self-portrait.

"In him there was no repentance," said Ham. "Like *Ponce de Leon* he chased a fleeting phantom to the grave."

Edward haunted the victims he left behind, including the Schutts. There is a local legend that Harriet Schutt can be seen walking slowly along the shore of Cayuga Lake on June 23, the anniversary of her death. The Schutts died wondering about the truth behind the deaths of four of their loved ones. Even Edward's own family seemed cursed after his death. His youngest brother, William Rulofson, fell to his death on November 2, 1878, from a roof in San Francisco. It was unclear whether it was an accident or suicide when he yelled in the air: "My God, I'm killed." Newspapers reported that when his pockets were searched, police made a morbid discovery: a photo of his older brother Edward's head.

Edward Rulloff's malignant, manipulative words echoed in Hamilton Freeman's mind long after his death at the gallows in 1871. For the rest of the author's life, Ham would remain fixated not only on the influence of Edward's criminal mind on others, but also his penchant for violence to achieve a goal; Ham searched his interview notes, struggling to locate the root of Edward Rulloff's malevolence—something other behavioral experts grapple with centuries later with contemporary psychopaths.

"I see him in my dreams," Ham wrote at the conclusion of the book. "If not insane, he was the incarnation of all that is wicked."

Acknowledgments

The evolution of this story has been astounding—from underdeveloped book idea, to hit podcast, to a (finally) successful book idea. I've loved writing this book, and no small part of that is because of the Schutts and their generosity with information about family history.

I've visited Dryden, New York, three times . . . and each time I discover more information. There are many folks who helped me along the way.

Kathy Chadwick and Craig Schutt, both relatives of Harriet Schutt, provided me with private papers and family history. Dr. Michael Weiss, professor of linguistics at Cornell University, helped me decipher Rulloff's convoluted theory and was an apt guide on the trail of linguistics.

For the neurology behind psychopathy, I interviewed Dr. Nigel Blackwood, a clinical academic in forensic psychiatry, King's College London. For information on Rulloff's gigantic brain, I talked with Dr. Barbara Finlay, professor of psychology at Cornell University.

For guidance on the mindset of a psychopath, I spoke with Dr. William Winslade, a professor of philosophy of medicine,

University of Texas Medical Branch; Dr. Craig Neumann, a professor of psychology at University of North Texas; and Dr. Katherine Ramsland, a professor of forensic psychology at DeSales University.

Dr. David Price, a professor of developmental neurobiology at the University of Edinburgh, knows seemingly everything about phrenology, while Esther Crain's expertise is Gilded-Age New York.

Archivists and historians are my heroes and there were several who saved me: Donna Eschenbrenner, Director of Archives and Research Services, the History Center in Tompkins County; Fred Muratori, reference librarian, Olin & Uris Libraries, Cornell University; David Blake and David Wren at Halsey House, Trumansburg, New York; Jude T. Corina at Rare Manuscripts, Kroch Library at Cornell; and Gerry Smith at the Broome County Public Library.

There are some other folks who deserve accolades:

My incredible fact-checker, Benjamin Kalin, who seemingly questioned *everything*, thank goodness.

Big thanks to some folks at the University of Texas, particularly the dean of the Moody College of Communication, Jay Bernhardt, and School of Journalism director Kathleen McElroy.

Thanks to Becka Oliver, the executive director of the Writers' League of Texas, who was a fantastic cheerleader from the beginning—and her organization is outstanding.

I'm thrilled to be with G. P. Putnam's Sons for the second time. Huge thanks to Ivan Held, president; Sally Kim, publisher; Katie Grinch, associate director of publicity; Ashley McClay, director of marketing; Brennin Cummings, senior manager of marketing; and Ashley Di Dio, editorial assistant.

ACKNOWLEDGMENTS

I'm astounded by the generosity and care that executive editor and good friend Michelle Howry offers me time after time. I'd be lost without her.

I'm thrilled to be on the Exactly Right Media team and I'm grateful for the support of Danielle Kramer, Karen Kilgariff, and Georgia Hardstark.

As always, my literary agent, Jessica Papin, with Dystel, Goderich & Bourret, is my patient partner in the maddening world of publishing—and I'm so grateful for her.

To my Texas girls (Angie, Leticia, Lorena, Monica, Robbynn, Tina, and Valeri), whose wit and charm have endless capacity.

To my late father, Robert Oscar Dawson, who was a brilliant professor of law at the University of Texas and who would have LOVED this book.

And finally, to my family, who have supported me whether I stood tall, or leaned, or fell. They've always helped me stand up again.

Bibliography

BOOKS/ARTICLES

"A Sermon on Rulloff, the Condemned." *New York Herald*, April 28, 1871.

Aamodt, Michael G., Terence Leary, and Larry Southard. *Radford/FGCU Annual Report on Serial Killer Statistics: 2020*. Radford, VA: Radford University, 2020.

Alcott, William A. *The Young Wife, or Duties of Woman in the Marriage Relation*. Boston: Waite, Peirce and Company, 1846. https://www.loc.gov/resource /dcmsiabooks.youngwifeordutie00alco/?sp=11&r=-1.21,-0.412,3.421,2.0 06,0.

Appleseed, Joannie. *Quill Pen, Caldwell One-Room School*. https://files.eric .ed.gov/fulltext/ED458080.pdf

Asbury, Herbert. *The Gangs of New York: An Informal History of the Underworld*. New York: Garden City Publishing, 1928.

Bailey, Richard W. *Rogue Scholar: The Sinister Life and Celebrated Death of Edward H. Rulloff*. Ann Arbor: University of Michigan Press, 2003.

Bonn, Scott A. "Organized Versus Disorganized Serial Predators: The Basis of FBI Criminal Profiling." *Psychology Today*, June 17, 2018.

Burr, George. "Edward H. Rulloff." *Phrenological Journal and Science of Health* 53, no. 3 (Sept. 1871). American Periodicals.

Burr, George. *Medico-Legal Notes on the Case of Edward H. Rulloff with Observations Upon, and Measurements of, His Cranium, Brain, etc*. Binghamton, NY: Appleton, 1871. https://collections.nlm.nih.gov/bookviewer?PID =nlm:nlmuid-28321460R-bk

Burr, George. "The Head of Rulloff." *American Eclectic Medical Review*. New York: J. F. Trow & Co, 1871.

Burrell, Brian. *Postcards from the Brain Museum: The Improbable Search for Meaning in the Matter of Famous Minds*. New York: Broadway Books, 2006.

Chan, Sewell. "Mailer and the Murderer." *New York Times*, November 12, 2007.

Clemens, Samuel Langhorne. "A Substitute for Rulloff." *New York Tribune*, May 3, 1871.

Crain, Esther. *The Gilded Age in New York, 1870–1910*. New York: Black Dog & Leventhal Publishers, 2017.

Crapsey, Edward. *The Man of Two Lives*. New York: American News Company, 1871.

Crapsey, Edward. "Rulloff. The Condemned Obdurate and Sullen to the Last." *New York Times*, May 18, 1871.

Crapsey, Edward. "Rulloff, The Murderer." *New York Times*, May 17, 1871.

Crapsey, Edward. "Rulloff. The Sentence of the Law Executed Upon the Murderer." *New York Times*, May 19, 1871.

Cuba, Nan, and Joel Norris. "The Two Faces of Henry Lee Lucas." *D Magazine*, October 1985.

Dawson, Kate Winkler. *Death in the Air: The True Story of a Serial Killer, the Great London Smog, and the Strangling of a City*. New York: Hachette Books, 2017.

DeLisi, Matt, Michael G. Vaughn, Kevin M. Beaver, and John Paul Wright. "The Hannibal Lecter Myth: Psychopathy and Verbal Intelligence in the MacArthur Violence Risk Assessment Study." *Journal of Psychopathology and Behavioral Assessment* 32, no. 2 (2010): 169–77. https://doi.org/10.1007/s10862-009-9147-z.

Desmond, Thomas C. "New York Smashes the Lunacy Commission Racket." *Journal of Criminal Law and Criminology*, January–February 1940.

Douglas, John E., and Mark Olshaker. *The Killer Across the Table: Unlocking the Secrets of Serial Killers and Predators with the FBI's Original Mindhunter*. New York: HarperCollins Publishers, 2019.

Dyer, Oliver. "The Modern Eugene Aram." *Sun* (New York), January 25, 1871.

Eagleman, David. "The Brain on Trial." *Atlantic*, July/August 2011.

East 17th Street /Irving Place Historic District Designation Report, NYC Landmarks Preservation Commission, 1998. http://s-media.nyc.gov/agencies/lpc/lp/1976.pdf

"Edward Hamilton Freeman, Former Binghamton Editor, Dies at Age of Eighty-Eight." *Binghamton Press*, October 21, 1930.

Farahany, Nita A. "Neuroscience and Behavioral Genetics in US Criminal Law: An Empirical Analysis." *Journal of Law and the Biosciences* 2, no. 3 (Nov. 2015): 485–509. https://doi.org/10.1093/jlb/lsv059.

"Farm Wives," from an unknown newspaper at the Tompkins County Public Library.

Fjell, A. M., and K. B. Walhovd. "Structural Brain Changes in Aging: Courses, Causes and Cognitive Consequences." *Reviews in the Neurosciences* 21, no. 3 (2010): 187–222.

Fouts, David P. "Schutt, The First Six Generations," no known publisher, 1938.

Freeman, Edward Hamilton. *Edward H. Rulloff: The Veil of Secrecy Removed*. Lowood Press, 1871.

BIBLIOGRAPHY

Gray, John P. "Report of the Commission Appointed to Determine the Mental Condition of Edward H. Ruloff, under Sentence of Death (since hanged) for Murder." *Psychological Medicine: A Quarterly Review of Diseases of the Nervous System, Medical Jurisprudence and Anthropology* (1871).

Gray, Nicola S., Kathrin Weidacker, and Robert J. Snowden. "Psychopathy and Impulsivity: The Relationship of Psychopathy to Different Aspects of UPPS-P Impulsivity." *Psychiatry Research* 272 (Feb. 2019): 474–82.

Greeley, Horace. "What Should be Done with Rulloff?" *New York Tribune,* April 25, 1871.

Greenberg, Melanie. "Are Narcissists Actually Covering Up Insecurity?" *Psychology Today,* March 29, 2021.

Gregory, Sarah, Dominic ffytche, Andrew Simmons, et al. "The Antisocial Brain: Psychopathy Matters: A Structural MRI Investigation of Antisocial Male Violent Offenders." *Archives of General Psychiatry* 69, no. 9 (2012): 962–72.

Goodrich, George E. "The Centennial History of the Town of Dryden, 1797–1897." Dryden, NY: Dryden Herald Steam Printing House, 1898.

Halliday, Samuel D. *Rulloff: The Great Criminal and Philologist.* Ithaca, NY: Ithaca Democrat Press, 1906.

Hancock, Jeffrey T., Michael Woodworth, and Rachel Boochever. "Psychopaths Online: The Linguistic Traces of Psychopathy in Email, Text Messaging and Facebook." *Media and Communication,* 2018.

Hare, Robert D., and Craig S. Neumann. "The PCL-R Assessment of Psychopathy: Development, Structural Properties, and New Directions." In *Handbook of Psychopathy,* edited by C. J. Patrick, 58–88. New York: Guilford Press, 2006.

Hartley, Cecil B. *The Gentlemen's Book of Etiquette and Manual of Politeness.* Boston: DeWolfe, Fiske & Co, 1860.

Hawthorne, Nathaniel. "The Canal Boat." *New-England Magazine,* no. 9 (December 1835): 398–409. https://www.eriecanal.org/texts/Hawthorne/canalboat.html.

Herbeck, Dan. "The Serial Killers' Confidant FBI Agent Bill Hagmaier Hears Some Terrible Truths." *Buffalo News,* July 12, 1990.

Holmes, Ronald M., and Stephen T. Holmes. *Profiling Violent Crimes: An Investigative Tool.* SAGE Publications, 2008.

"In the Human Brain." *Evening Star,* August 4, 1906.

Janik, Erica. "The Shape of Your Head and the Shape of Your Mind." *Atlantic,* January 6, 2014.

Jensen, Kelly. "Viral Story of Edmund Kemper's Audiobook Narration Tells Bigger Story." *Book Riot,* October 19, 2019.

"John Perdue Gray (1825–1886)." *Dickinson College Archives* (2005).

Johnson, Micah. "How Responsible Are Killers with Brain Damage?" *Scientific American,* January 30, 2018.

Johnson, Scott A. "Understanding the Violent Personality: Antisocial Personality Disorder, Psychopathy, & Sociopathy Explored." *Forensic Research & Criminal International Journal* 7, no. 2 (2019).

Lang, Susan B. "A Case for Brains: Cornell's Cerebral Display Gets Refurbished Home." *Cornell Chronicle*, May 5, 2006.

Lawyer, William S. *Binghamton, Its Settlement, Growth and Development and the Factors in its History, 1800–1900.* Century Memorial Publishing Co., 1900.

Lewis, Tayler. "The Murderer Rulloff." *New York Times*, May 4, 1871.

Life, Trial and Execution of Edward H. Rulloff, The Perpetrator of Eight Murders, Numerous Burglaries and Other Crimes, Who Was Recently Hanged at Binghamton, N.Y. Philadelphia: Barclay, 1871. https://cdm16694.contentdm.oclc.org/digital/collection/p16694coll8/id/523/.

"Lynch Law in New-York." *New York Times*, March 16, 1859.

"Map of Dryden, NY, 1869." Dewitt Historical Society archive.

Mather, Richard. "A Learned Murderer." *American Educational Monthly* 8. New York: J. W. Schermerhorn & Co., 1871.

McLeod, Saul. "Mind Body Debate." *Simple Psychology* (2018).

"Medical Jurisprudence." *Journal of Psychological Medicine* 5 (1871).

Michaud, Stephen G., and Hugh Aynesworth. *Ted Bundy: Conversations with a Killer: The Death Row Interviews.* New American Library, 1989; Sterling, 2000.

Miller, Julie. "Is This Why Ted Bundy Became a Murderer?" *Vanity Fair*, November 20, 2020.

Monkkonen, Eric H. "Homicide in New York, Los Angeles and Chicago." *Journal of Criminal Law and Criminology* 92, nos. 3 & 4 (Spring/Summer 2002): 809–22.

Muller, Robert T. "Death Penalty May Not Bring Peace to Victims' Families." *Psychology Today*, October 19, 2016.

Murray, John F. *The Gentleman's Companion, New York City.* 1870.

Neumann, Craig S. "Will the Real Psychopath Please Stand Up?" Blog, November 4, 2017. https://craigsneumann.weebly.com/blog/archives/11-2017.

O'Brien, Frank M. *The Story of the Sun, New York 1888–1918.* New York: George H. Doran Company, 1918.

Osowski, Kaylee. "Investigating a Serial Killer: The Development of the FBI's Role Told Through Public Documents." *DttP: Documents to the People* 46, no. 4 (Winter 2018).

"Overlooked History: Burt Green Wilder Debunked Biased Claims about Brain Size and Pioneered Neuroscience Outreach to Children." *Berkeley Neuroscience*, November 9, 2018.

Parker, Amasa Junius. *Reports of Decisions in Criminal Cases Made at Term, at Chambers, and in the Courts of Oyer and Terminer of the State of New York.* Volume 3. Albany: W. C. Little and Co., Law Booksellers, 1858.

Pérez-Peña, Richard. "Why Do Killers Represent Themselves? Ego, Ideology, Paranoia." *New York Times*, January 5, 2017.

"Pop Culture: 1840." United States Census Bureau.

Rafter, Nicole Hahn. "Biological Theories of Crime: A Historical Overview." Curator essay in catalog for *Searching the Criminal Body: Art/Science/ Prejudice, 1840s to Present*, an exhibit co-curated by Susan Erony and Nicole Rafter, September 26 to November 5, 2000. University Art Museum, State University of New York at Albany.

Ramsland, Katherine. *Confession of a Serial Killer: The Untold Story of Dennis Rader, the BTK Killer.* Lebanon, NH: University Press of New England, 2016.

Ramsland, Katherine. "Women Who Love Serial Killers." *Psychology Today,* April 20, 2012.

Rosenberg, Charles E. *The Trial of the Assassin Guiteau: Psychiatry and the Law in the Gilded Age.* Chicago: University of Chicago Press, 1968.

"Rulloff Case Stirred Tompkins County, Nation Just 100 Years Ago; Master Criminal Never Punished for Murder of His Wife and Child." Paper unknown but stored at the History Center in Tompkins County, NY, June 23, 1945.

"Rulloff Execution Invitation." Rulloff execution invitation, #1677. Division of Rare and Manuscript Collections, Cornell University Library.

"Rulloff's Petition." *New York Times,* April 29, 1871.

Savin, Jennifer. "A Forensic Psychologist on Why We Need to Stop Glamourising Serial Killers." *Cosmopolitan,* May 20, 2021.

Sawyer, George C. "Edward H. Rulloff." *American Journal of Insanity,* April 1872.

Seelye, Julius. Letter from Edward Rulloff to Seelye; *Julius Hawley Seelye Papers,* Amherst College Library.

Hewitt, W. T. *History of Lansing, NY: Landmarks of Tompkins County, New York, Including a History of Cornell University.* Edited by John H. Selkreg. D. Mason & Company, 1894. https://archive.org/stream/cu31924073798476 /cu31924073798476_djvu.txt.

Serial Killers, parts 1–8. FBI.gov News, September 10, 2013–October 10, 2014. https://www.fbi.gov/news/stories/serial-killers---part-1-the-fbis-role-takes -shape.

"Shorthand's Father in America Is Dead." *Pitman's Journal,* February 9, 1907.

Smith, Laura. "History Lesson: Area's One-Room Schoolhouses Preserve the Past." Ithaca.com, September 18, 2002; Eight Square Schoolhouse, the History Center in Tompkins County.

"Supreme Court, The People agt. Edward Rulloff." 1856 trial transcript. (Ithaca, NY: Ithaca Journal Steam Press, 1856).

"Suspected Murder." *Milwaukie Daily Sentinel,* January 7, 1846.

"Ted Bundy Multiagency Investigative Team Report 1992." U.S. Department of Justice, Federal Bureau of Investigation.

"The Development of Industrial United States (1870–1900)." Smithsonian, National Museum of American History. https://americanhistory.si.edu /presidency/timeline/pres_era/3_657.html.

BIBLIOGRAPHY

Torrey, E. Fuller. "The Year Neurology Almost Took Over Psychiatry." *Psychiatric Times,* January 1, 2002.

Torreyson, Blanche Schutt. A supplement to an application for the *Daughters of the American Revolution,* found in Schutt family papers (1914).

Treaster, Joseph B. "Former Teacher Admits to Killing of Brownie, 7." *New York Times,* June 20, 1974.

"Unsolved Mystery." *Ithaca Journal,* June 17, 1995.

Watts, Sarah. "What One Researcher Discovered about America's True Crime Obsession." *Forbes,* February 28, 2019.

Serial Killers, part 5: "Wayne Williams and the Atlanta Child Murders." FBI .gov News, February 7, 2014.

Wilford, John Noble. "How Epidemics Helped Shape the Modern Metropolis." *New York Times,* April 15, 2008.

INTERVIEWS

Dr. Nigel Blackwood, clinical academic in forensic psychiatry, King's College London

Kathy Chadwick, Rulloff relative

Esther Crain, author and expert in Gilded-Age New York

Dr. Barbara Finlay, professor of psychology at Cornell University

Dr. Craig Neumann, professor of psychology, University of North Texas

Dr. David Price, professor of developmental neurobiology, the University of Edinburgh

Dr. Katherine Ramsland, professor of forensic psychology, DeSales University

Craig Schutt, Rulloff relative

Dr. Michael Weiss, professor of linguistics at Cornell University

Dr. William Winslade, professor of philosophy of medicine, University of Texas Medical Branch at Galveston, Texas

MEDIA

"Conversations with a Killer: The Ted Bundy Tapes," a docuseries on Netflix.

"Frontier Life: Homestead History," *American Experience,* PBS.

"John White Webster (1793–1850)," *American Experience,* PBS.

"How notorious serial killer Ted Bundy was able to escape from custody not just once, but twice," ABC News.

"Terror on Trial," CNN.

"What Type of Criminal Are You? 19th-Century Doctors Claimed to Know by Your Face," History Channel.

Index

Note: Page references followed by an "n" indicate footnotes.

Abbott, Jack Henry, 77n
Adams, Nehemiah, 245
alienists, defined, 208–210. *See also* forensic psychiatrists; Gray, John
Allegheny College, 137–138
Allen, John, 84–85
American 19th-century culture
  country towns and, 20–21
  farm life, 20, 25–26
  following Civil War, 165–166
  hospitality and, 20
  marriage of first cousins, 43n
  one-room schoolhouses, 27
  putting the devil on trial, 127n
  rural families, 20–21
  school curriculum, 28
American Journal of Insanity, 209
American Philological Association annual conference, 153–155
Andrews, Judson Boardman, 165
antisocial personality disorder, 7, 113, 115–116, 192, 276
appeals. *See* New York Court of Appeals
Aram, Eugene, 164–165

Asbury, Herbert, 85
Auburn Plan, 124n
Auburn State Prison, Edward at
  as carpet designer, 108–109
  description of, 107–108
  Dyer interview, 112–116
  prison life, 108
  refining philology theory, 110–111
  reigniting passion for philosophers, 109
  release from, 123–124, 144
  revelation on origin of language, 109–111
  Seelye and, 111–112
  speculating on language of Homer, 111–112
  teasing belief in God, 115
  transfer from Tompkins County jail to, 142–143
  unified language theory, 113
Augustus, Charles (alias), 178
Aynesworth, Hugh, 211n, 238, 261

Balcom, Ransom, 125, 179–180
Barker, John, 137
Battle of Gettysburg, 224

Becker, George
  Burr and, 263–264
  Dyer and, 79, 85–86
  with Edward at execution,
    227–228
  Edward rarely listening to advice
    from, 205–206
  Edward's verbal abuse, 206, 229
  Ham's admiration for, 230
  requesting psychiatric
    assessment, 207
  using personal funds for legal
    expenses, 230
Binghamtom Jail, Edward at
  affront to Christianity, 256–257
  Crapsey's observations of,
    224–227
  denouncing everyone, 229
  Edward-Ham suicide scheme,
    246–247
  facade stripped away, 230
  growing anxious, 243–244
  leading up to execution, 201–204,
    241–247, 256–257
  transfer to Elmira prison, 195–196
biological psychiatric theory,
  212–214
Blackwood, Nigel, 274–275
Bradley & Rulofson, 137
"the brain defense," 266, 284
brain size and morality, 269–270.
  See also Edward's brain
Brookfield Farm, 22–27
BTK. See Rader, Dennis
Bull, Henry W., 42–46, 48, 53–55,
  60, 70
Bundy, Ted
  in days approaching execution,
    245–246
  FBI profiling of, 5
  on insanity defense strategy, 211n
  journalist's relationship with, 19n,
    87n, 238
  mental state, evaluation of, 276

on modifying behavior as a
    charade, 239
  narcissism of, 44n
  preventing emotions from
    derailing goals, 226
  representing himself in court, 134
  resentful of Al Carlisle, 235–236
  scheduled execution of, 261–262
  as self-defeating, 91
Burdick, John F., 98
Burr, Drs. Daniel and George, 232,
  235, 259–260, 264–265
Burrows, Gilbert, 173–175, 185, 197

Caldwell, Michael, 192–193
canal work, 22–23
capital punishment, 242–243, 261
Carlisle, Al, 134, 235–236
Chadwick, Kathy, 9–10
character disorders, 115–116
Chenango River, 173–174
Christian Union editorial, 200
Civil War, 165–166
Clark, Guy Carlton, 57
Clarke, Daniel, 164
Clemens, Samuel Langhorne,
  202–203
Cleveland, Ohio, 100
Commission on Lunacy, 207
Comte, Auguste, 33–34
Cornell University, 1–2, 11, 267,
  277–278
Crapsey, Ed, 15–16, 130–132, 149,
  224–227, 231–232, 243
criminal psychology, 233, 263
criminal psychopathology, 234–235
criminal trial(s) for Rulloff. See also
    execution
  for daughter's death, 129–130
  double jeopardy and, 125
  female audience at, 15–16, 16n
  Freeman's attendance at, 14–15
  guilty verdict, 186
  lynch mob, 186

manuscript as key evidence, 185–186
for Merrick's murder, 179, 183–184
as a spectacle, 15
for wife's murder, 124–129
criminality, 220, 234–235
criminals
"born criminal" theory, 84
fascination of place where crime committed, 94–95
intentional vs. unintentional, 270
motives of, 270
organized vs. disorganized, 95
representing themselves, 134, 185
Wilder's research on, 273–274
Crockett, David, 142
Cushing, S. B., 106

Darwin, Charles, 272
Daynes, Kerry, 235
death penalty, 242–243
Desmond, Thomas C., 207
Dexter, John, 182
Dexter, William "Billy," 149–150, 171–176
disorganized criminals, 95
Divine Providence, 115, 119
double jeopardy, 125
Douglas, John, 95, 113, 184
Dryden, John, 24
Dryden, New York, 9, 24–26. See also Brookfield Farm
DSM (Diagnostic and Statistical Manual of Mental Disorders), 115–116
dualism theory, 233–234
Dyer, Oliver
Allen exposé, 84–85
assessment of Edward, 281–282
background of, 79–80
Becker and, 85–86
"born criminal" theory, 84
Edward interview, 85–87, 112–116
entering Binghamton jail, 79

first impressions of Edward, 87–88
legitimizing Edward's theories, 114
against lynch mobs, 116
motives for interview, 80–81
as ordained minister, 116
potency of the pen, 84–85
as prolific innovator, 82
religious beliefs, 85
on saloons and brothels, 84
Sawyer's reaction to, 164

Edward's brain
"the brain defense" and, 266
Burr's assessment of, 264–267
in Cornell University collection, 1–2, 277–278
defined and defied brain science, 283
as enormous, 264–265, 269
formation of, 266
proving Hammond's theory as incorrect, 269
Wilder acquiring, 271–272
Wilder's analysis of, 274–275
Edward's remains. See also Edward's brain
Becker accepting Burr's proposal for, 263
Burr detaches head and skull, 263
funeral procession and burial of, 263–264
medical men and women vying for, 262–263
medical students invading grave, 264
public viewing of, 262–263
requesting brother to claim body, 253–254
Elmira prison, 195–196
Erie Canal, 21–22
Esquirol, Jean-Étienne Dominique, 157
execution. See also Binghamtom Jail; Edward's remains

execution (*cont.*)
  appeals for stay, 197, 251
  Becker's visit, 252–254
  citizens' enthusiasm for, 241–242
  citizens' invitations for, 223
  desertion of Edward's family, 254
  Edward's death, 258–259
  Edward's mood prior to,
    225–226, 257
  final words, 257–258
  gallows construction, 240
  Greeley suggested a delay in, 202
  growing crowd for, 255
  Ham refuses to help with
    suicide, 256
  Ham's visit, 250–256
  hope for final reprieve, 227–228
  petitioning governor for delay
    of, 194
  public's reaction to, 260–262
  request for surrogate for, 203
  Schutt family requesting audience
    with Edward, 249
  support for delay in, 201–204

FBI (Federal Bureau of
    Investigation), 4–6, 95
Finlay, Barbara, 272
forensic psychiatrists, 71, 208, 212,
    213–214, 220, 274–275
forensic psychologists, 16n, 114n,
    226, 235

Gacy, John Wayne, 95
Garfield, James A., 271
Garfield County Jail, 134
General Term of the Supreme Court
    in Elmira, 195
Genesee River Killer. *See* Shawcross,
    Arthur
Geneva Medical College, 232
genius psychopaths, 159–160
A Gentleman's Directory (pamphlet),
    83–84

Gilded-Age America. *See* American
    19th-century culture
Graham, Maggie, 151, 182
Grant, Ulysses S., 166
Gray, Hiram, 104, 105, 107–108
Gray, John
  as an alienist, 268
  as *American Journal of Insanity*
    editor, 209
  assessment of Edward, 207–210,
    214–220
  biological psychiatric theory and,
    212–214
  convinced of Edward's sanity,
    216–217
  hostile rivalry with Hammond,
    221, 266–269, 271
  reputation of, 208–209, 220
Greeley, Horace, 201–202
Guilfoyle, John, 239
Guiteau, Charles, 271

habeas corpus, 125
Hagmaier, Bill, 245–246
Halbert Brothers dry goods store
    robbery
  Balcom recognizing Edward,
    179–180
  detailed planning, 169–170
  Dexter's bloated body, 175–176,
    178
  Edward charged with murder,
    182
  Edward jailed for, 178–179
  Edward's recapture for, 181
  grand jury indictment, 179
  Jarvis's bloated body, 175–176, 178
  pretrial hearing, 181
  Reilley as investigator in, 182
  search for third suspect, 177
Hale's Store, 92
Hall, Tammany, 166–167
Halliday, Samuel, 94, 106, 133,
    141–142, 154

Hamilton Freeman, Edward "Ham"
  background of, 17
  on Becker's defense, 205–206, 230
  believing Edward murdered
    Priscilla, 72
  biased description of a killer, 18
  dazzled by Edward, 76–77, 237
  dismissing accusations from the
    Schutts, 66
  earning Edward's trust, 187
  Edward confronting Ham on
    insanity defense, 218–219
  as Edward's biographer, 14, 194
  at Edward's criminal trial, 14–15
  on Edward's dedication to the
    Jarvises, 139
  at Edward's execution, 250–256
  Edward's interview with, 19,
    30–31, 37, 42–43, 45, 64, 67–72
  Edward's suicide assistance
    request, 246–247
  on Edward's true character,
    31–32, 206
  as emotionally depleted, 227
  empathy for Edward, 15
  evaluation of Edward, 65–66,
    236–237
  faithful to Edward, 206–207
  first impressions, 18–19
  fixated on Edward, 285–286
  on insanity defense, 218–219
  reflecting on what he knew about
    Edward, 240–241
  repelled by Edward's true
    face, 230
  reporting on Halbert Brothers
    store robbery, 176
Hammond, William, 221, 267–271
Hannibal Lecter Myth, 160n
Hare Psychopathy Checklist, 7–8
Hawthorne, Nathaniel, 21–22
Hernandez, Aaron, 283–284
Hoffman, John T., 197, 202, 207,
  227–228, 251

human language theory (Edward
  Rulloff). *See also* manuscript on
  comparative philology
  examples of, 110–111
  Greeley's endorsement of, 200–201
  inconsistencies in, 188–189
  in its nascent period, 110
  Mather debunking, 158
  Mather fascinated with, 118
  Sawyer's assessment of, 163,
    187–189, 193–194
  used in petition for delayed
    execution, 194
hybristophilia, 16n

insanity. *See* mental illness
insanity defense, 211n, 218, 234
Irving Place apartment, 11, 147, 152,
  167–170, 182

Jack the Ripper, 96
Jakob, Pauline, 146–147
Jarvis, Albert
  assisting in Edward's prison
    escape, 133–134
  background of, 132–133
  Edward recognizing potential in,
    138–139
  Edward recruiting help from,
    148–150
  Edward tutoring, 130–132
  finding dead body of, 175–176
  Halbert Brothers store robbery,
    171–174
  ingratiating himself to Edward,
    133
Jarvis, Jacob, 131–132, 135, 139
Jarvis, Jane, 131–132, 134, 138,
  151–152
Johnson, Thomas, 243–244
Journal of Psychological Medicine,
  266–267
journalists, reciprocal relationship
  with psychopaths, 87n

Katsaris, Ken, 226
Kemper, Edmund, 5, 44n, 91, 95n, 109n

Lee, Robert E., 224
Leurio, E. (alias), 153
Lewis, Dorothy, 276
Lewis, Tayler, 199–202
Liberal Republican Party, 201
Lincoln, Abraham, 166
Livingston, Chauncey, 177–178
Lombroso, Cesare, 234–235
lunacy commissions, 207
lynch mob, 141–143
Lynds, Elam, 124n

Mailer, Norman, 77n
Mallard, Jack, 184
manipulative psychopaths, 58
manuscript on comparative
    philology. See also human
    language theory
  in brother's hands, 252
  Crapsey as impressed with volume
    of, 225
  Dyer's request to examine, 86
  Edward's fixation on, 238
  in Hamilton Freeman's paper, 86
  as key piece of evidence,
    185–186
  might warrant a delay in
    hanging, 200
  as precious, 169
  revisions to, 126, 183
  rush to complete, 224, 243
Mather, Richard
  assessment of Edward, 157–159
  on Edward's ideas on existence of
    God, 119
  on Edward's linguistic theories,
    117–118, 158
  on Edward's reaction to
    sentencing, 105
  enamored of Edward, 122

  fascinated with Edward's use of
    language, 122
  interviewing Edward, 120–123,
    156–160
  invited to petition Edward's
    execution delay, 194
  pondering Edward's character,
    159–160
  Sawyer as skeptical of, 162–164
  Seelye and, 118
  traveling to interview Edward, 118
McLeod, Saul, 234
McVeigh, Timothy, 241–242
Meade, George, 224
Meadville, Pennsylvania, 135–136
Mendota Juvenile Treatment Center,
    193
mental illness, 115–116, 192, 208,
    212–214, 220, 234, 273
Merrick, Frederick, 173–175
Michaud, Stephen G., 238
Military Tract of Central New York,
    24–25
mindhunters, 5–7
monomania, 154–155, 157, 237, 238,
    282
Montgomery, David, 268
moral responsibility, 217–218
moral teaching, 192
morality, brain size and, 269–270
Mukunth, Vasudevan, 260
Muller, Robert T., 242

NAACP, 271
narcissism, 44, 211
The Nation, 153
natural method, Sawyer on, 162
Nelson, James. See Rulloff, Edward,
    as escaped murderer
Nelson, James (alias), 137–138
Neumann, Craig, 8, 90–91, 192–193
neurologists, 209, 268. See also
    Hammond, William
neuropsychology, 265

neuroscience, 12, 272, 274, 277, 282–283, 284–285
New York City, Edward in
 brothels, 83–84
 cholera infestation, 167
 as "civilized society," 83
 Draft Riots, 167
 as easy place to get lost in, 144–145
 Edward's ambition of being a gentleman, 151
 Five Points neighborhood, 145
 Irish mob, 167
 Irving Place apartment, 11, 147, 152, 167–170, 182
 low crime rates per capita, 82–83
 Manhattan, 145
 population of, 82
 as Professor E. Leurio (alias), 153–155
 recruiting Al Jarvis, 148–149
 rise of corporate titans, 166
 robbing silk merchants, 150
 sordid side of, 83–84
 as a tutor, 150
New York Court of Appeals, 129, 141, 144, 195
New York Tribune, 201
Nilsen, Dennis, 235
19th-century culture. See American 19th-century culture

Oakley, S., 207
O'Brien, Jane, 57, 59
one-room schoolhouses, 27
onomatopoeia, 189–190
Oregon Trail, 20
organized killers, 95

Pérez-Peña, Richard, 185
personality pathology, 91
philology theory, 110–111
phrenology, 49–50, 233–234, 265
providence. See Divine Providence

psychopaths
 ability to adjust countenance, 71
 academic vs criminal intelligence, 90–91
 aggressive type of, 58
 as antagonistic, 122
 antisocial personality disorder and, 7, 113, 115–116, 192, 276
 brain of, 269–270, 274–275
  (see also Edward's brain)
 bravado/brashness outweighing common sense, 96
 as brilliant masterminds, 90–91
 categories of, 58
 constant manipulation by, 239
 debilitating insecurities, 44–45
 deception of, 132
 difficulty in controlling panic, 181–182
 emulating emotions, 42, 91
 excellent at subterfuge, 236
 false contrition, 75n
 genius psychopaths, 159–160
 glamorized by movies, 160n
 goals, 96
 Hannibal Lecter Myth and, 160n
 inflated sense of self-worth, 73
 journalist's relationship with, 87n, 238
 manipulative type of, 58
 masking emotions, 105
 narcissistic behavior, 44, 211
 online communication and, 121–122
 poor behavioral controls, 155
 preventing emotions from derailing goals, 226
 reaction to insanity assessments, 211n
 reduced gray matter and, 274–275
 rehabilitation response of, 8
 remorse, lack of, 149, 275

psychopaths (*cont.*)
  as self-defeating, 91, 211
  self-preservation, compulsion for,
    68, 96, 105, 113, 138–140, 165,
    174, 210, 276
  self-sabotage acts, 96
  self-serving complaints of, 114n
  study of, 7–9
  superficial charm of, 77
  treatment for, 192–193
  using intimidation to regain
    control, 71

racialist brain science, 269, 271,
  276–277. *See also* phrenology
Rader, Dennis (aka BTK), 4, 44n,
  87n, 91, 96, 235
Ramsland, Katherine, 16n, 96,
  114n, 235
Reid, Whitelaw, 203
Reilley, Philip, 182
Remshaw, Henry, 220
Ressler, Robert, 95
Richmond, A. B., 135–136
Robertson, Smith, 143
Robertson, Thomas, 73–74
Rockefeller, John D., 166
Rulloff, Edward. *See also* human
  language theory
  academic life, 33–35
  attending Philological Conven-
    tion, 153–155
  attorney for (*see* Becker, George)
  background of (*see* Rulloff,
    Edward, early life)
  Becker and (*see* Becker, George)
  at Binghamtom jail (*see* Bingham-
    tom Jail)
  biographer for (*see* Hamilton
    Freeman, Edward "Ham")
  botanical medicine studies, 48–49
  Bull, Henry W. and (*see* Bull,
    Henry W.)
  as canal worker, 23

  celebrity status of, 4
  consulting on legal cases, 152
  as contradictory, 114–115
  daily routine, 146–147
  death mask of, 11
  despised being undermined,
    204–205
  disdain for Schutt family, 249–250
  disdain for the Shutts, 249–250
  in Dryden village, 9, 23–24, 26–29
  enamored of international news,
    168–169
  as escaped murderer, 135–141
  execution of (*see* execution)
  gifted at reading his audience,
    139–140
  Gray's examination of, 209–210,
    214–218
  Hare Psychopathy Checklist and,
    7–8
  inflated sense of self-worth, 73
  intellectual examination of, 6
  lack of emotional awareness, 91
  in Lansing, 47–51, 62–63, 70–74
  learning phrenology, 49–50
  mindhunters researching, 6–7
  as monomaniac, 238, 282
  moral responsibility philosophy,
    217–218
  in New York City (*see* New York
    City)
  as organized and disorganized
    killer, 95–96
  remains of (*see* Edward's remains)
  reputation as a multiple murderer,
    186–187
  reputation of, 210
  Sawyer interview, 187–191
  self-destructive impulses, 171
  self-preservation skills, 174
  surviving relatives of, 9–10
  trial (*see* criminal trial(s) for
    Rulloff)
  as unique specimen for study, 3

violent outbursts, 44–45
wife's relationship with [see
    Rulloff, Harriet (Schutt)]
yearning for academic life, 50–51
Rulloff, Edward, early life
    Comte's theories influencing,
        33–34
    languages obsession, 34–35
    as law office clerk, 36
    parents of, 32–33
    reinventing himself, 37–38
    in Saint John jail, 37
    as store clerk, 36–37
Rulloff, Edward, post murder,
    89–93
Rulloff, Harriet (Schutt)
    dragging Cayuga Lake for body
        of, 148
    Edward's confession to killing,
        70–72
    Edward's determination to
        marry, 42
    as Edward's student, 27–28
    family's concern for, 29–30
    giving birth to Priscilla, 59
    kissing Bull on wedding day, 43
    as local legend, 285
    marriage to Edward, 39–40
    offering reward for discovery of
        body, 106
    refusing to abandon Edward,
        29–30
    refusing to move to Ohio, 68–70
    relationship with Edward, 39–40,
        45, 46, 56–58
Rulofson, John Edward. See Rulloff,
    Edward
Rulofson, Priscilla (mother),
    32–33, 40
Rulofson, Rulof (brother), 31, 38, 40,
    107, 136–137, 183–184, 228
Rulofson, William (brother), 109,
    136–137, 183–184, 285
Rulofson, William (father), 32

Saint John, New Brunswick,
    Canada, 32
Saint John's academy, 33
Salem witch trials, 127n
Sawyer, George C.
    assessment of Edward, 161,
        190–191, 193–194
    attack on "natural method," 162
    as career educator, 161–162
    criticisms of Edward's intellect,
        189–190
    Edward livid with, 253
    mistrust between Edward and, 187
    on moral learning in schools, 192
    questioning Edward's theories,
        187–189
    reaction to Dyer's report, 164
    reputation as a scholar, 162
    skeptical of Mather's conclusions,
        162–164
scheduled execution. See Bingham-
    tom Jail; execution
Schutt, Aaron, 249–250
Schutt, Amelia, 61–63, 142
Schutt, Craig, 10
Schutt, Ephraim (Harriet's brother)
    believing Harriet is dead, 101
    concerns for Harriet, 51–52
    confronting Edward, 52–53, 92–93
    Edward's capture and return
        home, 100–103
    at Edward's execution, 249–250
    at Edward's trial, 128
    on Harriet's relationship with
        Edward, 29–30
    requesting character references
        from Edward, 30
    searching/tracking Edward,
        98–100
    terrified for Jacob Jarvis, 132
    uneasy with Edward, 29
Schutt, Hannah, 61, 63, 128, 181–183
Schutt, Henry (Harriet's brother),
    22–24

Schutt, James, 25
Schutt, Jane (Harriet's sister), 55–56, 89–90, 97–98, 128
Schutt, John (Harriet's father), 25, 26–27, 142, 170–171
Schutt, Mary (Harriet's sister), 57–58
Schutt, William (Harriet's brother)
    asking Edward for medical help, 61–62
    confronting Edward, 92–93, 96–97
    Edward complaining of Bull to, 53–55, 60
    Edward disgusted with, 59
    Edward unexpected arrival, 89
    Edward's relationship with, 53–54
    at Edward's trial, 128
    ejecting Edward from Brookfield Farm, 59
    marrying Amelia, 45
    securing warrant for Edward's arrest, 98
scientific racism, 269, 271, 276–277, 284–285
Seelye, Julius Hawley, 111–112, 118
self-preservation, 68, 96, 105, 113, 138–140, 165, 174, 210, 276
Shawcross, Arthur, 87n, 283
Sing Sing Prison, 148
Six Mile Creek. *See* Dryden, New York
skulls. *See* Edward's brain; Edward's remains
sociopaths, 274
"Son of Sam," 96
sphygmograph, 215–216
Standard Oil, 166
Stone, William, 48, 49
strangulation, 260
stressor, defined, 46
The Sun (newspaper), 81–82. *See also* Dyer, Oliver
superficial charm, 77

Terre Haute, Indiana, 241–242
Tompkins County jail, 129–130, 133–135
trial(s) of Edward Rulloff
    appeals (*see* New York Court of Appeals)
    for Harriet's death, 104–108
    for Priscilla's death, 126–130
Trump, Donald, 284
Twain, Mark, 202–203
Tweed, William "Boss," 145–146, 166

University of North Carolina at Chapel Hill, 138
University of Washington, 239
Utica Free Academy, 161–162
Utica Lunatic Asylum, 207–208, 209

Vanderpoel, Dr., 208
The Veil of Secrecy Removed (Freeman), 76, 77
vigilante justice, 88, 108
violent psychopaths, 58
Vollum, Scott, 242

Webster, John White, 75
Weiss, Michael, 109, 158
well-bred men, defined, 83
Whicher, Larry, 242
Whitman, Charles, 283
Wilbur, Sarah, 83
Wilburn, Kathy, 242
Wilder, Burt Green, 271–273, 276–278
Williams, John A., 125–126, 130
Williams, Wayne B., 184–185
Wolfe, Charles, 264
women, attraction to high-profile killers, 16n